Stewardship in Motion

Leadership Lessons from the CIO's Seat

Francis Mushi, PhD, MBA

Copyright

First Edition

This book is grounded in lived enterprise leadership experience across strategy, governance, execution, data, modernization, digital workplace transformation, cybersecurity, and operational resilience. Some names, identifying details, and contextual elements have been modified to respect privacy while preserving the integrity of the lessons.

Dedication

This book is dedicated to the leaders who choose stewardship over visibility and continuity over applause.

To the technology leaders and executives who understand that some of their most important work goes unnoticed because, when it is done well, nothing breaks.

To those who protect trust, enforce discipline, and build systems that outlast their own tenure.

And to the teams who execute quietly every day, whose professionalism allows organizations to move, change, and grow without losing themselves.

May the work endure longer than the credit.

Contents

Preface

This book was written from the conviction that leadership is most clearly revealed when conditions are demanding, the path is not obvious, and the institution still has to keep moving. Over the years, my journey carried me from accounting into ERP work during the Y2K period, through outsourcing and my layoff at a global electronics components manufacturer, into consulting and ERP leadership, across coatings and manufacturing environments, through internationally funded development work, and eventually into the CIO seat at a global automotive and industrial coatings company. Each chapter of that journey taught me something different about pressure, governance, trust, continuity, and the real cost of getting leadership wrong. Taken together, those experiences formed the larger lesson that runs through this book. Leadership is stewardship under pressure.

I wrote this book for practicing CIOs, IT leaders, consultants, faculty, facilitators, instructors, and graduate students who want something more useful than slogans and more honest than polished leadership mythology. I wanted the language to stay human, but I also wanted the material to be serious enough for the classroom, the boardroom, and the real work of executive life. That is why the book returns to case studies, discussion questions, application for practice, teaching notes, and instructor summaries. I wanted the book to be readable, but also teachable. I wanted it to sound lived, because it was.

Instructor Note

This book is designed to work well in graduate leadership courses, executive education, CIO forums, technology leadership seminars, and facilitated discussion settings. Instructors can teach the chapters in sequence or assign them thematically around governance, trust, transformation, resilience, succession, organizational memory, and stewardship. The case studies are intended to stimulate discussion beyond technology and into executive judgment, operating-model design, cross-functional leadership, and institutional consequence. Readers should be encouraged to compare the situations in these pages with their own organizations, because the real value of the book is not only in the stories themselves, but in the conversations they can provoke about how leaders build institutions that last.

Introduction

I wrote this book as a practical guide to modern CIO leadership, shaped by real work in execution, governance, trust, AI accountability, and institutional resilience. It is grounded in lived enterprise experience and written for leaders, students, and practitioners who want a clearer view of what durable leadership actually looks like under pressure. I did not write it to romanticize the role or to make leadership sound cleaner than it is. I wrote it because too much of the conversation about leadership still skips over the daily realities that determine whether an institution becomes stronger or weaker over time. This book is meant to serve practicing CIOs, other IT leaders, consultants, and graduate leadership programs with equal seriousness, which is why it returns repeatedly to case studies, discussion questions, application for practice, facilitator guidance, and teaching value without losing the voice of lived executive work.

Why This Book

Over the years, I have learned that the CIO role is often misunderstood. People see projects, platforms, budgets, security, and roadmaps. Those things matter, but they do not fully explain the role. The deeper work is helping an enterprise think clearly, move together, and maintain trust while change is happening. It is helping leaders make better decisions, helping teams execute with fewer surprises, and helping organizations modernize without losing discipline, continuity, or common sense.

Why Stewardship Matters Now

Stewardship matters now more than it has in a very long time. Enterprises are moving through overlapping waves of pressure all at once. AI is accelerating expectations. Cybersecurity risks are more constant. Data is everywhere, but trust in data is still uneven. Transformation programs are expected to move faster, cost less, and create fewer disruptions, even as the business becomes more dependent on stable systems and clean execution. In that kind of environment, what holds is structure, clarity, trust, and disciplined execution.

Opening

This book comes from experience. It was shaped in real businesses, under real pressure, where systems matter, people matter, and timing is rarely convenient. The lessons in these pages were forged through enterprise transformation, platform modernization, cloud migration, stronger data foundations, cybersecurity improvement, AI adoption, and the steady work of helping the business move with greater clarity and less friction. I want this book to feel useful to the person reading it in a boardroom, in a graduate classroom, or late in the evening after a hard week of executive work. That is why it is written with both practicality and teachability in mind.

Leadership is often explained in ways that make it sound either more glamorous or more controllable than it really is. Some books lean heavily on theory. Others lean on dramatic success stories that feel so unusual they become difficult to apply. But most leaders do their real work somewhere in the middle. They are not standing on stages every day. They are carrying responsibility inside institutions that must continue operating whether conditions are favorable or not. They are making decisions with incomplete information, balancing change with continuity, trying to improve the future without breaking the present, and carrying the emotional weight of choices that affect other people's work, trust, and stability. That is the version of leadership I know best, and it is the version this book is written to serve.

From Y2K to the CIO Seat

My path into technology did not begin with a grand plan to become a CIO. It began with a problem the business could not ignore. During the Y2K era, while my foundation was still in accounting, I was asked to help with ERP work because the organization needed people who could understand both the numbers and the systems that produced them. At the time, I did not see that moment as the beginning of a career arc. I saw it as an assignment that mattered. But looking back now, I can see that it changed the direction of my professional life. It taught me something that has stayed with me ever since: technology is never only technical. It is operational. It is financial. It is human. And when it fails, the business does not experience it as an IT issue. The business experiences it as disruption.

That early shift from accounting into ERP and enterprise systems work shaped the way I learned to see organizations. I was not only learning software. I was learning how process, control, reporting, and execution all converge in the real life of a company. Over time, that view deepened through work across manufacturing, automotive, chemicals, ERP consulting, project delivery, and enterprise leadership. It carried me from analyst work into project leadership, from project leadership into broader IT management, and eventually into the executive responsibility of leading an enterprise technology function. Along the way, I learned that the best leaders are not the ones who make systems sound sophisticated. They are the ones who make the business steadier.

That perspective became even more important once I began leading large-scale transformation work. In the environments I inherited, the problems were rarely confined to technology. Weak governance, low morale, fragmented platforms, inconsistent priorities, and poor project success all tend to arrive together. When that happens, leaders have a choice. They can chase urgent fixes and create temporary relief, or they can begin the slower and more demanding work of rebuilding the operating model underneath the visible problems. In my own journey, that meant clarifying roles, creating accountability, improving communication rhythms, reinforcing governance, standardizing execution, and then modernizing the platforms that support the business. That order mattered. It still does.

The Assignment That Taught Me I Could Endure More Than I Knew

There was an early assignment in my journey that changed the way I understood both leadership and endurance. At the time, I still thought of growth mostly in terms of skill. Learn the system. Solve the problem. Improve the process. But the assignment demanded something more personal than competence. It required long stretches of focus, unfamiliar pressure, and a level of sacrifice that began reaching into life beyond the office. I was away more than I wanted to be. The pace was harder than I had imagined. And there were moments when the work seemed to ask more of me than I was sure I could sustain. Looking back, I can see that this was one of the first times leadership stopped being an aspiration and started becoming a test of character.

What stayed with me from that experience was not a sense of toughness for its own sake. It was the realization that leadership often grows in the seasons that feel least glamorous while you are living through them. Hard assignments expose your habits. They show you whether you can stay steady when comfort disappears, whether you can keep respecting people when the pressure is high, and whether you can keep learning even when the conditions are not ideal. That early hardship did not make me invincible. It made me more honest about what serious work can cost and more intentional about the kind of leader I wanted to become in the middle of it.

The Night I Realized Leadership Was About More Than Being Right

I still remember a long night early in my career when I knew the technical answer was correct, but the room around it was not ready to follow. I had done the analysis. The logic held. The recommendation made sense. Yet the people carrying the work were tired, unconvinced, and dealing with pressures I had not yet fully learned to read. That was the first time I understood that leadership was not only about being right. It was about helping people trust the path enough to move with it. The answer by itself was not enough. The conditions around the answer mattered just as much.

That realization changed the way I lead to this day. It taught me to pay attention to the emotional and organizational state of the room, not only the strength of the argument. People do not move because leaders have the smartest answer. They move when the answer is clear enough, credible enough, and grounded enough in their reality that they can take ownership of what comes next. In that sense, some of the most formative lessons in leadership begin the moment technical correctness stops being enough.

The Meeting Where I Saw Fatigue Before Failure

I remember another meeting from those early years when the project status still looked manageable, but the people in the room told a different story. No one was openly raising a red flag. The update was technically acceptable. The work was still moving. But the energy had changed. The questions were shorter. The confidence behind the answers was thinner. People were complying with the process while quietly losing trust in whether the pace, support, and expectations around them were still realistic. That was one of the first times I realized failure rarely begins with the formal signal. It begins in the room, in the small signs leaders miss when they are looking only at status instead of at the people carrying it.

That moment stayed with me because it taught me that leadership has to notice fatigue before the system turns it into failure. By the time people are willing to say openly that something is breaking, the cost is already higher than it needed to be. Good leaders learn to see the quieter indicators first: the hesitation, the defensive answers, the drop in useful challenge, the increase in polite silence. In later years, that lesson became one of the ways I tried to lead transformation differently. People are not obstacles around the work. They are the work. And when leaders fail to read the human condition of a project early enough, the operating issues that follow are rarely a surprise.

Learning the Business Before Leading the Technology

One advantage of beginning in accounting before moving into technology is that it taught me to see business consequences before I ever carried a technology title. Numbers were never abstract to me. They represented inventory, margin, timing, quality, forecasting, and decision discipline. When I later moved into ERP and broader enterprise systems work, that perspective stayed with me. I was not looking at software as a self-contained technical object. I was looking at the way a system could either strengthen or weaken the business's ability to understand itself. That changed the kind of technology leader I became. It made me care deeply about process integrity, reporting clarity, operational rhythm, and whether the business could trust what it was seeing.

Over time, that same foundation helped me move across very different environments without losing the thread. Automotive, chemical, manufacturing, ERP consulting, project delivery, and executive leadership all look different on the surface, but they share a common reality: the business needs clarity, discipline, and systems that support execution instead of complicating it. That is why my view of the CIO role was never shaped by technology alone. It was shaped by watching how businesses actually succeed or struggle when governance is weak, when information is fragmented, when priorities are unstable, and when leaders do not yet have an operating model strong enough to carry the pressure placed on it.

That is also why I have never believed a career path needs to be perfectly straight to be meaningful. Some of the most defining leadership lessons come through detours, not plans. What matters is whether a leader uses those moments to learn how organizations really work, how people experience change, and how trust is built in the middle of uncertainty. In my own journey, the shift into technology was not simply a new function. It was an invitation to see the enterprise more completely. Looking back, I can say with confidence that the detour was part of the preparation. It taught me to respect humble beginnings, to value steady progress over perfection, and to believe that leadership grows strongest when it stays close to the real work of people and process.

The First Time I Had to Carry Confidence for the Room

There was a stage in my journey when I realized that one of the leader's quiet jobs is to carry confidence for the room before the room can generate enough of its own. I do not mean false reassurance. I mean the steadiness required when the facts are incomplete, the pressure is real, and people are waiting to see whether the person responsible still believes the work can move. I remember feeling that weight acutely in assignments where the path was not yet proven and the people around me were looking for some evidence that discipline, patience, and effort would still lead somewhere worth going. In those moments, leadership felt less like explanation and more like borrowed stability.

That lesson became especially important later when I was leading larger transformation work. Confidence cannot be demanded from teams that have already seen disappointment. It has to be earned slowly through consistency, honesty, and visible follow-through. But before that trust is fully rebuilt, leaders often have to carry a little more of the emotional weight themselves. They have to stay credible before the results are fully visible. They have to protect the possibility of progress long enough for the organization to believe in it again. That is one of the more difficult forms of leadership, and one of the least visible. But in my experience, it is often what makes real change possible.

The Week I Realized Change Needed Language

There was a week early in my journey when I realized that change does not move simply because the plan is sound. It moves when people can name what is happening clearly enough to follow it. Up to that point, I had been focused mostly on analysis and process. But in that season, I watched good work stall because the people carrying it did not yet have language strong enough to hold the transition. Some thought they were being asked to do more with less. Others thought the process was changing only because leadership had lost patience. A few were waiting quietly to see whether this was another short-lived adjustment that would disappear as soon as attention shifted. The work itself was not the only challenge. The meaning around the work was unstable, and that instability was slowing trust.

That experience taught me that leaders do not only guide change through decisions. They guide it through language. They help people understand what is ending, what is beginning, what is being protected, and what is being asked of them now. Without that clarity, even intelligent change can feel arbitrary. With it, people begin to locate themselves inside the transition instead of standing outside it waiting to be convinced. In later years, that lesson became one of the ways I approached every major transformation. If I wanted people to move with the change, I had to give them language strong enough to carry it.

Author's Note to Students, Faculty, and Practitioners

I wrote this book for people who carry responsibility inside complex organizations. Some readers will come to it as CIOs, technology leaders, or executives. Others will come to it as graduate students, faculty members, facilitators, or rising leaders trying to make sense of how real leadership works when the environment is demanding and the decisions matter. My hope is that this book serves all of them well. I did not write it as a technical manual. I wrote it as a leadership book grounded in lived enterprise experience, because I have seen how governance, trust, clarity, and disciplined execution shape outcomes far beyond the IT function. I also wrote it intentionally as a teachable book. That is why, throughout the book, you will find case studies, discussion questions, application exercises, teaching notes, instructor summaries, and practical playbooks. These are not add-ons. They are part of the book's design.

If you are reading this book in a classroom, I hope you treat it as an invitation to think, question, and apply. If you are reading it in the middle of active leadership work, I hope it gives language to challenges you already feel and perspective for decisions you still need to make. And if you are teaching from it, I hope the case studies and discussion questions help connect theory to the realities of organizations under pressure. At its core, this book is about stewardship. It is about what leaders build, what they protect, and what they leave behind. That question matters in every boardroom, every plant, every classroom, and every institution serious about preparing leaders for work that truly endures.

How to Read This Book in Leadership Programs

This book can be read in more than one way. It can be read as a leadership book for practicing executives. It can be read as a reflection on the modern CIO role. It can also be used as a classroom text for graduate leadership programs, executive education, technology leadership seminars, and organizational change courses. Readers in academic settings will notice that many chapters include enterprise case studies, discussion questions, application for practice, teaching notes, and instructor summaries. That structure is intentional. The book is designed to support both reflection and facilitation. My aim is to keep the language human and grounded while making the material strong enough for serious classroom use, cohort discussion, board preparation, and executive development.

The arc of the book follows the same arc I lived. It begins with the formation years, where Y2K, early ERP, accounting discipline, and enterprise systems work taught me that technology is never only technical. It moves through harder seasons, including outsourcing, my layoff at a global electronics components manufacturer, consulting and ERP work at a global consulting firm, operating experience in coatings and manufacturing, and the cultural education that came through internationally funded development work across different parts of Africa. From there, the book turns toward the modern CIO seat: governance, data, AI accountability, resilience, enterprise integration, organizational memory, and the disciplined work of leaving institutions stronger than we found them. I want readers to feel that this is not a theory-first book. It is a field-tested leadership text written by someone who has had to make the call, carry the consequence, and keep going when the path was not yet obvious.

Why This Book Belongs in Graduate Leadership Education

Most books about technology leadership either stay too technical or become too general. They explain platforms, trends, and frameworks, but they do not always show what leadership looks like when the stakes are real and the environment is complex. I wanted this book to be different. I wanted it to sit where real enterprise leadership actually happens, at the intersection of strategy, execution, governance, trust, communication, and organizational design. That is why the lessons in these pages are written not only for CIOs, but also for leaders studying change, culture, accountability, operating models, executive decision-making, and institutional resilience.

In a graduate classroom, leadership becomes stronger when students can see how ideas behave under pressure. They need more than slogans. They need examples of what happens when governance is weak, when data cannot be trusted, when transformation fails quietly, when calm matters more than charisma, and when leadership is measured by what endures after the visible win. That is the contribution I hope this book can make. It offers a leadership model grounded in enterprise transformation, but broad enough to matter well beyond the CIO role. At its core, this is a book about stewardship. And stewardship is relevant wherever leaders are responsible for leaving systems, teams, and institutions stronger than they found them.

That is also why I believe this book belongs in graduate leadership education. It helps readers examine how executive judgment is formed across time, pressure, disappointment, recovery, and institutional responsibility. It invites students and practicing leaders to study how governance, trust, sequencing, communication, and operating-model design interact in real organizational life. In other words, the book does not treat leadership as a collection of slogans. It treats leadership as a discipline shaped by consequence. That is the level of seriousness I want the reader to feel from the beginning.

Introduction Conclusion

The CIO is not there to make technology louder. The CIO is there to help the enterprise move with more clarity and less confusion. That is where stewardship begins, and where durable leadership often becomes visible first. The chapters that follow are an invitation to examine that leadership closely and to ask what kind of institution your own choices are helping to build.

Leadership Lessons

- Technology decisions are leadership decisions.
- Trust grows through discipline repeated over time.
- The best leadership makes the business steadier.
- Continuity matters more than noise.

Chapter 1: Leadership in the Age of AI Accountability

Opening

AI will continue to improve. That is not the most important part. The more important question is what happens to leadership when information begins moving faster than judgment. AI can compress synthesis, reduce the time between question and summary, and produce first drafts, patterns, and historical context quickly. It can help a leadership team prepare for a board discussion, summarize a long thread of updates, compare options, and bring structure to complexity in minutes instead of hours. That matters. In many executive environments, time has been one of the scarcest resources. But AI still cannot carry accountability. Decision ownership does not move. Consequence does not move. Moral responsibility does not move. A leader may use AI to improve preparation, but the leader still has to stand behind the decision when the room gets quiet and the outcome begins to unfold. That is why this chapter matters not only for practicing CIOs, but also for graduate leadership programs, executive education, and consultants trying to understand how modern leadership changes when intelligent tools enter the room.

That is why the arrival of AI is not only a technology story. It is a leadership test. It asks whether the people entrusted with decisions can remain disciplined when the tools around them become more persuasive, more immediate, and more capable of making unfinished thinking look complete. In many organizations, the pressure to move quickly is already high. Board conversations are shorter. Expectations are higher. Teams are overloaded. The temptation to accept a polished answer without interrogating its underlying quality is real. But leadership does not become more mature simply because the summary becomes faster. Leadership becomes more mature when the leader knows when to trust the assistance, when to verify the output, and when to slow the room down enough to make sure the recommendation still belongs to a human being who understands the consequence.

I have found that the most useful way to think about AI in leadership is as an amplifier. It amplifies preparation when discipline is healthy. It amplifies confusion when ownership is vague. It amplifies insight when the data is governed. And it amplifies risk when the enterprise still has weak standards, loose access, and too much dependence on informal workarounds. Mature leaders therefore do not ask only whether the tool is powerful. They ask what kind of environment the tool is entering. They ask whether the operating model can absorb faster synthesis without losing clarity, and whether the people using the tool understand that assistance is not the same thing as authority.

This is also why I have chosen to open the book here, with accountability, rather than with technology. The chapters that follow move through the parts of the work that defined my journey, including modernization, governance, security, talent, and the discipline of execution. But all of it rests on one idea. Leadership is stewardship in motion. It is the act of carrying responsibility for people, decisions, and outcomes while the ground keeps shifting underneath you. AI raises the stakes of that idea rather than retiring it. The faster the tools become, the more clearly we will see which leaders were holding real accountability all along and which were relying on the appearance of it. That is the test this chapter is built around, and it is the test every chapter after it returns to in a different form.

What I Learned Early About Tools and Judgment

Long before anyone was speaking about generative AI in boardrooms, I was already learning a simpler version of the same lesson. Tools can help people work faster, but they cannot think on their behalf. In the early years of enterprise systems work, the excitement often centered on capability. What can the platform automate. What can the new process accelerate. What can the system standardize. Those are important questions. But even then, the deeper question was always about judgment. Who understands the consequence of the choice. Who owns the trade-off. Who remains accountable when the polished output collides with real operations. The technology has changed dramatically since those days. The leadership question has not.

That is why I am careful not to treat AI as a category error in leadership. It is important. It is powerful. It is changing the pace and shape of knowledge work. But it is still a tool entering an enterprise that already has habits, blind spots, incentives, politics, strengths, and weaknesses. If those conditions are weak, AI will not neutralize them. It will expose them faster. If the operating model is fragmented, AI may summarize fragmented reality more elegantly, but it will not make it truer. I saw this begin to take shape very quickly in practice.

That lesson was reinforced again and again as my career moved from hands-on ERP work into broader enterprise modernization. In my earliest ERP environments, I watched how easily leaders could assume that better software would automatically create better discipline. It never worked that way. Strong outcomes came when ownership was clear, process design was respected, reporting logic held together, and the business was willing to standardize what no longer needed to vary. That same pattern followed me into BI, HRIS, Data-Lake modernization, and now AI adoption. The tool changes. The stewardship requirement does not. The enterprise still needs leaders who can separate speed from judgment, convenience from trust, and polished output from real accountability.

If data is inconsistent, AI may present the inconsistency with more confidence, but confidence is not the same thing as trustworthiness. If ownership is vague, AI may accelerate recommendations in a room where no one is ready to absorb the consequence. In that sense, AI is not only a new productivity layer. It is a revealing layer. It shows leaders whether the enterprise beneath the tool is mature enough to use acceleration without confusing it for wisdom.

That is one reason I have always been cautious about leaders becoming too attached to the tool itself. The tool matters, but the people around it matter more. A strong platform in the hands of an unclear, fearful, or overloaded team will not create the result leaders hope for. The deeper work is helping people use capability well by building trust, making complexity understandable, and creating enough clarity that the technology serves judgment rather than distracting from it. In my experience, leadership gets stronger when it remembers that systems do not transform organizations on their own. People do. That principle has stayed with me through ERP modernization, analytics work, cybersecurity improvement, digital workplace change, and now AI adoption. The pattern is consistent. The strongest results come when leaders build operating discipline first, then let the tool amplify what is already becoming healthier inside the enterprise.

That pattern became even clearer as the enterprise moved through multiple waves of change at once. Modernization, cybersecurity, analytics, carve-out work, AI adoption, and daily operational support were all competing for leadership attention. In that kind of environment, the quality of the operating model matters even more than the quality of the tool. If governance is weak, every new capability becomes another source of ambiguity. If standards are strong, new capability can be introduced without destabilizing the whole system. I saw this repeatedly in our own work. The gains we made in project performance, service reliability, and benefit realization did not come from excitement alone. They came from structure, communication rhythms, clearer ownership, and a willingness to build discipline before scale.

The Seat Changes, the Question Does Not

I did not arrive in the CIO seat by starting there. I arrived by spending years closer to the work, first as a consultant configuring and implementing ERP systems, then as a project manager accountable for delivery, then as a leader responsible for whole portfolios of change. Each seat gave me a different view of the same enterprise. From the consultant seat, I learned how often a beautifully designed process fails the moment it meets the habits of the people who have to live inside it. From the project seat, I learned that a plan is only as honest as the conversations happening underneath it. From the leadership seat, I learned that the higher you sit, the more your decisions depend on information you did not gather yourself, which means your judgment increasingly rests on how much you trust the people and the systems feeding it to you.

That progression is the reason AI does not feel like a stranger to me. It feels like the next entry in a long line of tools that promised to make the work easier and, in the process, quietly tested whether the work was disciplined enough to be made easier safely. The seat changed many times across my journey. The underlying question never did. Who owns this. Who understands the consequence. Who will still be accountable when the recommendation becomes a real decision affecting real people. I have asked those questions while standing in front of a configuration screen, in front of a steering committee, and in front of a board. The tools in my hands kept getting more capable. The questions in my mind stayed exactly the same.

For practicing leaders, this is worth sitting with. The skills that carried you into a leadership role are not the same skills that keep you trustworthy once you are there. Earlier in a career, value comes from what you can build and deliver yourself. Later, value comes from the quality of judgment you bring to decisions you can no longer verify firsthand. AI lands directly on that shift. It hands every leader a steady supply of confident output about things they did not personally examine. The leaders who thrive will be the ones who already learned, somewhere along the journey, how to hold accountability for work they did not do with their own hands.

The Briefing That Looked Complete

I remember an executive briefing that looked complete on paper. The summary was polished, the options were laid out cleanly, and the language gave the impression that the thinking was already finished. But as the discussion unfolded, it became clear that what was missing was not information. It was ownership. No one had fully worked through the operational consequence of the recommendation, and no one was yet prepared to stand behind the trade-off once it left the room. That moment stayed with me because it showed how easily a strong-looking output can create false confidence. The document looked ready. The judgment was not.

Experiences like that shaped the way I think about tools, intelligence, and leadership preparation. A well-formed summary can be valuable. It can save time, sharpen dialogue, and reveal patterns quickly. But it can also tempt leaders into moving past the harder work of owning the decision. In my experience, that is where mature leadership shows up. Not in whether the material looks finished, but in whether someone is ready to absorb the consequence of what the material is recommending. That distinction matters even more now, because the more capable our tools become, the easier it is to confuse coherent language with completed thinking. A briefing assembled in seconds can carry the same polish that once signaled days of careful work, and the leader who cannot tell the difference will keep mistaking speed for rigor.

The Recommendation I Was Not Ready to Own

There was an early recommendation in my career that taught me more about leadership than many formal training sessions ever could. On the surface, the analysis was sound. The numbers were right. The proposed path made sense. But when the moment came to stand behind it in front of others, I felt a hesitation I could not ignore. It was not because the logic had failed. It was because I had not yet carried the consequences far enough in my own thinking to own them fully in the room. That experience forced me to confront something important. Analysis can be correct long before a leader is ready to absorb the responsibility attached to acting on it.

That moment stayed with me because it changed the standard I used for preparation. I stopped asking only whether the recommendation was persuasive. I began asking whether I was ready to own what would happen if people trusted it and moved. That is a different kind of readiness. It requires more than intelligence. It requires moral and operational seriousness. In later years, especially as tools became faster and information more abundant, I returned to that lesson often. A recommendation is not mature because it reads well. It is mature when the leader behind it is ready to stand in front of the consequence with clarity, accountability, and enough courage to remain present once the decision leaves the page. I have come to believe that the hesitation I felt that day was not weakness. It was judgment doing its job, telling me that ownership had not yet caught up to analysis.

When Fluency Looks Like Finished Thinking

There is a particular risk that comes with tools that write well. Fluency is persuasive. When a recommendation is expressed in clean, confident language, the mind tends to grant it more authority than it has earned. We are wired to associate clear expression with clear thinking, and most of the time that association serves us. AI breaks the link. It can produce language that is fluent without being grounded, structured without being verified, and confident without being correct. The danger is not that the output is always wrong. The danger is that it is wrong in a tone that sounds exactly like being right.

This is why I tell leaders that the skill the moment requires is not faster reading. It is slower trusting. When a polished answer arrives, the disciplined response is to ask where it came from, what data it rests on, what it quietly assumes, and who would be affected if it were acted on and turned out to be incomplete. None of those questions are about the technology. They are about the standards a leader holds before allowing information to shape a decision. A team that has learned to ask them will use AI as a genuine accelerant. A team that has not will use the same tool to reach the wrong conclusion more quickly and with more conviction.

The practical answer is to build verification into the workflow rather than leaving it to individual willpower. In our environment, that meant being explicit about which outputs could inform action directly, which required a human check before they traveled any further, and which had to be traced back to a governed source before anyone relied on them at all. The point was never to slow people down for its own sake. The point was to make sure that the speed AI offered was attached to something solid underneath it. Acceleration is only an advantage when the thing being accelerated is sound.

Why This Chapter Matters

AI is arriving in organizations that are not equally prepared for it. Some enterprises already have strong governance, disciplined execution, trusted data, and clear ownership. Others still struggle with fragmented systems, weak standards, duplicated process, shadow reporting, and too much dependence on informal workarounds. In that kind of environment, AI does not fix weak leadership habits. It exposes them faster. It reveals whether the business knows where truth lives, who owns the process, what data can be trusted, and how decisions move. If those questions are still unsettled, the risk is not only technical. It is executive. Leaders may begin making faster decisions on top of conditions that still need discipline more than acceleration.

My own CIO journey reinforced this point because the turnaround did not begin with acceleration. It began with structure. The IT organization I inherited needed more than new tools. It needed clarity, accountability, stronger governance, and a healthier operating rhythm. The work started with role clarity, weekly staff meetings, regular town halls, clearer performance expectations, steering discipline, PMO structure, and more visible accountability. Over time, that operating maturity translated into measurable performance. Project success rose from the mid fifties to above ninety five percent. Delivery performance strengthened across schedule, budget, scope, and benefit realization. Enterprise uptime stayed above target even during major transformation work. Those outcomes mattered to me because they were evidence of something deeper than activity. They showed that disciplined leadership had begun to make the system steadier. That is the real lesson for AI. Intelligent acceleration works best in environments that already know how to absorb responsibility.

Those execution outcomes matter in this chapter because they help distinguish real maturity from rhetorical maturity. It is easy for organizations to say they are ready for AI because the technology is available. It is much harder to demonstrate readiness through operating behavior. In our case, readiness showed up through measurable project performance, a service level mindset, and a culture that began learning how to make decisions with more clarity and less drama. Over time, project success moved into the mid nineties, uptime held close to the high nines, and the business realized stronger benefits across approved initiatives. Those are not abstract indicators. They are signs that the enterprise is learning how to change without losing itself. That is exactly the kind of foundation AI needs if it is going to serve leadership rather than destabilize it.

I have written this chapter with several kinds of readers in mind, because the same lesson lands differently depending on where you sit. For the practicing CIO and the IT leader, the message is operational. Build the discipline before you scale the capability, and treat AI readiness as a question about your operating model rather than your tool list. For the consultant, the message is diagnostic. When you walk into a client preparing to adopt AI, the maturity of their governance and data will tell you more about their odds of success than the sophistication of the platform they have selected. And for the faculty member, the facilitator, and the graduate student, the message is conceptual. This is a chance to study accountability as something that does not transfer, no matter how capable the tools around a decision become. Each of these readers is looking at the same truth from a different seat. Accountability is the part of leadership that technology cannot carry.

A Real Leadership Lesson

One of the clearest lessons from my experience is that disciplined leadership has to come before intelligent acceleration. In one of our more demanding transformation years, the IT organization maintained a project success rate above ninety five percent while supporting parallel carve-out work, core platform changes, and enterprise readiness activities. Delivery stayed strong on schedule, budget, and scope. System uptime remained above service objectives. Business benefits were realized at a high rate, showing that the work was producing value, not just motion. Those results did not come from speed alone. They came from governance, accountability, sequencing, and the kind of execution discipline that allows the enterprise to change without feeling like it is coming apart. That is exactly the environment in which AI becomes useful instead of risky.

That is the right lesson for AI. The strongest organizations are not the ones that simply adopt tools quickly. They are the ones that know how to absorb those tools without weakening judgment. AI works best in environments where leaders already know how to lead. It improves preparation. It does not replace responsibility. It can help summarize a position, shape a first draft, compare scenarios, and provide historical context for a decision. But the leader still has to ask the harder questions. Is the information trustworthy. Is the trade-off visible. Is the recommendation aligned to business reality. Are the data sources governed. Who owns the consequence if this choice creates friction later. Those questions remain stubbornly human. They are part of the moral architecture of leadership, and no tool can carry them for us.

One reason I call this a moral architecture is that accountability cannot be delegated to a workflow. It sits with the person who accepts the recommendation and uses it to shape real outcomes for real people. That is true in finance, operations, HR, cybersecurity, manufacturing, and executive decision making. A tool can help a leader gather context faster. It can improve first drafts, summarize meetings, and compare scenarios. But the leader still has to decide whether the recommendation is fair, whether it fits the business reality, whether the trade-off is visible, and whether the people affected by the decision will experience it as disciplined leadership or careless acceleration. Those questions are not technical. They are questions of stewardship.

There is a conviction I have carried through every role, and AI has only deepened it. Transformation does not fail because of technology. It fails when leadership becomes personality driven instead of system driven. The strongest organizations are not built on heroes who happen to be in the room at the right moment. They are built on clarity, discipline, and the kind of structure that keeps working when any one person steps away. This matters enormously in the age of AI, because a persuasive tool in the hands of a personality driven culture is dangerous in a way that is easy to miss. It makes the confident voice even more confident and the unexamined decision even faster. A system driven culture uses the same tool differently. It runs the output through shared standards, names the owner, and checks the decision against reality before anyone acts. The difference is not the intelligence of the tool. The difference is the maturity of the leadership the tool is entering.

Boardroom Perspective: The Questions Leadership Should Ask Before AI Scales

Boardrooms do not need the CIO to arrive with exaggerated certainty about AI. They need the CIO to bring disciplined clarity. In practice, the most useful executive questions are not about the novelty of the tool. They are about ownership, exposure, value, and consequence. What enterprise data is being touched. Which use cases actually create measurable business value. What decisions remain fully human. How is the organization validating outputs before they influence action. Who is accountable when a recommendation is wrong, incomplete, or based on unstable information. Those are governance questions, not curiosity questions. And they matter because an enterprise can become excited about AI long before it becomes disciplined enough to use AI responsibly.

When I think about the boardroom in this era, I do not think of it as the place where leaders approve technology adoption in principle. I think of it as the place where the enterprise should force itself to become honest about what it is actually ready to govern. The board does not need to know every feature. It does need confidence that the organization understands where AI belongs, where it does not belong, and how trust will be protected as capability expands. That is one reason I believe the CIO must speak about AI in the language of institutional strength. Not only productivity. Not only automation. Institutional strength. Because if AI adoption weakens trust, weakens governance, or weakens accountability, then the organization has not really progressed. It has only accelerated into a more fragile form of modernity.

In our own environment, a handful of quiet signals told me that adoption was maturing in the right direction. They were not dramatic, but together they showed that capability and discipline were growing at the same time.

- Governance discussions began to include AI use as a standing topic rather than an afterthought
- Data classification and sensitivity labels were reinforced before access was widened
- Training focused on the principle that AI assists while humans decide
- Teams used AI more confidently, but also more carefully, because they understood the boundaries
- Leadership decisions remained clearly owned by people, with the tool informing rather than deciding
- Security posture held steady or improved even as adoption increased across the enterprise

From the CIO's Desk

One discipline has served me more than any framework as AI has entered serious enterprise work. I treat every machine recommendation as an input to judgment, never as a replacement for it. The tools in our environment are genuinely useful. They summarize faster than we do, they draft faster than we do, and they surface patterns we might miss. But usefulness is not the same as ownership. When a decision reaches my desk wrapped in confident, fluent language, my first question is not whether the answer sounds finished. It is whether a person I trust has examined the reasoning, tested it against what we actually know, and is prepared to stand behind the consequence. If no one can say yes to that, the decision is not ready, no matter how polished it appears.

I hold that line because accountability is the one thing the enterprise cannot delegate to a model. Boards do not accept a system as the responsible party. Regulators do not. Customers do not. Neither do the employees whose work is shaped by what leadership approves. So in my own seat, AI has not lowered the standard for judgment. It has raised it. The faster the answers arrive, the more deliberate the ownership behind them has to become. That, to me, is what accountable adoption looks like from the CIO's desk. Welcome the speed, keep the responsibility, and never confuse fluency with finished thinking.

Five Leadership Rules for AI Accountability

These are the rules I keep returning to. They are simple to state and demanding to live, which is usually the mark of a principle worth keeping.

First, define ownership before expanding use. If no one can clearly explain who owns the output, the organization is not ready to scale the use case. Ownership is not a formality. It is the name of the person who will answer for the decision once the recommendation becomes action. When that name is missing, expansion only spreads ambiguity faster.

Second, govern the data before trusting the answer. AI cannot create trustworthy output from weak definitions, unstable sources, or poorly governed information. An answer is only as sound as the data underneath it, and a confident tool will happily build a polished conclusion on a shaky foundation. Governing the data first is what makes the speed worth having.

Third, train for judgment, not only for prompts. The real issue is not whether people can use the tool. It is whether they know when to question it. Prompt skill teaches people how to get an answer. Judgment teaches them whether to believe it. The second skill is rarer, harder to build, and far more valuable as capability spreads across the workforce.

Fourth, keep accountability visible in every workflow. A polished response still needs a human owner who is willing to stand behind its consequence. The goal is to design processes where it is always clear who reviewed the output, who approved the decision, and who carries the result. Accountability that is visible tends to stay strong. Accountability that is assumed tends to quietly disappear.

Fifth, evaluate AI by institutional value, not by novelty alone. If the tool does not improve clarity, reduce friction, or strengthen decision quality without weakening trust, then the enterprise should be honest about that and move more carefully. Excitement is not a strategy. The right question is never whether a capability is impressive. It is whether the organization is genuinely stronger for having adopted it.

Stewardship in Motion

I called this book Stewardship in Motion because leadership has never felt to me like a fixed position. It is something you carry while everything around you keeps moving. The tools change. The pressures change. The pace changes. AI is simply the most capable and most persuasive of the many forces that will test whether a leader is holding real responsibility or only the appearance of it. The leaders I respect most are not the ones who move the fastest. They are the ones who stay accountable while moving, who can absorb new capability without losing their judgment, and who understand that their job is not to be the smartest presence in the room but to leave the organization stronger and steadier than they found it.

That is the spirit that runs through every chapter ahead. We will talk about modernization, governance, security, talent, communication, and the discipline of execution. We will look at what worked, what did not, and what I learned standing in the seat while the decisions were live and the outcomes were still unknown. But underneath all of it is the idea this chapter has tried to make plain. Intelligence can be borrowed. Speed can be purchased. Accountability cannot. It stays with the leader, and in the age of AI, that is not a burden to escape. It is the part of the work that still makes leadership matter.

Leadership Lessons

- AI should improve preparation, not replace judgment.
- Governance matters more, not less, when tools begin to move faster.
- Trusted data is a precondition for trusted AI, never an afterthought to it.
- Strong operating models make AI useful instead of risky.
- Decision ownership does not move, even when the output is polished.
- Fluency is persuasive, so disciplined leaders learn to slow their trust, not their reading.
- System driven cultures absorb new capability safely, while personality driven cultures are exposed by it.
- The leader's real task is to leave the enterprise stronger and steadier, not to be indispensable to it.

Discussion Questions

- Why does AI make accountability more visible rather than less important?
- How should leaders distinguish between a polished answer and a well owned decision?
- What would responsible AI use look like in a boardroom, a leadership team, or a consulting engagement?
- Where is the line between using AI to prepare for a decision and allowing it to quietly make the decision for you?

- How can an organization tell the difference between being genuinely ready to govern AI and merely being eager to adopt it?
- If you were teaching this chapter, what evidence would you ask students to look for in a real organization to judge its AI readiness?

Application for Practice

- For the practicing leader: identify one current AI use case in your organization. Name the person who owns the consequence of the output, and decide whether that ownership is visible enough to others.
- For the IT leader: review one decision process in your environment that AI could accelerate. Mark the specific step that must remain fully human, and explain why.
- For the consultant: imagine assessing a client about to scale AI. List the three questions about their governance and data you would ask before evaluating their tools at all.
- For the faculty member or facilitator: design a short seminar exercise in which students must defend a recommendation produced by AI and then identify what they would need to verify before owning it.
- For any reader: write a short leadership principle explaining how your team should balance the usefulness of AI with the responsibility that cannot be delegated to it.
- For reflection: think of a moment when you stood behind a decision whose consequences you had not fully carried in your own mind. What did that teach you, and how would AI have made that moment easier or harder?

Chapter 2: Data as Institutional Memory

Opening

Organizations forget faster than they realize. They forget why a standard was introduced, what conditions led to a policy, and what reasoning shaped a decision that once felt obvious. Over time, they repeat debates, revisit trade-offs, and pay again for lessons they have already learned. In most enterprises, memory is fragmented, incomplete, and inconsistent. That is why this chapter matters. This is not just a data problem. It is a leadership problem. For CIOs, consultants, and graduate leadership programs alike, the real question is whether the institution can remember clearly enough to act with confidence instead of renegotiating the truth every time pressure rises.

The danger is not only that information gets lost. It is that organizations begin mistaking repeated rediscovery for normal work. A question that should have been settled returns to the agenda. A definition that once felt clear becomes negotiable again. A report that should support decision-making becomes the beginning of a new debate about what the numbers really mean. When that pattern repeats, the enterprise is no longer compounding learning. It is relearning at great cost. That cost shows up in slower decisions, lower trust, more defensive meetings, and too much dependence on the loudest interpretation in the room. That is why I think of data as institutional memory. It is one of the main ways an organization remembers what it has already learned well enough to act with confidence.

Leaders should care about this because memory determines whether the institution gets stronger with time or simply older. Mature organizations do not only collect data. They protect meaning. They define what matters, preserve context, and make it easier for the next decision to start from clarity rather than confusion. In my experience, that work is not glamorous, but it is one of the most practical forms of stewardship a leader can practice. A business with strong memory moves faster, argues less about basic truth, and is more capable of carrying its lessons forward into the next challenge.

I have seen this most clearly in organizations that were trying hard to grow, modernize, or integrate while still carrying fragmented reporting habits from an earlier era. The business may be improving in real ways, but if the reporting environment cannot preserve those lessons faithfully, the institution keeps acting as though it is starting over. Leaders revisit settled questions. Teams rebuild reports that should already exist. Side spreadsheets become temporary memory devices for a business that has not yet learned how to remember together. Over time, that weakens more than efficiency. It weakens confidence. People become less sure that the enterprise can explain itself consistently, and once that confidence slips, decision-making becomes heavier than it needs to be.

There is also a reason this chapter follows directly after a chapter on accountability in the age of AI. The two ideas are connected at the root. The first chapter argued that intelligent tools amplify whatever already exists inside the enterprise. This chapter is about what those tools will be amplifying. If the institution remembers clearly, AI will help it act on that memory faster. If the institution remembers poorly, AI will reproduce the confusion with more polish and more speed. Trusted memory is therefore not a side concern that sits beneath the technology. It is the foundation the technology stands on. Stewardship in this chapter means protecting that foundation so the enterprise can keep building rather than constantly rebuilding.

When Data Becomes Argument Instead of Memory

I have sat in more leadership meetings than I can count where the discussion appeared to be about performance, but the real discussion was about which number everyone trusted. That is one of the most expensive forms of organizational weakness because it hides in plain sight. People still meet. Reports still circulate. Dashboards still look impressive. But beneath the surface, the enterprise is no longer building on shared memory. It is negotiating competing versions of reality. Once that happens, decision-making slows down, confidence drops, and the organization begins paying twice for what it should have learned the first time.

That lesson was reinforced for me repeatedly over the years because data problems are rarely only data problems. They usually reveal something else. Unclear ownership, inconsistent definitions, weak governance, or a culture too comfortable with informal workarounds. When data becomes argument instead of memory, the business loses more than efficiency. It loses continuity. It loses the ability to compound learning. It loses the quiet confidence that comes from knowing the enterprise can still explain itself clearly under pressure. That is why I treat this chapter as a leadership chapter first and a data chapter second.

I have learned to watch for a particular moment in executive meetings. It is the moment when the conversation is no longer really about performance, even though everyone is still speaking as if it is. The room begins circling around the numbers themselves. Someone asks which version is current. Someone else explains a calculation differently. A third person wants to reconcile a source before agreeing to move. Once that happens, the business is not using data as memory anymore. It is using data as argument. That shift matters because argument consumes confidence. It teaches people to come prepared to defend their version instead of building from a shared one. Over time, that weakens the institution more than many leaders realize.

What makes this more expensive is that informal workarounds often feel helpful in the short term. A private spreadsheet can seem faster. A local definition can feel practical. A manually corrected report may appear more responsive than waiting for the governed version to catch up. I understand why people do it. But every workaround that survives too long teaches the organization that memory can remain personal instead of institutional. It shifts trust away from the enterprise and back toward the individual who knows how to patch the gap. Over time, that is unsustainable. The business becomes too dependent on who remembers, who adjusts, and who happens to be in the room. That is not resilience. It is fragile memory wearing the appearance of productivity.

What Finance Taught Me About Truth

My early grounding in finance shaped the way I think about truth inside organizations. In finance, ambiguity has a cost. A number means something specific or it does not. A control exists or it does not. A process reconciles or it does not. That discipline stayed with me when I moved into systems and later into executive leadership. It made me less tolerant of environments where numbers could be adjusted by interpretation depending on who was speaking. It also made me appreciate how much energy organizations waste when they cannot trust their own reporting. Once truth becomes negotiable, decision-making becomes slower, politics become louder, and leadership spends too much time clarifying what should already be clear.

That is one reason I have always believed that data governance is as much about respect as it is about control. It respects the time of executives who should not have to renegotiate definitions in every meeting. It respects the effort of teams who need a stable basis for action. And it respects the enterprise itself by insisting that institutional memory should not depend on who happens to be in the room. Finance taught me that truth is not only something you report. It is something you protect.

Finance also taught me something else that stayed with me as I moved into leadership. Clarity is one of the most underestimated forms of care in an organization. When definitions are stable, people do not waste energy second-guessing the ground beneath them. When truth is protected, teams can focus on solving the problem instead of debating the meaning of the problem. That is why I now think of clarity not only as a reporting virtue, but as a leadership one. It reduces friction, lowers anxiety, and gives people a fairer chance to do their best work.

I have even come to describe well-governed data as a form of organizational kindness. When the truth is clear, people do not have to protect themselves with side notes, private spreadsheets, or repeated verification. They can do their work with more confidence because the enterprise has reduced one of the most exhausting forms of friction, which is uncertainty about what is true. In a healthy environment, clarity becomes ordinary enough that people forget how much energy ambiguity used to consume. I see that as a leadership outcome. It reflects discipline, respect for people's time, and a commitment to leaving the institution easier to trust than it was before.

This is one reason Chapter 2 matters so much in leadership education. Many students and executives are taught to think of data as a technical capability, a reporting layer, or a support function for decision-making. All of that is true, but incomplete. Data also preserves institutional learning. It protects the enterprise from having to depend on memory by personality, memory by role, or memory by who happens to be strongest in the room. In that sense, governing data is part of governing continuity. It is one of the ways leaders make the institution fairer, steadier, and more capable of carrying what it knows into the next quarter, the next transition, and the next generation of leaders.

I learned this even more deeply through global ERP and project work, where the same organization could appear competent on paper yet still lose continuity through poor knowledge transfer, weak definitions, or inconsistent local practice. In large multinational and internationally funded project environments, for example, continuity could not depend only on who happened to be present that month. It had to survive distance, role changes, local constraints, and different cultural rhythms around authority and communication. Later, in manufacturing and coatings environments, the same truth appeared in a different form. If reporting, process logic, and business definitions were not preserved clearly, the enterprise kept paying again for lessons it had already earned. That is why I describe data as institutional memory rather than as a reporting layer. It helps the organization remember well enough to act with confidence.

The Month-End Meeting That Changed My View

I still remember a month-end meeting early in my career when the numbers were on the screen, the room was full, and confidence was supposed to be high. Instead, what I felt was hesitation. A total looked reasonable, but no one could explain one part of it with enough certainty to let the decision move. One person believed the variance was timing. Another thought it was classification. A third was quietly checking whether the underlying report had changed since the last cycle. The discussion became less about performance and more about whether anyone trusted the ground beneath the discussion. That moment stayed with me because it revealed how much leadership energy gets consumed when truth is present only in pieces.

What changed my view was not the existence of the discrepancy. It was what the discrepancy did to the room. It introduced caution, slowed confidence, and forced people to negotiate meaning before they could make a decision. From that point forward, I began to see reconciliation as more than a finance routine. It was a lesson in leadership trust. If people cannot rely on the numbers, they cannot move with conviction. And if they cannot move with conviction, even strong leaders begin spending too much of their time recovering clarity that should already exist.

That insight stayed with me well beyond finance because every executive function eventually depends on the same discipline. Operations needs numbers it can act on. Commercial teams need metrics they do not have to reinterpret every week. HR needs reliable data to support decisions about people, capacity, and compliance. Boards need confidence that the story behind the performance is not changing depending on who is presenting. In that sense, reconciliation is not only about closing a book or resolving a variance. It is about protecting the credibility of the enterprise itself.

That room dynamic matters more than many leaders realize. When credibility in the data is strong, meetings focus on action, trade-offs, and next steps. When credibility is weak, the room becomes cautious before it becomes useful. People protect themselves with qualifiers. They soften their confidence. They delay commitment while waiting for one more confirmation. That pattern may look prudent, but repeated often enough it changes the culture of decision-making. The organization becomes slower, not because people lack intelligence, but because the ground beneath the conversation keeps moving. Protecting institutional memory is one of the ways leaders stop that drift and restore confidence in the room.

Enterprise Case Study: Data Truth, Memory, and the Operating Model

A strong case for graduate leadership classrooms in this chapter is the shift from fragmented information to governed enterprise memory. In the transformation work I led, we did not treat data as a reporting afterthought. We treated it as a strategic asset connected to governance, project discipline, quarterly audits, and the reduction of shadow IT. That same discipline linked better data practice to stronger project outcomes, stronger stakeholder confidence, better executive decisions, and a more unified organization. Over time I came to position self-service analytics and governed data democratization as a leadership issue, not merely a tooling issue.

What makes this an academic case rather than just an IT success story is the underlying leadership problem. When truth is fragmented, organizations cannot compound learning. They revisit decisions, negotiate numbers, and lose time arguing over what should already be clear. Students can use this case to explore how governance, definitions, ownership, and reporting discipline shape decision quality over time. It is especially useful in leadership programs because it shows that memory is not passive. Leaders choose whether an enterprise remembers clearly or relearns expensively.

What made this lesson especially practical for me was seeing how governed analytics changed the tone of leadership meetings. When BI and Data-Lake work were disciplined through certified sources, shared KPI definitions, training, and clearer reporting standards, the room spent less time debating whose number was right and more time deciding what the business should do next. That shift matters because it changes the emotional quality of decision making. People become less defensive. They prepare differently. They trust the discussion more. In my experience, that is one of the quiet signs that data has stopped behaving like private interpretation and started behaving like institutional memory.

The Discipline of Defining Truth

Defining truth sounds more philosophical than operational, but in practice it is one of the most concrete disciplines in enterprise leadership. Someone has to decide what a KPI means. Someone has to determine which source is authoritative. Someone has to own the standard when different functions want the metric to support different narratives. Those decisions may not feel dramatic, but they shape everything that follows. Once a business agrees on what is true, it can move. If it does not, it spends its energy renegotiating what should already be settled.

I have come to believe that this discipline is one of the clearest marks of mature leadership. Mature leaders do not only ask for more data. They ask whether the enterprise is disciplined enough to trust what it already has. They build governance around definitions, ownership, and usage because they understand that memory is not formed accidentally. It is formed when the organization decides that truth matters enough to be protected.

In practice, this means leaders must be willing to ask very plain questions. What exactly does this metric mean. Which source is authoritative. Who owns the definition. How is it governed when the business changes. Those questions may sound basic, but they are foundational. In our own roadmap and steering conversations, the move toward stronger BI discipline included user training, data audits, shared service expectations, dashboard standards, and a longer-term commitment to making self-service possible without making truth optional. Mature organizations do not only publish dashboards. They create conditions under which the dashboard can be trusted as a continuation of enterprise memory rather than a fresh interpretation every time it appears.

For leaders, that means the discipline of defining truth should never be delegated entirely downward and then forgotten. Data teams, analysts, and BI developers play essential roles, but senior leaders also shape whether definitions will hold under pressure. They decide whether the organization will tolerate competing narratives, whether a dashboard can be published without real ownership, and whether convenience will outrun consistency. Graduate leadership programs should teach this plainly. The quality of data governance is not separate from the quality of leadership. It is one of the places leadership becomes visible in operational form.

Building Memory That Outlives People

The hardest test of institutional memory is not whether it works while the people who built it are still in their seats. It is whether it survives their departure. Every enterprise eventually loses the person who knew why a number was calculated a certain way, where the authoritative source lived, and which exception had a good reason behind it. When that knowledge walks out the door undocumented, the organization does not simply lose an employee. It loses a piece of its memory, and it usually does not notice until the next time that knowledge is needed and cannot be found.

I have come to believe that one of the quietest responsibilities of leadership is making the institution resilient without any single person, including the leader. That conviction has shaped how I think about data. Memory that lives only in one person's head, one analyst's spreadsheet, or one manager's habits is not institutional memory at all. It is personal memory that the organization has agreed to depend on, which is a risk dressed up as a convenience. The work of leadership is to move that knowledge out of individuals and into shared definitions, documented ownership, governed sources, and standards that a new person can inherit and trust. This is not glamorous work, and it rarely earns applause, but it is one of the truest forms of stewardship a leader can practice.

This is also where transitions deserve far more attention than they usually receive. Knowledge is most often lost not in a dramatic failure but in an ordinary handoff. A role changes. A system is replaced. A project closes and the team disperses. In each of those moments, the enterprise quietly assumes that memory will transfer on its own, and it almost never does. Leaders who take memory seriously treat these transitions as carefully as they treat the transactions that get all the attention. They ask what context must be captured before it disappears, who will own it next, and how the next person will know where to look. An institution that manages its transitions well is an institution that keeps its memory. One that manages them carelessly relearns the same lessons again and again, paying full price each time.

Why This Chapter Matters

For students, faculty, and practicing executives, that is the deeper value of this chapter. Data is not simply a technical asset sitting in a warehouse or dashboard. It is one of the ways an institution remembers itself. It preserves what the business has learned, protects meaning across time, and allows leaders to make decisions without renegotiating the same truths in every room. When memory is weak, organizations become more political, more repetitive, and less confident. When memory is strong, leadership becomes steadier because the enterprise no longer has to keep rediscovering what it already knows. That is why the discipline of data governance belongs at the heart of leadership education. It teaches leaders how to protect continuity in a world that forgets quickly.

I have written this chapter with the same range of readers in mind that the book is built to serve, because the lesson lands differently depending on where you sit. For the practicing CIO and the IT leader, the message is operational. Treat data governance as a leadership system, not a technical project, and measure its success by whether the organization argues less about basic truth over time. For the consultant, the message is diagnostic. When you assess a client, the number of meetings that quietly turn into debates about whose figure is correct will tell you more about the health of their operating model than any architecture diagram. And for the faculty member, the facilitator, and the graduate student, the message is conceptual. This is a chance to study memory as something a leader actively protects or carelessly loses, rather than something an organization simply has.

The leadership move in this chapter is practical and durable. Define truth clearly, standardize definitions, assign ownership, enforce governance, and make knowledge usable beyond the individual. That is how memory becomes institutional rather than personal.

The deepest lesson of this chapter is simple. Institutions do not become wiser merely by accumulating more information. They become wiser when they can preserve meaning, protect definitions, and carry what they have learned into future decisions without having to rediscover it each time. That is why I keep returning to data as memory rather than data as storage. Memory implies continuity. Memory implies stewardship. Memory implies that what the organization learned yesterday should still be usable tomorrow. In a time when information is abundant and attention is fragmented, that may be one of the most important leadership disciplines an enterprise can build.

When Memory Meets AI

Everything in this chapter becomes more urgent the moment an enterprise begins applying AI to its own information. AI does not bring its own understanding of the business. It works from whatever the organization has recorded, defined, and stored. That means it inherits the institution's memory, with all of its strengths and all of its gaps. If the memory is clear, governed, and consistent, AI can become a genuine accelerant, surfacing patterns and answers from a foundation the enterprise can trust. If the memory is fragmented, AI will reproduce the fragmentation, only faster and in more confident language. The tool does not repair weak memory. It scales whatever memory it is given.

This is why I told the board, in different words, that the readiness question for AI is really a readiness question for our data. A model asked to summarize performance will summarize whatever sources it can reach, including the inconsistent ones. A system asked to recommend an action will reason from definitions that may never have been agreed upon. The polish of the output can easily hide the weakness of the foundation underneath it, and a leader who has not protected that foundation will find it harder, not easier, to tell the difference. The discipline that protects institutional memory is the same discipline that makes AI trustworthy. They are not two separate programs. They are the same stewardship applied at different layers.

There is a hopeful version of this as well. An organization that has done the patient work of defining truth, assigning ownership, and governing its sources is unusually well positioned for this moment. It has already built the foundation that makes intelligent tools safe to use at scale. In that sense, the unglamorous work of the last several years, the data audits, the shared definitions, the reporting standards, the reduction of shadow systems, turns out to be the very thing that lets an enterprise adopt AI with confidence rather than anxiety. Memory built carefully in quiet times becomes an advantage exactly when the pace of decision-making accelerates.

Boardroom Perspective: Why Trusted Data Is a Leadership Asset

Boards rarely ask for better data in abstract terms. They ask for clearer decisions, stronger forecasting, fewer surprises, and more confidence in the institution's ability to explain itself. That is why trusted data should never be treated as an IT concern alone. It is a leadership asset. It shapes how quickly executives can act, how confidently risk can be discussed, and whether the enterprise can maintain a coherent story about performance across functions, regions, and time. When the board is hearing multiple versions of the truth from different parts of the organization, the issue is not reporting alone. The issue is institutional memory under stress.

A mature board should therefore ask questions that go deeper than dashboard aesthetics. Who owns the most important definitions in the business. What happens when a critical data owner leaves. How often are leaders still debating numbers instead of acting on them. Where does truth still depend too heavily on local files, legacy habits, or individual memory. These are governance questions because they determine whether the enterprise can keep learning or whether it will keep rediscovering the same problems with slightly better charts. Trusted information is not simply a reporting advantage. It is one of the quiet ways an institution proves that it knows how to remember.

From the CIO's Desk

One of the most practical leadership lessons of my career is that organizations become calmer when they stop arguing with their own memory. Meetings improve. Trust improves. Decision quality improves. Not because people suddenly become smarter, but because the institution no longer forces them to keep renegotiating what should already be known. I have seen the difference directly. When data is governed, defined, and trusted, teams spend less time defending numbers and more time improving outcomes. The atmosphere changes. The business feels steadier because the ground beneath the discussion stops shifting.

That is why I have come to see data stewardship as one of the most human parts of enterprise leadership. It respects people's time. It reduces unnecessary friction. It protects the future from having to rediscover what the past already learned through cost, effort, and experience. Good leaders do not only ask whether the dashboard works. They ask whether the institution can still explain itself clearly a year from now, after roles have changed, projects have moved on, and the people who once carried the context are no longer in the room. That, to me, is what it means for data to become institutional memory rather than personal memory wearing business language.

Five Leadership Rules for Protecting Institutional Memory

These are the rules I keep returning to. Like most principles worth keeping, they are easy to say and demanding to practice.

First, define truth before you scale access. Shared access without shared definitions only multiplies confusion. The instinct to give everyone a dashboard is understandable, but access without agreed meaning simply lets more people disagree more quickly. Define what the numbers mean first, then widen the door.

Second, make ownership explicit. The most important data in the business should never be ownerless. Every critical definition needs a name attached to it, a person who is responsible for keeping it accurate and answering for it when it is questioned. Ownerless data is memory waiting to decay, because no one is accountable for keeping it alive.

Third, preserve context, not just output. Reports and dashboards need traceable meaning, not only attractive presentation. A number without its context is an invitation to misread it. The enterprise should be able to explain not only what a figure is but why it is calculated that way and where it comes from, so the meaning travels with the metric.

Fourth, govern transitions as seriously as transactions. Knowledge is most often lost when people change roles, systems change hands, or the institution assumes memory will somehow transfer on its own. Build the handoff into the plan. Capture the context before the person leaves, name the next owner, and make sure the next person knows where to look.

Fifth, treat reporting discipline as a form of stewardship. When the organization can still explain its numbers clearly across time and functions, it is proving that it knows how to learn instead of merely react. Reporting discipline is not bureaucracy. It is the practice of keeping the institution's memory honest, so that what was learned at real cost is not quietly lost to convenience.

Leadership Lessons

- Data is institutional memory, not just storage, and memory is something leaders actively protect.
- When data becomes argument instead of memory, the enterprise pays twice for what it should have learned once.
- Clarity about what is true is a form of care, because it spares people the friction of defending the ground beneath them.

- Truth that depends on who is in the room is fragile memory wearing the appearance of productivity.
- Knowledge is lost most often in ordinary transitions, so transitions deserve as much discipline as transactions.
- Trusted data is the precondition for trusted AI, because intelligent tools scale whatever memory they are given.
- The clearest sign of healthy memory is a leadership room that argues less about basic truth over time.

Discussion Questions

- Why is fragmented data ultimately a leadership problem rather than only a reporting problem?
- How does institutional memory affect decision quality, speed, and accountability over time?
- What role should governance, ownership, and shared definitions play in establishing a single source of truth?
- Why does weak institutional memory become more dangerous, rather than less, once an organization begins adopting AI?
- As a consultant or adviser, what signals in a leadership meeting would tell you that an organization is negotiating truth rather than acting on it?
- If you were teaching this chapter as a case, what would you identify as the hidden cost of allowing organizational truth to remain negotiable?

Application for Practice

- For the practicing leader: choose one performance metric in your organization that is frequently discussed. Name who owns its definition, and assess how consistently it is interpreted across teams.

- For the IT leader: identify one place where people are still negotiating truth rather than working from shared understanding. Decide what specific governance action would reduce that ambiguity.
- For the consultant: review a client environment and list the three questions about data ownership and definitions you would ask before evaluating their reporting tools at all.
- For the faculty member or facilitator: design a short exercise in which students examine a disputed report and must identify whether the real problem is the data, the definition, or the ownership.
- For any reader: create a short action plan for strengthening one element of institutional memory in your environment, such as definitions, documentation, reporting standards, or decision traceability.
- For reflection: think of a meeting where numbers were debated rather than acted on. What did that reveal about ownership, standards, or trust, and how might better memory have changed the outcome?

Chapter 3: What CIOs Get Wrong About Speed

Opening

Speed is one of the most celebrated words in leadership. It is also one of the most misunderstood. Most organizations talk about speed in terms of activity: move faster, deliver sooner, increase output. This chapter challenges that instinct. Speed without sequence creates rework. Speed without governance creates instability. Speed without clarity creates a permanent state of escalation. Movement is not the same as progress, and motion without coherence eventually turns into drag. For CIOs, consultants, and graduate leadership programs alike, the deeper question is not whether the organization is busy. It is whether the organization is moving in a way that can still be trusted.

In my experience, leaders often ask for speed when what they really need is less ambiguity. They need fewer unresolved dependencies, fewer competing priorities, fewer half-made decisions, and fewer places where the organization is quietly improvising because no one has clarified the sequence. That is why I do not think of speed as a personality trait in leadership. I think of it as a design outcome. When the design is weak, urgency becomes noise. When the design is strong, the organization begins moving faster almost without talking about speed at all.

That distinction matters because speed has a human cost when leaders misuse it. Teams can survive hard pushes. They cannot live indefinitely inside a system that treats interruption as normal and sequencing as optional. Over time, that kind of environment erodes confidence, increases rework, and teaches people to protect themselves with local shortcuts. Leaders who understand this do not only ask how to go faster. They ask what kind of operating model would make sustainable speed possible without quietly exhausting the people carrying the work.

What often gets missed in these conversations is that urgency has a habit of hiding its own waste. A leader can feel responsive while quietly creating a trail of partial work, late-discovered conflicts, and exhausted teams who are still trying to look committed. The organization keeps moving, but the movement becomes more expensive than it appears. That is why I have learned to ask a different question when speed is on the table. Not only how quickly can this begin, but what will this do to the system that must still finish everything else already underway.

This is the third idea in a connected argument. The first chapter said that intelligent tools amplify whatever already exists. The second said that the enterprise has to protect its memory so there is something trustworthy to amplify. This chapter is about the tempo at which all of it moves. Stewardship is not only about what an organization knows and how accountable it is. It is also about whether the pace of change respects the people and the system carrying it. A leader can damage a healthy enterprise simply by asking it to move faster than it can move honestly. Designed speed is therefore a form of stewardship in motion, because it protects both the work and the people doing it from the quiet harm of urgency without order.

The Cost of Motion Without Sequence

One of the most common leadership mistakes I have seen is mistaking visible motion for actual progress. Teams get busier. Meetings multiply. More initiatives begin. More updates circulate. On the surface, it can look like a high-energy organization. But if the work has not been sequenced honestly, that energy eventually turns against the system. People begin solving around each other. Dependencies are discovered late. Priorities compete for the same capacity. And what looked like speed starts producing friction, fatigue, and avoidable rework. That is why sequence matters so much. It protects momentum from turning into waste.

I learned this lesson most clearly in turnaround environments. When an organization is struggling, the instinct is often to accelerate. Solve more. Launch more. Respond faster. But weak operating models do not become stronger through urgency alone. They become stronger when leaders decide what has to happen first, what must wait, and what the business can no longer afford to keep pretending is manageable. Real speed begins when the sequence becomes honest. That honesty is not bureaucratic. It is respectful. It gives teams a chance to finish meaningful work instead of living permanently inside interruption.

This is one reason I became wary of organizations that celebrate busyness too quickly. Output can be high while coherence remains low. Teams can produce updates, close tasks, and respond rapidly while the underlying system is still paying a hidden tax in context switching, dependency collisions, and incomplete decisions. From a distance, that can look like commitment. From inside the work, it often feels like drag. Sustainable speed begins the moment leaders become willing to distinguish what is merely moving from what is truly advancing.

This became especially visible once we began naming a familiar problem more directly: surprise work. Surprise work is not simply unplanned effort. It is work introduced late through informal decisions, missed coordination, or weak escalation discipline. It interrupts flow because the organization has not treated the change as a real decision with visible impact. In our own leadership conversations, this became an explicit issue. The answer was not heavier bureaucracy. It was lighter but clearer discipline. Capture what changed, why it changed, who owns it, and what it affects. That small amount of structure protects speed because it prevents teams from being asked to absorb quiet changes without the sequence ever being reset honestly.

Turnaround Work Changed My View of Speed

Turnaround work changed my view of speed because it forced me to separate urgency from progress. In a struggling environment, everything feels late, everything feels important, and every stakeholder can make a reasonable case for why their issue should move first. That atmosphere can easily trap leaders into thinking that the answer is simply to push harder. But once I had lived through enough inherited dysfunction, I realized that speed created under those conditions is often borrowed from the future. Teams absorb too much. Sequencing gets hidden under pressure. Dependencies are ignored until they become visible through failure. And what looked fast on a slide begins slowing the organization down in practice.

What began to matter more to me in those environments was not how quickly the organization could start things. It was how honestly it could finish them. That meant clarifying the sequence, reducing hidden work, building governance before adding more demand, and helping leaders understand that discipline was not delay. It was the only reliable path out of perpetual rework. Some of the most meaningful improvements I have seen in enterprise technology did not come from acceleration first. They came from restoring order, rebuilding confidence, and creating an operating rhythm strong enough to support real movement again.

That experience also changed the way I think about leadership pressure. In difficult environments, it is easy to lead with urgency because urgency feels strong. But the most useful leaders I have seen do something harder. They lead with purpose instead of pressure. They slow the room down enough for people to think clearly, tell the truth about trade-offs, and rebuild confidence through disciplined execution rather than through noise. In my experience, that is what gives teams the courage to keep moving without becoming chaotic.

Consulting sharpened this lesson for me because clients often wanted speed before the institution had earned the right to move that quickly. In ERP consulting, it was common to hear urgency described as strategy. But once you have seen enough projects struggle, you realize that urgency by itself is not an operating model. It is a pressure condition. The better question is whether the enterprise has enough shared understanding, governance, capacity, and decision discipline to move without quietly creating tomorrow's problems today. Later, in executive leadership, that same lesson became even more important because the boardroom often sees ambition first while teams below feel sequence first. A mature CIO learns to honor both realities without letting one destroy the other.

That became even clearer during the IT turnaround journey. Early conditions included weak governance, unclear roles, inconsistent standards, poor project performance, and teams carrying too much without enough structure. The answer was not simply to push harder. It was to reorganize the environment so execution could become credible again. I framed this plainly from the start: role clarity, enterprise prioritization, operational excellence, and governance were prerequisites for restoring trust. Later, PMO discipline and governance routines gave that structure operational teeth. The result was not theoretical. Project success moved from the mid-fifties to above ninety percent and later into the mid-nineties because the organization finally had a stronger sequence for how work should move.

What I appreciate now is that this was not only a turnaround in project metrics. It was a turnaround in how the organization thought about speed itself. Earlier conditions rewarded reaction. Later conditions began rewarding sequence. I watched that evolution happen clearly, as the work moved from basic control and discipline into optimization, decision clarity, demand management, and enterprise value delivery. That shift matters because mature speed does not come from asking teams to care more. It comes from giving them an environment where decision ownership, intake discipline, and trade-offs are visible enough that effort is not constantly being scattered.

The Week Everything Was Urgent

I remember one stretch of turnaround work when every conversation seemed to begin with the same word: urgent. A failing issue in one area was colliding with a delayed deliverable in another. A leader needed an answer for a meeting. A team needed support for work already behind. New requests were arriving faster than the existing backlog could stabilize. On paper, it looked like a period of high responsiveness. In reality, it was a system being pushed to solve too many things at once without enough agreed sequence to support the effort. People were working hard, but the work was no longer moving in a way that felt ordered.

What I learned from that week was that overload often masquerades as commitment in struggling environments. Leaders interpret visible effort as progress because they want to believe the team is meeting the moment. But effort without sequence eventually becomes its own source of drag. Questions get answered out of order. Dependencies surface too late. Teams begin protecting themselves with local shortcuts. The turning point did not come when people worked harder. It came when we were finally willing to say that not everything urgent could move at once and still be done well. That honesty created the first real sense of speed.

I came to see capacity protection as a form of respect. It respects the fact that people do their best work when the sequence is believable. It respects the reality that every new urgent request changes the quality of what is already underway. And it respects the business enough to tell the truth early rather than offering optimistic reassurance that will later be paid for through delay and rework. In high-pressure environments, that kind of honesty may sound slower in the moment. In practice, it is one of the few ways to create speed that the organization can actually sustain.

This is where demand management becomes more than a PMO practice. It becomes a leadership truth-telling practice. Demand almost always outpaces capacity in a growing enterprise. The question is whether leaders will acknowledge that reality early enough to protect execution quality. We later made this explicit. Demand visibility, prioritization, quarterly review, and capacity balancing were not side conversations. They were core to keeping the organization from confusing desire with readiness. Once leaders accept that every new request changes the shape of the system, prioritization becomes less political and more honest.

The Project Review No One Wanted to Hear

I remember a project review where the hardest thing I had to bring into the room was not a technical issue, but the truth about capacity. Everyone wanted progress. Everyone wanted improvement. And everyone had a reasonable explanation for why their initiative should keep moving. But the system underneath the ambition was stretched past what it could carry responsibly. Saying that out loud changed the temperature of the room immediately. No one likes hearing that effort alone will not be enough. But pretending otherwise would have created the kind of false momentum that looks productive for a few weeks and then unravels under the weight of its own unfinished work.

That review stayed with me because it reminded me that leadership sometimes means disappointing the room in order to protect the work. There are moments when the most responsible thing a leader can do is tell the truth about sequence before the organization pays for denial through delay, rework, and quiet exhaustion. In my experience, some of the best turning points in a struggling environment begin when someone is willing to say, with clarity and calm, this cannot all move at once and still be done well. That kind of honesty can feel unwelcome in the moment, but it is often the first real step toward speed that lasts.

This is exactly why mature leaders learn to separate strategic ambition from operational sequencing. Both matter, but they are not the same conversation. Strategy identifies what the business should become. Sequencing determines what the current system can carry responsibly on the way there. When leaders collapse those two conversations into one, teams pay the difference. They inherit timelines built from aspiration instead of readiness. Honest project reviews help prevent that. They force the organization to face the current condition of the system before it mortgages trust for the appearance of momentum.

What sharpened this lesson for me was the rise of what we eventually began calling surprise work. Surprise work is not simply unplanned effort. It is work introduced late through informal decisions, weak escalation, or stakeholder habits that bypass sequence and force teams to absorb change without enough warning. In our own governance work, this became one of the clearest pressure points because it looked small in the moment but carried a larger cost over time. It disrupted focus, weakened predictability, and made good teams feel slower than they really were. That is why I came to see sustainable speed as a leadership discipline. It is the protection of sequence before hidden interruptions turn motion into drag.

I also learned that sequencing becomes more credible when the organization is willing to compare actuals with estimates and value with activity. Otherwise, leaders can keep believing a portfolio is healthy simply because the updates are frequent. Maturing our project discipline changed that by focusing on throughput, predictability, and enterprise value rather than output alone. Re-baselining plans against actual effort, tightening escalation paths, and making trade-offs visible were all forms of respect for the truth of the system. They helped the business stop asking whether teams were busy enough and start asking whether the current sequence could still deliver what mattered.

Enterprise Case Study: Governance, Prioritization, and Designed Speed

This chapter lends itself naturally to a leadership case about the relationship between governance and speed. The transformation I led moved through a three-phase journey: reorganization, governance and culture, and strategic execution. That sequencing matters. It suggests that sustainable speed was not created by urgency alone, but by first clarifying roles, establishing communication rhythms, forming a steering committee, standardizing project management practices, and reinforcing performance accountability. The results were measurable. Project success rose above ninety percent, budget and scope performance strengthened, and stakeholder trust improved. Our governance reviews steadily added decision review, demand management discussion, metric refinement, and cross-functional accountability for what moves forward and why.

This is exactly the kind of case graduate programs can use to examine leadership trade-offs. Students can discuss when governance accelerates rather than delays, how prioritization protects execution capacity, and why clarity is a more durable form of speed than pressure. They can also test a deeper proposition: in mature organizations, speed is rarely the result of doing more. It is the result of reducing ambiguity early enough that the work does not need to be done twice.

I saw this reinforced repeatedly. We built the PMO around the idea that projects fail not only because of technical issues, but because of weak approval paths, poor demand visibility, limited resource planning, inconsistent governance, and the habit of letting urgent tasks continuously interrupt important work. Over time, the opposite pattern took hold: clearer demand management, executive review, resource allocation, quarterly progress reviews, and stronger project delivery metrics. That is why I describe governance as designed speed. It reduces the energy the organization wastes discovering too late what should have been clarified earlier.

Financial discipline reinforces the same lesson. Some of the most mature signals I tracked were not only project metrics, but the willingness to defer non-critical work, retime spend, and protect the core operating model rather than pretending every initiative should launch now. That is another form of speed design. It keeps the organization from overcommitting financially and operationally at the same time. In that sense, designed speed is not only a PMO concept. It is also a stewardship concept. Leaders protect future execution when they are disciplined enough to hold some work back until the system is truly ready to carry it.

What Changed When Governance Became Normal

There is a point in every transformation when governance stops feeling like a separate exercise and starts feeling normal. That shift is more important than many leaders realize. In the beginning, governance can feel formal, even intrusive, especially in environments used to moving by instinct or personality. But when it is designed well, it eventually fades into the operating rhythm of the business. Decisions become clearer. Escalations become more meaningful. Prioritization becomes easier to explain. Teams begin to trust the sequence because they can see why it exists. That is when governance stops being perceived as drag and starts being experienced as support.

In my experience, that normalization is one of the strongest indicators that the operating model is maturing. People no longer need to be persuaded that priorities must be visible. They no longer treat demand management as resistance. They no longer assume every new request deserves immediate execution. Instead, they begin to understand that governance protects execution quality, team health, and the credibility of leadership itself. When that understanding takes hold, the enterprise moves faster without feeling more chaotic. That is the kind of speed worth building.

When governance becomes normal in that way, something else improves besides delivery. Team health improves. Trust improves. Leaders spend less time rescuing work from preventable collisions and more time helping the business think clearly about what comes next. The emotional temperature of execution changes. The organization becomes less reactive, less theatrical, and more capable of carrying pressure without turning every difficult season into chaos. That is one reason I believe designed speed is an act of stewardship. It protects both the work and the people doing it.

When Speed Meets AI

The arrival of AI raises the stakes of everything in this chapter, because AI lowers the cost of starting almost to zero. It can generate a plan, a draft, an analysis, or a proposal in moments. That sounds like pure acceleration, and in a disciplined environment it can be. But in an environment that already confuses motion with progress, AI becomes an engine for producing even more things to start, more options to consider, and more polished proposals competing for the same limited capacity to finish. The bottleneck in most enterprises was never the ability to begin work. It was the ability to sequence and complete it. AI does not relieve that bottleneck. It pushes harder against it.

I have come to think of this as the difference between generation and completion. AI is extraordinary at generation. It is indifferent to completion, because completion depends on human capacity, governance, and the discipline to finish one thing before starting the next. A leader who hands a team faster generation without strengthening their ability to sequence and absorb is not giving them speed. They are giving them more surprise work, arriving faster and dressed more convincingly. The same demand discipline that protected execution before AI is what will protect it now, except that the volume of plausible-looking initiatives will be higher and the temptation to launch them all will be stronger.

There is a healthier version of this as well. An organization that has already built designed speed, with honest sequencing, visible capacity, and governed intake, is unusually well positioned to use AI as a genuine accelerant. It can let the tool generate freely while the operating model decides calmly what actually moves. In that environment, AI compresses the early work of thinking without disturbing the discipline of finishing. The lesson holds exactly as it did before. Real speed is not created by producing more. It is created by reducing ambiguity early enough that the work, however it is generated, only needs to be done once.

Why This Chapter Matters

For students, faculty, and practicing executives, this chapter offers a practical reframing of speed. Speed is not mainly an acceleration problem. It is a sequencing problem, a governance problem, and often a courage problem. It asks whether leaders are willing to tell the truth about capacity, dependencies, and readiness before the organization pays for denial through wasted motion. The deeper lesson is simple. Sustainable speed is not created by urgency alone. It is created when leaders reduce ambiguity early enough that people can move with confidence, finish meaningful work, and trust that the operating model will not quietly betray their effort.

The lesson lands differently depending on where the reader sits. For the practicing CIO and the IT leader, the message is operational. Treat sequencing, capacity, and demand management as the real levers of speed, and be willing to disappoint a room in order to protect the system. For the consultant, the message is diagnostic. When a client asks how fast they can move, the more useful read comes from how honestly they sequence work and how much surprise work their teams are quietly absorbing. And for the faculty member and the graduate student, the message is conceptual. This is a chance to study speed as a property of the operating model rather than a trait of energetic leaders, and to examine why governance, properly designed, accelerates rather than delays.

The leadership move here is straightforward. Decide clearly, sequence honestly, protect focus, and remove ambiguity early. Real speed is not about doing more. It is about doing the right things once, in the right order, with enough clarity that the work does not need to be done again.

Boardroom Perspective: Why Sustainable Speed Starts with Governance

Boards often ask a fair question: how quickly can the organization move. Mature CIOs learn to answer that question with a better one close behind: how well can the organization move at that pace without weakening execution, trust, or resilience. That distinction matters because speed without control is not acceleration. It is borrowed confidence. It can make the enterprise look more responsive for a season while quietly increasing rework, changing priorities midstream, and asking teams to absorb more ambiguity than the operating model was built to carry. Boards should therefore care not only about how fast a roadmap appears to advance, but about whether governance is strong enough to keep movement from becoming instability.

In practical terms, boards should ask where overload is hiding, where work is being approved faster than it can be absorbed, and where teams are still relying on effort to compensate for weak sequencing. They should ask whether the organization is getting faster at finishing meaningful work or simply faster at starting more work than it can close. They should ask whether prioritization is clear enough that trade-offs are visible before commitments are made, rather than after disappointment begins to surface. Those are not project management questions alone.

They are enterprise stewardship questions, because they determine whether speed is strengthening the institution or quietly exhausting it.

From the CIO's Desk

One of the clearest lessons of my career is that organizations rarely fail because people do not care enough. More often, they struggle because leaders ask committed people to carry too much ambiguity at once. In those moments, speed becomes a kind of pressure language. Everyone says yes. Work starts everywhere. Energy rises. But the system underneath the work is still weak, and weak systems turn urgency into drag surprisingly quickly. That is why I no longer admire movement by itself. I admire sequence, finishing power, and the kind of governance that allows teams to keep their confidence because the work around them still makes sense.

If I had to summarize my own view simply, it would be this. Speed is earned through clarity, not demanded through urgency. Teams move well when they can trust the sequence, understand what matters now, and believe that current commitments will not be quietly weakened by every new request that sounds important. Designed speed matters so much to me for exactly that reason. It protects people from avoidable overload, protects the business from false momentum, and protects leadership credibility by making sure promises are made inside an operating model strong enough to keep them.

Five Leadership Rules for Sustainable Speed

These are the rules I keep returning to. Like most rules worth holding, they are easy to state and demanding to live.

First, sequence before you accelerate. Starting more work is easy. Protecting the order in which meaningful work can actually finish is harder and far more valuable. A clear sequence is what turns effort into progress instead of collisions.

Second, make capacity visible. Speed becomes believable when teams are not expected to absorb unlimited demand through effort alone. When capacity is visible, prioritization becomes an honest conversation rather than a hidden negotiation that surfaces only when something slips.

Third, govern surprise work aggressively. Unplanned requests, late changes, and quiet interruptions create hidden drag long before they appear in delivery metrics. Treat every late change as a real decision with a visible owner and a visible impact, not as a small favor the team can simply absorb.

Fourth, measure completion rather than motion. Organizations often confuse activity with progress because motion is easier to see than finished value. Track what the enterprise actually finishes and the value it produces, not how busy the calendar looks.

Fifth, protect trust while you pursue pace. Sustainable speed strengthens confidence because commitments still mean something after the meeting ends. When people learn that a promise made under pressure will be honored rather than quietly weakened, they move faster because they trust the system around them.

Leadership Lessons

- Motion is not progress, and the difference is usually a question of sequence.
- Speed is a design outcome of the operating model, not a personality trait of energetic leaders.
- Urgency hides its own waste, so a leader can feel responsive while quietly creating rework.

- Surprise work is one of the largest sources of hidden drag, and it deserves real governance.
- Telling the truth about capacity is a form of respect, even when it disappoints the room.
- Governance, designed well, eventually feels normal, and that normalization is a sign of maturity.
- AI accelerates generation but not completion, so disciplined sequencing matters more, not less.

Discussion Questions

- Why do leaders often confuse urgency, activity, and speed, and what damage does that confusion create?
- How did sequencing, governance, and prioritization create designed speed in the enterprise case study for this chapter?
- What are the trade-offs between moving quickly with ambiguity and moving deliberately with clarity?
- How can leaders tell whether their organization is progressing faster or simply generating more motion?
- Why might AI make the discipline of sequencing more important rather than less, even as it makes starting work easier?
- As a consultant or adviser, what signals would tell you that a client is generating more work than its operating model can responsibly finish?

Application for Practice

- For the practicing leader: list the top five active priorities in your organization. Decide whether they are sequenced honestly, or whether teams are being asked to carry too much ambiguity at once.

- For the IT leader: identify one area where activity is high but progress feels slow. Determine what part of the issue is really about sequence, governance, or clarity rather than effort.
- For the consultant: review how new work enters a client environment. Identify which decisions are made early enough and which are delayed until rework becomes likely.
- For the faculty member or facilitator: design a short exercise in which students must decide what to defer in an overloaded portfolio, and then defend the sequence they chose.
- For any reader: design one governance improvement that would help your team move faster by reducing confusion before work begins.
- For reflection: think of a time you pushed for speed and created rework instead. What sequencing truth, told earlier, would have changed the outcome?

Chapter 4: The CIO as Enterprise Integrator

Opening

When most people think about a CIO, they think about systems, security, and projects. That is part of the role, but it is not the whole role. The real work is integration. The CIO connects technology, people, process, risk, and strategy into a single operating model that allows the business to move as one enterprise. Without that integration, organizations do not move together. They move in parallel, and parallel motion is not the same as alignment. That is why this chapter matters for practicing CIOs, technology leaders, consultants, and graduate leadership programs alike. The more complex the enterprise becomes, the more valuable integration becomes as a leadership discipline.

That larger view of the role was shaped over time, not all at once. My own path into enterprise integration did not begin with a CIO title. It began during the Y2K era, when I shifted from accounting into ERP work and started seeing how finance, operations, process, and systems all converged in the real life of a business. Later, I learned another hard lesson when outsourcing moved work offshore and I experienced the shock of seeing roles disappear and eventually being laid off. That season changed me. It taught me that enterprise systems are never only technical. They are tied to people's livelihoods, to organizational trust, and to how leaders navigate change when the cost is no longer theoretical. From there, global ERP implementations, consulting work, automotive environments, coatings, internationally funded development projects, ERP leadership, and cross-border travel all deepened the same lesson. The CIO's greatest value is often helping the enterprise understand itself across boundaries it would otherwise keep experiencing as separate worlds.

That lesson kept repeating across the arc of my career. At a global electronics components manufacturer, when IT work moved offshore and I experienced my first and only layoff, I learned how global operating decisions can change the meaning of leadership overnight. At a large coatings company, I was introduced to an industrial world where product, process, and operations had to align with equal seriousness. Through global consulting and broader ERP implementation work, I saw how consulting can teach pattern recognition across businesses while still demanding humility in each local context. International development project management taught me something even deeper. Culture matters, and leadership that works in one environment can fail quickly if it ignores how people experience authority, timing, and trust somewhere else. Later, through ERP work in Canada, major ERP consulting, and finally as CIO of a global automotive and industrial coatings company, the picture came full circle. The role was no longer simply to implement technology. It was to hold the enterprise together well enough that strategy, systems, people, and execution could finally reinforce one another instead of colliding.

What makes that arc meaningful to me is not simply that it spans many industries and roles. It is that each chapter added another layer to my understanding of integration. The electronics manufacturer taught me that enterprise decisions can reshape people's lives very quickly. Consulting taught me how to read patterns across organizations without assuming that every answer travels unchanged. The coatings world taught me that industrial reality has a rhythm of its own and that process discipline is not the enemy of innovation. International development work taught me to respect culture, patience, and local context when leading change across borders. By the time I reached my current role, the responsibility felt both broader and clearer. The role was to help strategy, systems, people, and execution reinforce one another in a business that needed coherence more than noise. In that sense, it really did come full circle.

Integration Is Translation Before It Is Technology

Over time, I came to see that integration is translation before it is technology. Finance, operations, HR, quality, and executive leadership can all be telling the truth at the same time from their own vantage point. The CIO has to help those truths belong to one enterprise instead of becoming separate realities. That is why integration is not only about connecting applications. It is about connecting meaning, timing, ownership, and consequence. When that work is done well, the business feels less fragmented even before every platform is fully aligned. When it is done poorly, the organization can look digitally connected while still behaving like disconnected departments sharing the same logo.

That lesson became especially practical in environments where ERP, HRIS, MES, BI, Data-Lake, service operations, and communications all had to move together across sites and borders. The challenge was never simply to launch a platform. The challenge was to help the enterprise absorb change as one system of work. That same point held across every part of the work. Cross functional progress became stronger when leaders made dependencies visible, aligned business readiness with technical readiness, and treated integration as an operating-model discipline rather than a tool-by-tool exercise. In that kind of environment, the CIO becomes one of the few leaders responsible for helping the business experience multiple changes as one more coherent enterprise becoming possible.

My Job Stopped Being About Systems Alone

There was a point in my own leadership journey when I realized my job had stopped being primarily about systems. That did not mean systems mattered less. If anything, they mattered more. But the center of gravity had shifted. The real challenge was no longer choosing technology in isolation. It was helping different parts of the business move together with less friction, less duplication, and more shared understanding. Finance was asking one question. Operations was feeling another pressure. HR had its own sequence, timing, and implications. The CIO role became more than technical stewardship. It became enterprise translation.

That is one reason I describe the CIO as an integrator. Integration is not only about connecting applications. It is about helping the enterprise understand its own interdependence. It is helping one function see the downstream consequence of another function's decision. It is making sure a platform choice, a process change, a reporting standard, or a governance decision still makes sense once it reaches the plant, the boardroom, the service desk, and the finance review. In real organizations, that kind of integration does not happen automatically. It is built through credibility, communication, and disciplined follow-through.

The longer I worked across these environments, the more I realized that integration is rarely won by architecture alone. It is won when people begin trusting that the change makes sense beyond their own function. That trust grows when leaders can explain not only what is changing, but why the change helps the wider enterprise hold together more intelligently than before. In my experience, that is where the integrator earns credibility. Not by sounding technical, but by making complexity feel more understandable and more shared.

From the Shop Floor to the Boardroom

One of the most valuable lessons I learned in leadership was that credibility has to travel across levels. It is not enough to speak well in the boardroom if the shop floor experiences the system as friction. It is not enough to solve a local operational problem if the executive team still cannot see the enterprise implication clearly. The CIO sits in the middle of those worlds and has to move between them without sounding abstract in one direction or too narrow in the other. That kind of translation takes more than technical knowledge. It takes listening, context, and the discipline to respect the reality of both the people doing the work and the leaders responsible for the larger enterprise.

I have always valued that part of the role. Some leaders are most comfortable at one level of the organization. My own experience taught me to pay attention to all of them. The executive suite needs clarity, discipline, and strategic framing. Plant operations need stability, practicality, and systems that respect the tempo of real work. Middle managers need sequence, decision support, and enough visibility to align their teams. When those levels stop understanding one another, technology becomes a point of tension instead of a source of coherence. But when the CIO can help connect them, integration becomes something the business can actually feel.

Language matters a great deal in that work. The boardroom usually needs synthesis, pattern, and implication. The plant needs clarity, practicality, and confidence that the system will not make the shift harder than it already is. The same initiative has to be described in ways that are faithful to both realities. If the language is too abstract, operations feels unseen. If it is too local, leadership loses the enterprise picture. The integrator learns to move between those levels without distorting either one. That is one of the quiet disciplines of the CIO role, and one of the reasons trust across levels matters so much.

That cross-level work also taught me something simple but important. Leadership is not climbing. It is carrying. It is carrying lessons from one level of the organization into another, carrying respect for people regardless of title, and carrying enough humility to keep learning from places others might overlook. Some of the best process insight I have ever received came far from the executive table. That is one reason I hold titles lightly. The enterprise becomes stronger when leaders learn to treat people at every level as builders of the future, not just participants in someone else's plan.

I came to see that cross-level credibility as one of the quiet tests of enterprise leadership. If the board believes the strategy but the plant experiences the system as disruption, integration is still incomplete. If a plant likes the local tool but leadership cannot see the enterprise implications, integration is still incomplete. Real integration happens when the language of the boardroom, the realities of the plant, and the rhythm of middle management begin reinforcing one another instead of competing for legitimacy. That kind of coherence takes more than authority. It takes trust built across levels over time.

When the Plant and the Executive Team Needed Different Things

One of the clearest expressions of the CIO role comes when two parts of the enterprise need something different at the same time and both are right from where they sit. I remember situations where the executive team needed clarity on timing, risk, and strategic implication while the plant needed something simpler and more immediate, a system that worked at the pace of operations without forcing people into unnecessary friction. Both perspectives mattered. The challenge was not choosing one over the other. It was helping each side understand the legitimate reality of the other without letting the conversation collapse into abstraction on one side or urgency on the other.

That kind of moment taught me that integration often depends on timing as much as logic. The boardroom wants signal. The shop floor wants usability. Middle management wants enough clarity to coordinate work without carrying avoidable confusion. If a leader speaks only one of those languages, somebody will feel unseen. But when the CIO can help the organization hear all three without losing the thread of the enterprise, people begin to trust that the work is being led from a place larger than one function's immediate concern. That is when integration becomes credible enough to hold.

Pacing becomes part of integration because different parts of the enterprise can absorb change at different speeds. The executive team may be ready for the broad strategic arc while the plant is still asking practical questions about workflow, cutover, and support. HR may need to communicate earlier to reduce anxiety while operations may need to see the process functioning before belief settles in. The CIO cannot simply broadcast one message and hope alignment appears. The role requires sequencing understanding as carefully as sequencing technology. That is what helps the enterprise move together rather than merely change at the same time.

That is also why empathy belongs in enterprise integration more than many executives realize. Integration does not ask leaders to flatten the differences between functions. It asks them to respect those differences without allowing the enterprise to fracture around them. Timing becomes part of that discipline. Sometimes the executive team needs the broad pattern before the plant is ready for the details. Sometimes the plant needs clarity and reassurance before leadership is ready to discuss the longer arc. The integrator has to know how to move that sequence well enough that each part of the enterprise receives what it needs without losing sight of the larger whole.

Enterprise Case Study: Integration Through Separation, Platform Strategy, and Shared Execution

A particularly strong case for leadership education in this chapter is the way enterprise integration was built across both separation work and platform modernization. In my own enterprise, multiple threads ran at once: a major ERP separation completed with stable operations, validated manufacturing execution after go-live, a business separation executed with no disruption, a stable manufacturing time-entry launch, a payroll stabilization period completed successfully, and foundational work for further expansion underway. The wider architecture around those moments treated ERP, MES, HRIS, BI, QMS, CMMS, intranet, AI, and governance all as parts of one operating model rather than disconnected projects.

That makes this a rich graduate-level case about enterprise integration, not just systems integration. Students can explore how a CIO helps multiple functions move together during periods of high change, how governance and communication support cross-border execution, and how platform decisions connect to culture, credibility, and strategic alignment. The deeper lesson is that integration is not a technical endpoint. It is a leadership discipline that allows the business to operate as one enterprise even while it is changing underneath.

The cross-border dimension makes this even more instructive. Stable execution across manufacturing, payroll, HRIS, and ERP workstreams requires more than project management. It requires a common operating language strong enough to travel across regions, time zones, local plant realities, and different functional incentives without losing coherence. In our own work, that meant the business could experience HRIS stability in one region, ERP readiness in another, manufacturing time-entry stability on the plant floor, and separation execution across the organization as parts of one leadership system rather than unrelated successes. That kind of coherence is one of the clearest signs that enterprise integration is becoming real.

I saw this in a concrete way. In the same operating environment, an ERP separation went live with stable operations across plants, manufacturing execution stations were validated after go-live, manufacturing time entry launched with no process disruption, and HRIS in one region concluded its stabilization period with stable payroll and system performance. These are not just technical milestones. They show what enterprise integration looks like when process, data, training, governance, and execution are aligned well enough that the business does not have to feel every internal seam. They also show why the CIO role is larger than a platform role. Someone has to hold the operating model together while multiple functions are changing at the same time.

What Integration Looked Like Across Borders, Plants, and Functions

A fuller view of the work shows that integration was not happening in one lane at a time. ERP separation, HRIS readiness, manufacturing stabilization, BI and Data-Lake integration, business applications governance, service model maturity, and executive steering all had to move in a way the business could still trust. That is what makes this chapter stronger for graduate leadership programs and executive education. It shows that integration is not simply technical architecture. It is the discipline of aligning business rhythm, communication rhythm, and execution rhythm so that multiple changes do not fracture the enterprise into isolated workstreams. Every part of the work pointed to the same deeper lesson. Integration becomes real when leadership reduces seams before the business has to feel them.

What made this work believable was not only technical coordination. It was the way the enterprise began to feel more coherent in practice. Plants experienced steadier operations. Leaders had clearer visibility into trade-offs. Functional teams could see more easily how their decisions affected the rest of the system. In my experience, that is when integration stops sounding like an architecture term and starts becoming a lived leadership reality.

In practice, integration rarely arrives as one dramatic moment. It shows up in the quieter work of making complexity more coherent across time. It looks like ERP decisions that still support operations once the plant is live. It looks like HRIS rollouts that respect local realities while still strengthening enterprise consistency. It looks like cross-border programs where technology, process, governance, payroll, quality, analytics, and communication all have to land together without the business feeling every seam. Those are not separate leadership acts. They are all expressions of integration.

That is also why integration demands more than formal authority. People do not align simply because a governance chart says they should. They align when they trust that the work has been thought through, that the trade-offs are visible, and that the leader can connect local pain points to enterprise priorities without dismissing either one. In my experience, the real power of integration is not that it makes the enterprise look organized. It is that it allows the enterprise to keep changing without tearing itself apart every time something important moves.

When Integration Meets AI

AI is about to test enterprise integration more severely than any platform before it, because AI does not respect functional boundaries and it does not wait for the operating model to be ready. A model can reach across finance, operations, HR, and quality data in a single query. It can produce an answer that spans the whole enterprise instantly, whether or not the enterprise has actually agreed on how those functions connect. That is both the promise and the danger. Where integration is real, AI can make the enterprise feel even more coherent, surfacing connections people had not seen. Where integration is only cosmetic, AI will expose the seams quickly, because it will confidently combine information from functions that never truly reconciled their definitions, their ownership, or their meaning.

This is why I have come to see integration as a precondition for using AI well, not a nice-to-have alongside it. An AI tool reasoning over a fragmented enterprise will produce fragmented conclusions wrapped in fluent language. It will treat a finance definition and an operations definition as interchangeable when they are not. It will assume a process is connected when it is only adjacent. The integrator's work, reconciling meaning, ownership, timing, and consequence across functions, is exactly the work that determines whether AI becomes a source of enterprise clarity or a faster way to act on hidden contradictions. The tool does not integrate the business. It assumes the business is already integrated, and it will reveal the truth either way.

The encouraging side is that the integration discipline a CIO builds in quieter times becomes an unusual advantage in this moment. An enterprise whose functions already share a coherent operating language, whose data already reconciles across boundaries, and whose leaders already understand their interdependence is an enterprise that can let AI work across the whole organization with confidence. The patient work of reducing seams turns out to be the very thing that makes intelligent tools safe to use at enterprise scale. Integration was always about helping the business act as one. AI simply raises the reward for having done that work and the cost of having skipped it.

Why This Chapter Matters

For students, faculty, and practicing executives, the central insight of this chapter is that integration is one of the purest tests of enterprise leadership. It asks whether a leader can reduce fragmentation without flattening complexity, create coherence without oversimplifying reality, and help multiple parts of the business move together without forcing them into artificial sameness. The CIO sits in that tension constantly. At its best, the role becomes a form of stewardship that helps the institution think more clearly, align more honestly, and change with less internal friction than it otherwise could.

The lesson reads differently depending on the reader's seat. For the practicing CIO and the IT leader, the message is operational. Treat integration as an operating-model discipline rather than a sequence of platform projects, and earn it through credibility and translation rather than authority. For the consultant, the message is diagnostic. When a client looks technologically modern but still feels fragmented, the seams between functions, not the architecture, are usually where the real work lives. And for the faculty member and the graduate student, the message is conceptual. This is a chance to study enterprise integration as distinct from systems integration, and to examine how a leader holds an organization coherent while it changes underneath.

The leadership move in this chapter is practical and durable. Connect people before connecting systems. Align priorities before launching execution. Define one version of truth. And translate local issues into enterprise impact. That is integration in practice, and it is one of the most important responsibilities of the CIO.

Boardroom Perspective: Integration as a Business Leadership Responsibility

Boards often speak about growth, resilience, customer experience, and operating performance as if they are separate executive topics. In practice, they are deeply connected through integration. The quality of the customer experience depends on how well systems, process, people, and information move together. The quality of risk oversight depends on whether one part of the organization can still see the consequence of decisions being made elsewhere. That is why the CIO's role in the boardroom is not simply to report on technology. It is to help leadership see whether the enterprise is functioning as one institution or as multiple well-intentioned fragments sharing the same brand.

A mature board should therefore ask questions that surface seams before those seams become costs. Where are decisions still being optimized locally but hurting the enterprise globally. Where do data, process, or accountability break as work crosses functions or regions. What dependencies are still invisible until a project reaches the point of friction. These are not only operational questions. They are institutional questions, because enterprise fragmentation eventually becomes a business performance issue whether leaders describe it in those terms or not.

That is why boards should care not only about whether systems connect, but about whether functions, regions, and leaders can still act from one coherent understanding of the enterprise. Integration is what turns separate initiatives into institutional capability. Without it, the organization remains busy but divided. With it, strategy, operations, people, and systems begin reinforcing one another in ways the business can actually feel.

From the CIO's Desk

One of the quiet truths of the CIO role is that integration often succeeds without drawing much attention to itself. People simply experience less friction. Reports align more easily. Systems feel less separate. Handoffs become smoother. What many leaders call transformation is often, at its best, the steady reduction of internal fragmentation. I have come to value that deeply because the enterprise rarely suffers from lack of effort alone. It more often suffers from lack of connection. Different teams are working hard, but not always in a way that still lets the organization move together. That is why integration matters so much to me. It protects the enterprise from becoming increasingly divided by its own complexity.

If I had to summarize my own view simply, it would be this. Integration is one of the clearest ways a leader makes an institution easier to trust. It reduces the amount of translation people must do just to understand one another. It shortens the distance between strategic intent and operational reality. And it helps future change land in an environment that is more coherent than the one that came before it. The CIO, in other words, cannot remain only a systems leader. The role keeps growing into enterprise stewardship because the business increasingly depends on someone being able to hold the whole pattern together.

Five Leadership Rules for Enterprise Integration

These are the rules I keep returning to. They are simple to name and demanding to practice, which is usually the sign of a principle worth keeping.

First, connect priorities before connecting platforms. Technology cannot unify an enterprise that still has conflicting assumptions about what matters most. Alignment on priorities is the foundation that makes integration of systems meaningful rather than cosmetic.

Second, make seams visible. Integration begins when leaders are willing to identify where process, data, or ownership still break as work crosses boundaries. You cannot reduce a seam you refuse to name, and the seams the business hides are the ones that become costs later.

Third, translate constantly. Strong integrators help finance, operations, HR, quality, and executive leadership understand one another without flattening their real differences. Translation is not a one-time briefing. It is the ongoing work of keeping different functions acting from one shared understanding.

Fourth, standardize what should no longer vary. Variation should earn its place. Otherwise it quietly becomes cost. The discipline is to protect the local differences that genuinely matter while retiring the ones that survive only out of habit.

Fifth, protect coherence as the business grows. The enterprise becomes stronger when change makes the organization feel more connected, not merely more digital. Every new initiative should leave the business more coherent than it found it, or the complexity will eventually outpace the leadership holding it together.

Leadership Lessons

- The CIO's deepest work is integration, which is translation before it is technology.
- Parallel motion is not alignment, and an enterprise can look connected while behaving like separate departments.
- Credibility has to travel across levels, from the shop floor to the boardroom, or integration stays incomplete.
- Leadership is not climbing, it is carrying, and the best process insight often comes far from the executive table.
- Integration is won through trust and visible trade-offs, not through a governance chart that says people should align.
- AI assumes the enterprise is already integrated, so it rewards real coherence and exposes the cosmetic kind.
- The quiet reduction of fragmentation is one of the clearest ways a leader makes an institution easier to trust.

Discussion Questions

- What is the difference between systems integration and enterprise integration, and why does that difference matter for senior leadership?
- In the enterprise case study for this chapter, how did separation work, platform strategy, and governance combine to support stable execution?
- Why does integration require credibility across functions rather than formal authority alone?
- If an organization appears technologically modern but still experiences friction, what evidence would suggest that true integration has not yet been achieved?
- Why might AI expose weak integration faster than earlier technologies, and what does that imply for how leaders prepare?

- As a consultant, how would you assess whether functions in a client organization truly share one operating language, beyond what the architecture diagram shows?

Application for Practice

- For the practicing leader: identify one initiative in your organization that crosses functions. Name the integration risks that exist beyond the technology itself.
- For the IT leader: review a recent decision that solved one department's problem but created friction elsewhere. Determine what stronger enterprise integration would have required.
- For the consultant: map the major systems, processes, and stakeholders involved in one cross-functional workflow in a client environment, and mark where the seams are most visible to the business.
- For the faculty member or facilitator: design a short exercise in which students must reconcile two functions that define the same metric differently and decide how a CIO would resolve it.
- For any reader: write a short reflection on where your role currently requires translation across functions, and what would help you build more credibility as an integrator.
- For reflection: think of a time when a technically successful project still left the business feeling fragmented. What seam was never actually closed?

Chapter 5: Why Digital Transformation Fails Quietly

Opening

Most transformations do not fail in a dramatic way. They fail quietly. Systems go live. Projects close. Initial excitement fades. And then, slowly, behavior returns to what it was before. That is where transformation begins to weaken, not because the technology failed, but because the operating habits around it never really changed. For CIOs, IT leaders, consultants, and graduate leadership programs alike, that is the more important lesson. Transformation is not proven at launch. It is proven when the new environment begins carrying ordinary work without the organization quietly protecting itself with the old one.

Quiet failure is dangerous precisely because it does not interrupt the calendar right away. The steering committee still meets. The dashboard still updates. The milestone still appears complete. Leadership can point to real activity and still miss the deeper truth that the organization has not yet crossed the behavioral threshold that makes the change durable. In that kind of environment, transformation becomes something the business can describe without yet being able to fully live. That is why I have learned to look beyond deployment status and ask a harder question: what has actually become normal in the daily life of the enterprise.

This chapter sits naturally alongside the ones before it. The first three argued that intelligent tools amplify what exists, that the enterprise must protect its memory, and that speed has to be designed rather than demanded. This chapter is about what happens after the change is supposedly done. It is about the gap between a system being available and a system being trusted, and about the patient stewardship required to close that gap. Quiet failure is what stewardship is meant to prevent. It is the slow leak of a change that was declared finished before the people carrying the work had actually decided to rely on it. Understanding why transformation fails quietly is, in the end, understanding why trust transfers slowly even when technology moves fast.

When Transformation Looks Busy but Stays the Same

Over the years, I have learned to be careful around the language of transformation because organizations can sound transformed long before they actually behave differently. New platforms create energy. Dashboards create visibility. Go lives create momentum. Executive updates create the impression that something significant has happened. But I have also seen environments where the language changed much faster than the operating habits did. That lesson stayed with me across very different chapters of my career, from the Y2K era when I moved from accounting into ERP work and first saw how systems reshape business process, to global ERP consulting and implementation work, to internationally funded development project environments where change had to respect culture as much as timeline, to manufacturing, coatings, automotive, and finally enterprise leadership as CIO. The pattern was consistent. Technology can move quickly. Human confidence, operating trust, and habit change move more slowly. Mature leaders learn to lead both.

That understanding was shaped not only by projects that succeeded, but also by the harder seasons that exposed what change really costs. The outsourcing period and my first and only layoff at a global electronics components manufacturer taught me that transformation is never only about systems. It touches identity, livelihoods, and the trust people place in leadership during periods of uncertainty. Global consulting and wider ERP implementation work taught me how easily organizations can confuse new architecture with real operating change. The coatings world introduced me to another industrial reality where process, product, and execution had to align tightly. International development project work added another layer by teaching me that culture can either strengthen transformation or quietly resist it if leaders fail to respect how people experience authority, timing, and change. By the time I reached my current role as CIO, those lessons had come full circle. I no longer saw transformation mainly as deployment. I saw it as the disciplined transfer of trust from the old world into the new one.

I want to be clear that this is not an argument against ambition or against moving quickly. New platforms genuinely matter, and the energy around a launch is not a problem to be suppressed. The point is narrower and, in my experience, more useful. The visible signals of transformation arrive early and the durable ones arrive late, and a leader who reads only the early signals will consistently overestimate how much has actually changed. Holding both timelines in view at once, the fast technical one and the slower human one, is one of the quiet disciplines that separates leaders who declare transformation from leaders who actually achieve it.

What I Learned About Trust After Go Live

One of the most practical lessons I learned in enterprise transformation is that trust is often tested after the project team has already declared success. During implementation, people pay attention because they know change is happening. Support is visible. Decisions are elevated. Leadership is engaged. But after go live, the organization begins asking a quieter question. Can I rely on this tomorrow when no one is standing next to me. That is when trust either settles into the system or slips back toward workaround behavior. If the answer is yes, adoption grows. If the answer is not yet, the old process begins returning one small exception at a time.

That is why I believe transformation leaders must stay close to behavior after the visible milestone has passed. They need to ask what people are still doing outside the official process, what they still do not trust, what still feels slower than it should, and where the organization is quietly carrying two systems instead of one. Those are not small questions. They are the real indicators of whether the transformation has taken root. Go live proves that something can run. Trust proves that people are willing to let it carry the work.

I have also learned that hypercare matters more than many leaders assume. Hypercare is not only a support window. It is a trust-building window. It shows whether leadership will stay close enough to the business after launch to make the new process feel reliable under real conditions. Stable support for payroll, manufacturing time entry, and major process transitions mattered because it gave users evidence, not slogans. It showed that the organization was serious about making the new environment work well enough that people could finally stop holding onto the old one for safety.

I learned to respect that trust window because I had seen too many organizations celebrate technical completion before operational belief had actually transferred. In consulting work, in manufacturing environments, and later in enterprise leadership, the same pattern kept appearing. A system could be live and still not be trusted. A dashboard could be admired and still not be believed. A workflow could be available and still not feel safe enough to replace the old one. That is why I have come to see post go-live stewardship as part of the transformation itself. It is the season when the business decides whether the future is truly dependable or whether the past still feels safer, even when the past was objectively weaker.

The Anatomy of a Quiet Failure

It helps to be precise about how quiet failure actually happens, because naming the mechanism is the first step to preventing it. A quiet failure almost never has a single cause. It is the accumulation of several ordinary ones. The first is that leadership attention tends to leave at exactly the wrong moment. The energy, sponsorship, and visibility that carried the project all peak at go-live and then move on to the next initiative, just as the business is entering the harder phase of deciding whether to trust the change. The second is that the behavioral threshold is never crossed. The system is available, but nothing has made the old way genuinely unavailable, so the organization quietly keeps both.

The third mechanism is unchanged incentives. If people are still measured, rewarded, and reassured by the metrics and routines of the old world, they will keep one foot in it no matter how good the new system is. The fourth is design friction that was treated as a training problem. When a workflow is genuinely slower or harder than what it replaced, no amount of training will move trust, because the resistance is rational. And the fifth is that parallel systems are allowed to live too long. Every shadow spreadsheet, every retained legacy approval path, every extra manual export is a small vote of no confidence, and when the organization tolerates them indefinitely, it teaches itself that the new environment is optional.

Understanding these mechanisms changes what a leader watches for. Instead of asking whether the project closed on time, the more useful questions become whether sponsorship stayed past go-live, whether the old path was deliberately retired, whether incentives reward the new behavior, whether friction was treated as feedback rather than resistance, and how long parallel systems were allowed to survive. None of those questions appear on a typical milestone report. All of them determine whether the transformation actually took root or merely went live. Quiet failure is rarely a mystery after the fact. It is usually a set of warnings that no one was assigned to read.

The Quiet Return of Old Habits

What makes this phase of transformation so difficult is that old habits rarely come back all at once. They return quietly. A manager asks for one extra export because they are not fully comfortable with the new report. A team keeps one shadow spreadsheet open during the first month, just to be safe. A legacy approval path is retained in parallel because no one wants to take responsibility for removing it too early. None of those choices sound dramatic in isolation. But taken together, they begin to recreate the same operating logic the transformation was supposed to replace. That is why successful go-live leadership is not only about stabilization. It is also about protecting the organization from its own instinct to retreat into familiar work.

I learned to watch for these quiet returns because they often say more than official status reports do. If the business keeps building side routes around the new system, the problem is rarely only training. It may be speed. It may be trust. It may be a deeper mismatch between the way the platform was configured and the way the work actually flows. Good transformation leaders stay close enough to those signals to interpret them honestly. They do not dismiss them as resistance too quickly, and they do not excuse them forever. They treat them as feedback from the operating model itself.

What I found useful was to ask a different question for each kind of quiet return, because the right response depends on the cause. If the workaround exists because the new path is genuinely slower, the answer is to fix the friction, not to lecture people about adoption. If it exists because people do not yet trust the output, the answer is consistency and visible reliability over time, not pressure. And if it exists because no one was ever made responsible for removing the old path, the answer is ownership, a named person accountable for retiring the legacy route once the new one has earned it. Lumping all three together under the word resistance is one of the most common mistakes I have seen leaders make after go-live. It treats a design problem, a trust problem, and an ownership problem as if they were the same failure of will, when in fact they call for three very different leadership responses.

The Dashboard Everyone Praised

I remember a rollout where the new dashboard earned immediate praise. The presentation went well. Leaders liked the visibility. The metrics looked cleaner than what the business had been using before. From a distance, it felt like a success story unfolding exactly as planned. But when I spent more time with the teams actually doing the work, I found something different. They were still cross-checking the numbers in old reports, keeping side notes, and using manual comparisons before trusting the dashboard enough to act from it. The dashboard was admired quickly. It had not yet become trusted enough to replace the habits beneath it.

That moment taught me to distinguish between adoption theater and operating change. Leaders can be impressed by the surface of transformation because the surface is easier to see. What takes longer is the transfer of trust from the old routines into the new system. That transfer only happens when the business experiences enough consistency to let go of its private safeguards. Until then, the official environment and the trusted environment are not yet the same thing.

Enterprise Case Study: When Transformation Became Trust

Context. A major enterprise transformation was declared technically successful. The system was functioning. Leadership had every reason to feel confident about the rollout. On paper, the work was complete.

Tension. In practice, teams began quietly returning to old habits. They exported data into spreadsheets, rechecked outputs manually, and kept familiar routines alive in parallel with the new system. The issue was not technical failure. The issue was confidence. The new environment had gone live, but trust had not yet transferred fully.

Leadership Decision. The response was not to dismiss those behaviors or force compliance through pressure alone. Hypercare was extended and structured more deliberately. Feedback from users was taken seriously. Workarounds were studied rather than ignored. Where the system created friction, improvements were made. Where old habits remained from the past, the organization was guided forward through clarity, responsiveness, and repetition. Leadership treated post go-live trust as part of the transformation itself, not as a support afterthought.

Outcome and Teaching Value. Over time, adoption increased. Manual workarounds began to reduce. Trust in the new environment improved. Most importantly, old processes were gradually retired because the system had become more believable in practice, not merely more available in theory. This case is valuable for graduate leadership programs, executive education, and CIO development because it shows that transformation is defined by behavior, not deployment. It invites discussion about trust, governance, post go-live stewardship, and the difference between technical success and real operating change. A useful classroom extension is to ask what leadership indicators, beyond the milestone report, would have revealed the gap between going live and being trusted, and who should have been accountable for watching them.

When Transformation Meets AI

AI deserves special attention in a chapter about quiet failure, because AI initiatives may be the most quietly failure-prone work an enterprise will undertake. The reason is that AI demonstrates beautifully. A pilot dazzles. A demo produces an impressive answer. Leadership sees the potential immediately and declares the future arrived. But the gap between a convincing demonstration and a trusted part of daily work is wider for AI than for almost any system before it, because trusting AI asks people to rely on output they cannot fully trace, produced by a process they cannot fully see. That is a steep trust hill, and a dazzling demo does almost nothing to climb it.

So the same pattern repeats, only more so. The tool goes live. People are impressed. And then, quietly, they keep doing the manual version anyway, just to be safe. They run the AI summary and then re-read the source. They accept the recommendation and then verify it the old way. They use the new capability for the visible work and keep their private judgment for the work that matters. From a distance it looks like adoption. Up close it is the same parallel-system behavior this chapter has described throughout, and if leaders measure AI success by usage statistics rather than by whether people have actually stopped maintaining the manual fallback, they will declare victory over a quiet failure.

The discipline that prevents this is the discipline this whole chapter has argued for. Stay close to behavior after the launch. Watch whether the manual fallback is actually being retired or merely hidden. Treat friction and distrust as honest feedback about whether the output deserves to be relied upon, rather than as resistance to be overcome. And be honest that trust in AI must be earned through consistency over time, not granted because the demonstration was persuasive. Transformation with AI is still proven the same way every transformation is proven. Not when the tool can run, but when the business is genuinely willing to let it carry the work without quietly protecting itself from it.

Why This Chapter Matters

This chapter changes what leaders measure, and that is its practical value. Most transformation scorecards are built around deployment, because deployment is visible and finite. But deployment answers the smaller question. The larger question is whether the enterprise has actually changed how it works, and that question is answered in behavior over time, not in milestones. A leader who learns to measure durable adoption rather than visible activity is a leader who can tell the difference between a transformation that took root and one that merely went live.

The lesson lands differently depending on the reader's seat. For the practicing CIO and the IT leader, the message is operational. Treat the period after go-live as part of the transformation, keep sponsorship and attention there, and retire the old path deliberately rather than hoping it fades. For the consultant, the message is diagnostic. The clearest sign of a quiet failure is a business still maintaining parallel systems long after a project was declared complete, and that is something you can look for directly. And for the faculty member and the graduate student, the message is conceptual. This is a chance to study transformation as a transfer of trust and a change of behavior, rather than as the installation of a system, and to examine why technical success and operating change are not the same achievement.

Boardroom Perspective: Why Quiet Failure Matters More Than Go Live Success

Boards are often shown launch dates, dashboards, and milestone completions because those markers are visible and easy to report. They matter, but they do not answer the deeper question boards should care about most. Has the organization actually changed how it works. A board that stops at go-live reporting may believe transformation risk has been reduced when in reality the more consequential phase has only just begun. Quiet failure matters because it leaves systems technically present but behaviorally optional. The platform is available, but people still protect themselves with legacy habits, local checks, and shadow processes. In that environment, the business appears transformed before it has actually become more coherent.

A mature board should therefore ask questions that reach past the launch. How long after go-live did leadership sponsorship remain. What old processes have actually been retired, and which are still running in parallel. Where is the business still maintaining manual fallbacks around a system that was declared complete. How is durable adoption being measured, as distinct from initial usage. Those questions matter because they tell the board whether it is being shown a transformation that changed the enterprise or one that simply changed the technology. The first reduces risk. The second only relocates it.

From the CIO's Desk

One of the clearest leadership lessons I have learned is that transformation is easiest to overestimate at the exact moment leaders most want to believe it has succeeded. The launch happened. The pressure eased. The room wants to celebrate. I understand that impulse. But over time I learned to stay close to behavior longer than celebration naturally lasts. I want to know what people still do when no one is watching, what they still export manually, what they still verify privately, and what old routine they still trust more than the new workflow. That is where transformation tells the truth about itself.

If I had to summarize my own view simply, it would be this. Leaders should not confuse visible movement with settled change. The real measure is whether the new environment can carry ordinary work without requiring people to quietly protect themselves from it. That is why post go-live stewardship matters so much to me. It is the discipline of staying close long enough for trust to transfer, habits to shift, and the institution to stop leaning on the old world for reassurance. When that happens, transformation becomes more than a project. It becomes part of how the enterprise now lives.

Five Leadership Rules for Making Transformation Stick

These are the rules I keep returning to. They are easy to say and hard to sustain, which is exactly why they matter after the launch.

First, treat go live as the beginning of proof. Deployment shows that the system can run. It does not yet prove that the business will rely on it. The harder and more important work begins the day after the milestone, when attention naturally wants to leave.

Second, watch behavior longer than the project plan suggests. Workarounds, side files, private checks, and quiet exceptions reveal where trust is still incomplete. Stay close enough to read those signals, because they tell the truth that status reports cannot.

Third, use hypercare to build confidence, not just to close tickets. Support after launch should help the business transfer belief into the new way of working. The goal is not only a working system but a trusted one, and trust is built through consistency under real conditions.

Fourth, retire legacy habits deliberately. Old routines do not disappear on their own just because a better tool is available. Someone has to take responsibility for making the old path genuinely unavailable, or the organization will quietly keep both worlds alive.

Fifth, measure durable adoption, not only visible activity. A transformation becomes real when the new process starts carrying ordinary work without constant protection from the old one. Usage statistics can hide a quiet failure. The truer measure is whether the manual fallback has actually been retired.

Leadership Lessons

- Transformation is proven by behavior over time, not by deployment at launch.
- Quiet failure does not interrupt the calendar, which is exactly why it is so dangerous.
- Trust is tested after the project team declares success, when people decide whether to rely on the system alone.
- Old habits return one small exception at a time, and parallel systems are votes of no confidence.

- Friction is often rational feedback about design, not resistance to be overcome with more training.
- Hypercare is a trust-building window, not only a support window.
- AI is especially prone to quiet failure, because a dazzling demo does little to build the trust daily reliance requires.

Discussion Questions

- Why do many digital transformations appear successful at go live but fail to create lasting behavioral change?
- What leadership actions distinguish deployment from true transformation?
- How do trust, governance, and the removal of workarounds affect long term adoption of new systems?
- Why might AI initiatives be even more prone to quiet failure than traditional system rollouts, and what would prevent it?
- As a consultant, what evidence of parallel systems or manual fallbacks would tell you a past transformation never fully took root?
- If you were teaching this chapter, what would you identify as the hidden leadership cost of allowing old habits to survive quietly underneath a new platform?

Application for Practice

- For the practicing leader: choose one transformation in your organization that was declared successful. Identify what behaviors actually changed, and what old habits quietly remained in place.
- For the IT leader: identify one workaround that still exists around a newer system or process. Determine what that workaround reveals about trust, design, or change adoption.

- For the consultant: in a client environment, list the parallel systems and manual fallbacks still running after a completed project, and assess what they reveal about whether trust transferred.
- For the faculty member or facilitator: draft a short set of post go-live leadership indicators that a class could use to judge whether a transformation took root, beyond the milestone report.
- For any reader: review how success was measured for a past transformation. Decide whether those measures focused more on deployment or on lasting behavior change.
- For reflection: think of a change you believed had succeeded until you looked closely at daily behavior. What was the first quiet sign that trust had not actually transferred?

Chapter 6: Legacy Systems vs Legacy Thinking

Opening

Most companies think their biggest problem is legacy systems. Old ERP. Old tools. Old platforms. Those can be real problems. But the harder problem is usually legacy thinking. Old assumptions, old exceptions, and old habits often survive long after the old systems are gone. That is why modernization can succeed technically and still disappoint operationally. A modern platform cannot produce modern outcomes if the organization keeps insisting on old patterns of work. For practicing CIOs, IT leaders, consultants, and graduate leadership programs alike, this chapter matters because it shows that modernization is not proven by a newer tool alone. It is proven when the business is willing to let old thinking lose its authority.

Experience has taught me to be careful when people describe modernization as a technology problem alone. The systems may be old, but the deeper issue is often what the organization has learned to protect around them. Old controls. Old exceptions. Old ways of proving that someone is still watching. Those habits may once have made perfect sense. But when they survive after the conditions have changed, they begin teaching the enterprise that the past still has more authority than the future. That is what makes legacy thinking so expensive. It quietly tells the organization to keep rebuilding yesterday inside tools that were meant to support tomorrow.

Legacy thinking is also emotional before it becomes operational. People do not hold onto old patterns simply because they are stubborn. They hold onto them because those patterns once reduced risk, preserved control, or made the work feel more understandable. A familiar report, an extra approval, a local variation, or a private check can feel like competence rather than drag. Leaders have to understand that emotional logic if they want modernization to become believable. Otherwise they will treat every legacy habit as resistance instead of seeing it as a signal about where trust has not yet fully transferred.

That is why legacy thinking often survives in organizations that sincerely want to modernize. The desire for improvement is real, but so is the pull of what once kept the business safe. Leaders can underestimate how much identity is embedded in old routines. Sometimes a local report is not only a report. It is a sign that someone knows how to protect the process. Sometimes an extra approval is not only an extra step. It is a sign that someone still cares enough to check what others might miss. If leaders rush past that meaning, modernization becomes a contest of will. If they understand it, they can begin replacing inherited reassurance with stronger institutional confidence.

This chapter extends a thread that has run through the book so far. Earlier chapters argued that tools amplify what already exists, that memory must be protected, that speed must be designed, that the enterprise must be integrated, and that transformation is proven by behavior rather than deployment. Legacy thinking is the common enemy of all of them. It is the gravity that pulls an organization back toward the past even as it invests in the future. Stewardship, in this chapter, means having the courage and the patience to retire thinking that has outlived its purpose, so that the modern tools an enterprise buys are actually allowed to produce modern outcomes rather than a more expensive version of the old ones.

Why Old Habits Survive New Platforms

Legacy thinking survives because habits often outlast the conditions that created them. A process may have started as a reasonable workaround years earlier when a system truly could not handle the requirement, when reporting was unreliable, or when teams lacked shared visibility. Over time, that workaround becomes normal. It gets explained as practical. It becomes part of how experienced people protect the business. Then a new platform arrives and removes the original limitation, but the habit remains because it no longer feels like a workaround. It feels like common sense. That is what makes legacy thinking so persistent. It no longer looks old to the people living inside it. I have seen this repeatedly across early ERP platforms, global ERP consulting, internationally funded development project environments, coatings, automotive, and finally as CIO. The systems changed. The harder work was always helping the institution release what it no longer needed to keep carrying.

That lesson became clearer through every major chapter of my career. The Y2K shift from accounting into ERP work taught me early that systems are never only technical. Outsourcing and the offshore transition at a global electronics components manufacturer taught me how quickly global operating decisions can redefine people's relationship to change, risk, and trust. Global consulting and broader ERP work exposed me to organizations that wanted modern tools but were still defending inherited exceptions as if they were strategic advantages. The coatings world introduced me to another industrial reality where process rigor mattered just as much as innovation. International development project leadership added the cultural lesson that modernization fails quietly when leaders ignore how people experience authority, timing, and control. Later, ERP work in Canada, major ERP implementation experience, and finally my current role brought the pattern full circle. The roadmap work around ERP, business applications, lifecycle management, master data, single sign-on, and enterprise standardization all reinforced the same point. Modernization succeeds only when the institution becomes disciplined enough to stop rebuilding the past inside the future.

I have seen this repeatedly in modernization work. Leaders invest in strong platforms and then wonder why complexity has not fallen the way they expected. The answer is often uncomfortable. The organization rebuilt too much of the old logic inside the new environment. It preserved too many exceptions, protected too many local variations, and treated standardization as a threat rather than a path to scale. When that happens, the technology may be modern, but the operating model is still negotiating with the past. That is why this chapter is not really about software age. It is about leadership willingness to let outdated thinking lose its authority.

I have found that organizations rebuild old logic inside new platforms for a simple reason. The old logic is familiar, while the new environment still has to earn credibility. If leaders are not disciplined, modernization becomes a technical transplant without an operating reset. The screens look newer. The platform is stronger. But too many decisions are still being made from habits designed for a different era. In that kind of environment, technical debt begins to reappear almost immediately because the business is not only carrying the new system. It is carrying the memory of the old one inside it.

One of the reasons this is so difficult is that legacy thinking rarely presents itself as outdated to the people closest to it. It presents itself as prudence, thoroughness, business knowledge, or earned caution. That is why leaders have to be both respectful and disciplined. Respectful enough to understand the history behind the habit. Disciplined enough to ask whether that history still justifies the cost. In my experience, modernization becomes more successful when leaders can say, with credibility, we are not dismissing the past. We are deciding what the future no longer needs to keep carrying.

That is one reason I have tried to write about legacy thinking with more sympathy than many modernization conversations allow. Old habits often began as rational protection. A manual check once prevented a costly mistake. A local variation once kept operations moving when the enterprise standard was not yet strong enough. A private spreadsheet once created visibility that the formal report could not yet provide. The problem is not that these habits ever existed. The problem is when the institution forgets to revisit whether the reason still holds. Mature modernization requires that kind of honest review. It asks the enterprise to respect its history without letting history keep governing the future after the conditions have changed.

The Leadership Work of Standardizing What Matters

Over time, I came to see standardization not as a restriction on the business, but as a form of stewardship. It protects the enterprise from having to solve the same variation repeatedly. It allows teams to support the environment more consistently. It makes reporting more comparable, training more effective, and change more manageable. Most importantly, it lowers the amount of unnecessary thinking required to keep the business operating. That may not sound dramatic, but it is a real form of leadership value. The most durable environments are often the ones where leaders had the courage to simplify what no longer needed to be debated.

I saw this play out in practical ways. Our ERP direction tied future scalability to master data management, stronger integrations, and operational standardization across sites, while our broader applications direction linked standardization to single sign-on, lifecycle management, integration frameworks, and the reduction of manual effort. These are not isolated technical improvements. They are signs that the enterprise is choosing coherence over local variation where variation no longer creates real value. That is one of the clearest ways leaders reduce legacy thinking. They stop treating every inherited difference as sacred and begin asking whether the business is still paying for complexity that no longer earns its keep.

Standardization also protects memory. When processes are cleaner and definitions hold across sites, the business no longer has to keep translating itself every time work crosses a boundary. The institution can learn once and reuse the lesson more broadly. That is why simplification is about more than efficiency. It is about preserving meaning across geography, function, and time. In a multi-site environment, that is one of the most practical gifts leaders can give the enterprise. They make the organization easier to understand, not only easier to support.

What Standardization Made Possible

One of the reasons I became more committed to standardization over time is that I saw what it made possible once the organization stopped treating every variation as sacred. Reporting became more trustworthy because definitions no longer shifted by site or function. Support became more stable because teams were no longer chasing dozens of local exceptions that added little value. Training became easier because the business could learn one stronger way of working instead of memorizing a patchwork of historical preferences. And change itself became more manageable because the enterprise had fewer moving parts to reconcile each time a new initiative was introduced. In other words, standardization did not reduce capability. It made capability more portable.

That mattered even more in multi-site and cross-border environments, where inconsistency compounds quickly. A small local exception in one place may seem harmless on its own, but multiplied across plants, teams, and processes, it turns into cost, delay, and confusion. I came to see standardization as one of the quiet enablers of scale. It gave the organization a better chance to grow, integrate, report, and improve without constantly renegotiating the basics. It also created a stronger platform for trust. People could rely more confidently on the output because the underlying process was no longer changing shape every time it crossed a boundary.

This matters because complexity is not only paid for in support cost or technical effort. It is also paid for in attention. Every unnecessary variation asks people to think harder than they should have to just to do ordinary work. Every overlapping tool asks them to remember one more exception. Every local process asks them to translate what should already be clear. When leaders simplify the environment, they are not merely removing clutter. They are returning cognitive capacity to the business. That is one reason simplification is so valuable. It lowers the invisible tax that complexity places on judgment every single day.

What Simplification Gave Back to the Business

One of the less obvious benefits of simplification is that it gives time and attention back to the business. When teams are no longer carrying unnecessary variations, duplicate approvals, scattered reports, and local exceptions that no longer create real value, they can spend more of their energy on judgment, improvement, and execution. That shift is easy to underestimate because simplification does not always look dramatic in a presentation. But in practice, it reduces cognitive load. It lowers support friction. It makes training more transferable and decisions more comparable. In other words, it allows the organization to use more of its energy on work that actually moves it forward.

I came to appreciate that deeply in multi-site environments, where even small inconsistencies multiply into real effort. A single unnecessary exception might not feel costly in one location. But across plants, teams, systems, and reporting cycles, it becomes part of the drag that leaders eventually mistake for normal life. Simplification changes that. It gives the business back some of the bandwidth it had been spending just to cope. And once that happens, the organization becomes more capable of absorbing change without feeling constantly burdened by its own complexity.

What I came to appreciate over time was that simplification also changes the emotional experience of work. When people no longer have to remember as many exceptions, reconcile as many side processes, or navigate as many overlapping tools, they become more confident in the environment itself. The work feels lighter because the organization has stopped asking people to carry complexity that no longer creates real value. In my experience, that is one of the quiet signs that modernization is becoming believable. The future feels easier to trust because the past is no longer being rebuilt everywhere people turn.

This is also where application rationalization becomes a leadership issue rather than an inventory exercise. A growing enterprise easily accumulates tools, exceptions, and overlapping processes that once solved a local problem but now increase support burden, confuse ownership, and fragment the user experience. In our own work, we moved toward a more integrated ecosystem with stronger governance, lifecycle management, single sign-on, and Data-Lake connectivity. That shift matters because it reduces the amount of legacy complexity users have to navigate every day. Simplification gives the business back more than time. It gives back clearer responsibility, fewer seams, and a stronger chance for the environment to make sense as one system rather than many partial histories.

The Process No One Wanted to Let Go

I remember one process that everyone agreed was inefficient, but no one was quite ready to let go. It had grown out of an earlier limitation and stayed alive long after the original reason for it had disappeared. People knew it created extra work. They knew it slowed the flow. They knew it duplicated effort that the newer system could now handle more cleanly. And still, when the conversation turned to retiring it, hesitation filled the room. The process had become more than a workaround. It had become familiar. It had become a private assurance that someone was still checking the system from outside the system. What looked like a simple cleanup on paper was really a trust conversation in disguise.

That moment taught me why simplification requires more leadership than people often expect. You are not only removing a step. You are asking people to release a habit that once protected them. If leaders treat that too casually, resistance hardens. But if they recognize the emotional meaning underneath the old process, they have a better chance to replace it with something stronger. In my experience, the most successful simplification happens when the business no longer feels that it is losing control. It feels that it is gaining a cleaner way to keep control in the right place.

That is why leaders have to interpret old processes with more patience than the process map may suggest. A duplicated check, local file, or manual approval may not survive because people love inefficiency. It survives because at some point it represented safety. Mature modernization does not shame that history. It learns from it. Leaders ask what fear the old process is still absorbing, what trust the new environment has not yet fully earned, and what evidence people need before they can release the extra layer without feeling exposed.

The Exception Everyone Defended

I remember one exception that almost everyone defended even though very few people still believed it was truly necessary. It had been in place for years, and over time it had become part of how the business reassured itself that the process was still safe. When we finally examined it closely, the logic underneath it had weakened, but the emotional attachment had not. People were not arguing mainly for efficiency. They were arguing for familiarity. The exception represented a layer of personal comfort in a system they had not yet fully learned to trust without it. That is why simplification is often harder than the process map makes it look. What leaders are really asking people to surrender is not always the step itself. Sometimes it is the emotional protection that step had come to symbolize.

This is exactly why lifecycle management matters. If leaders never return to old exceptions, customizations, and workarounds with enough discipline to ask whether they still belong, the environment quietly fills with historical residue. Technical debt is not only code or infrastructure. It is also every rule, process, and variation the enterprise keeps carrying because no one has yet created permission to retire it. Strong governance gives leaders a way to revisit those accumulated layers before they become permanent drag. In that sense, lifecycle management is stewardship applied to complexity. It helps the organization stop confusing inherited habit with enduring necessity.

I have also come to think of technical debt more broadly than the term is often used. It is not only aging code, unsupported platforms, or outdated infrastructure. It is also obsolete reports that no one retires, duplicate approvals that no one revisits, field definitions that no longer align with the business, and exceptions that continue because no one wants to reopen the conversation. Over time, that residue becomes part of the environment people assume they have to live with. But much of it survives not because it is still valuable. It survives because the organization has not yet created the discipline to clean up after its own history. Modernization, for all these reasons, requires more than investment. It requires periodic courage.

Legacy Thinking in the Age of AI

AI gives this chapter a sharper edge, because AI is where legacy thinking does its most expensive damage in two opposite directions at once. The first is treating AI as merely another tool to bolt onto the old way of working. Leaders approve an AI capability and then wire it into the same exceptions, the same manual checks, and the same fragmented processes the organization always had, expecting a different result. That is the purest form of rebuilding the past inside the future. The tool is new, the thinking is old, and the outcome is a faster, more expensive version of yesterday. The second direction is the opposite mistake, importing old fears wholesale and refusing to let AI change anything, so the organization pays for the capability and then governs it into irrelevance out of habit.

There is also a quieter danger that is specific to how these tools work. AI learns from what an organization has already done. If the enterprise feeds it years of accumulated workarounds, undocumented exceptions, and inconsistent definitions, the tool will faithfully learn that legacy logic and reproduce it with confidence and at scale. In that sense, AI can become the most powerful preservation engine for legacy thinking ever built, because it can take the residue of the past and make it look like the recommendation of the future. The discipline this chapter argues for, retiring exceptions that no longer earn their keep and standardizing what no longer needs to vary, is exactly what determines whether AI learns from a clean foundation or from a museum of old habits.

The healthier path is to treat AI adoption as an occasion for the operating reset that modernization always required and rarely received. Before automating a process, ask whether the process still deserves to exist in its current form. Before training a model on historical data, ask whether that history represents how the business should work or merely how it used to cope. AI raises the stakes of the central question in this chapter to their highest point yet. If the system can now support a simpler, stronger way of working, why would a leader teach it the old way instead.

Why This Chapter Matters

A practical shift happens during modernization. When technology removes old constraints, some long-protected habits lose their justification. The question becomes harder to avoid. If the system can now support a simpler, stronger way of working, why are we still doing it the old way.

For students, faculty, and practicing executives, that is the enduring leadership value of this chapter. It is not asking whether modernization is worthwhile. It is asking whether leaders are willing to modernize their thinking with the same seriousness they apply to the platforms themselves. They must decide what complexity still earns its keep, what exceptions still serve a real purpose, and what habits are now costing the institution more than they protect. In a world full of digital renewal, that may be one of the most overlooked leadership disciplines of all, the courage to stop rebuilding the past inside the future.

The lesson reads differently depending on the reader's seat. For the practicing CIO and the IT leader, the message is operational. Pair every platform investment with a deliberate operating reset, and treat standardization and lifecycle management as the tools that keep old logic from migrating into the new environment. For the consultant, the message is diagnostic. When a modernization disappoints, look first at the exceptions, workarounds, and definitions that survived the migration untouched, because that is usually where the old drag was preserved. And for the faculty member and the graduate student, the message is conceptual. This is a chance to study modernization as a change in thinking rather than a change in tooling, and to examine why technically successful projects so often fail to deliver the outcomes leaders expected.

Boardroom Perspective: Why Legacy Thinking Is a Leadership Risk

Boards often approve modernization with the assumption that replacing aging platforms will naturally reduce complexity, increase agility, and improve execution. Sometimes it does. But if old assumptions, local exceptions, and inherited workarounds are allowed to survive untouched, the business may invest heavily in new technology while preserving the same operational drag underneath it. That is why legacy thinking should be treated as a leadership risk, not merely a cultural inconvenience. It quietly turns modernization into migration without improvement, and it leaves the institution wondering why the new environment still feels so familiar in all the wrong ways.

A mature board should therefore ask questions that go beyond platform age. Which historical exceptions are still being treated as untouchable even though the original reason has faded. Where is the enterprise still carrying old reassurance behaviors inside new tools. What complexity is being preserved because no one has yet created permission to let it go. These are not only architecture questions. They are stewardship questions, because they determine whether modernization will strengthen institutional capability or simply relocate the same constraints into a more expensive environment.

From the CIO's Desk

One of the clearest lessons of my career is that modernization fails quietly when leaders replace the technology but protect too much of the thinking that made the old environment hard to live with in the first place. I have seen businesses spend real money, energy, and leadership attention on new platforms and still carry old fear, old exceptions, and old reassurance habits into the future as though those habits were part of wisdom rather than part of the burden. These days I no longer ask only whether the system is newer. I ask whether the business is now thinking more clearly, working more simply, and trusting the enterprise enough to stop rebuilding old complexity inside new tools.

If I had to summarize my own view simply, it would be this. Legacy thinking is rarely defeated by enthusiasm alone. It is replaced when leaders make the future easier to trust than the past. That takes explanation, standardization, visible governance, and enough patience to understand why people are still holding onto what once protected them. In my experience, the most durable modernization happens when the enterprise can finally let go of an old habit without feeling that it has lost control. That is when change becomes believable enough to last.

Five Leadership Rules for Replacing Legacy Thinking

These are the rules I keep returning to. They are simple to name and demanding to live, which is usually the mark of a principle worth keeping.

First, separate history from necessity. Respect the reason a habit began, but do not assume that reason still justifies today's cost. Many exceptions were once wise and have simply outlived the conditions that made them so. The discipline is to honor the history without being governed by it.

Second, standardize what should no longer vary. Every preserved exception should earn its place against the complexity it creates. Variation that adds real value deserves protection. Variation that survives only out of habit is a quiet tax on attention, support, and scale.

Third, interpret workarounds as signals. Old habits often reveal where trust, clarity, or design still need strengthening. Before treating a workaround as resistance, ask what fear it is absorbing and what the new environment has not yet earned, because the answer tells you what to fix.

Fourth, make simplification emotionally safe. People release legacy patterns more readily when leaders explain how the new environment will now protect what the old routine once guarded. The goal is for the business to feel it is keeping control in a better place, not losing it.

Fifth, treat modernization as a thinking shift, not only a platform shift. The technology has truly changed only when the institution begins living differently because of it. A newer screen over an older habit is migration, not modernization, and the difference shows up in whether the outcomes actually improve.

Leadership Lessons

- Legacy systems are a technology problem, but legacy thinking is a leadership problem, and it is the harder one.
- Old habits survive because they once represented safety, not because people are stubborn.
- Standardization is stewardship, because it returns attention to the business and makes capability portable.
- Technical debt is not only code, it is every report, approval, and exception no one was given permission to retire.

- Simplification is often a trust conversation in disguise, so it requires patience as well as discipline.
- AI can become the most powerful preservation engine for legacy thinking, because it learns whatever history it is given.
- Modernization is proven when the institution begins living differently, not when the platform is newer.

Discussion Questions

- What is the difference between a legacy system and legacy thinking, and why is that distinction important for leaders?
- How did cross-industry and cross-cultural experience reinforce the lesson that modernization is never only technical?
- What role do standardization, lifecycle management, master data, and governance play in preventing the organization from rebuilding old habits inside new platforms?
- Why might AI preserve legacy thinking rather than replace it, and what discipline would prevent that?
- As a consultant, how would you identify which inherited exceptions in a client environment still earn their keep and which have become pure drag?
- If you were teaching this chapter, what would you identify as the hidden cost of allowing inherited exceptions to survive after the original reason for them has disappeared?

Application for Practice

- For the practicing leader: identify one process in your organization that may still be shaped more by legacy thinking than by current business reality. Name the assumptions keeping it in place.

- For the IT leader: review one recent modernization effort. Assess the extent to which the organization changed its habits, standards, and decision-making along with the technology.
- For the consultant: in a client environment, list three recurring exceptions and judge which are truly necessary and which are preserving unnecessary complexity.
- For the faculty member or facilitator: design a short exercise in which students must decide whether to automate a flawed process as-is or redesign it first, and defend the choice.
- For any reader: write a short leadership note explaining why standardization in one area of your organization would be an act of stewardship rather than a loss of flexibility.
- For reflection: think of an old habit you personally defended longer than the reason for it survived. What evidence finally made it safe to let go?

Chapter 7: Stewardship and Organizational Trust

Opening

Trust is one of the most underestimated operating assets in enterprise leadership. By the time trust shows up clearly in a metric, it has usually been changing for a while. People start checking things twice. They keep local copies. They hesitate before relying on the official process. They verify more often, or they stop escalating as early as they should because they are unsure how leadership will respond. Those signals rarely appear first in a dashboard, but they matter. For practicing CIOs, IT leaders, consultants, and graduate leadership programs alike, this chapter matters because trust is not a soft side issue in technology leadership. It is one of the conditions that determines whether an institution can move with clarity, absorb pressure, and keep behaving responsibly when the room is under strain.

My own view of trust was shaped gradually across very different chapters of my career. The Y2K shift from accounting into ERP work taught me early that systems are never only technical. They either strengthen confidence in the business or quietly weaken it. The outsourcing and offshore transition at a global electronics components manufacturer taught me that change touches people's sense of security as much as their workflow. Global consulting and broader ERP work showed me how fragile trust becomes when leaders promise more than the operating model can honestly carry. International development project work reinforced that culture matters because people do not experience authority, timing, and accountability the same way everywhere. By the time I reached my current role as CIO, those lessons had come full circle. Trust was no longer an abstract leadership virtue. It was one of the most practical forces shaping whether systems, people, and decisions could hold together under pressure.

That is why I have come to think of stewardship as the work of making trust easier to justify. Leaders do that when they build environments where systems are stable, expectations are clear, ownership is visible, and people do not have to guess whether the organization will support them for doing the responsible thing. Trust becomes more believable when communication is disciplined, when awareness is reinforced, and when people know where the truth of the work lives and how to reach one another when it matters most.

Trust is also the quiet substrate beneath every other idea in this book. Accountability depends on it, because people will only own hard decisions in an environment where honesty is safe. Memory depends on it, because shared definitions only hold when people trust the source instead of their private copy. Speed depends on it, because teams move quickly only when they believe a commitment will be honored. Integration depends on it, because functions align through trust long before they align through architecture. And transformation depends on it, because adoption is finally a decision to rely on something new. It is the reason I treat trust as an operating asset rather than a sentiment. Stewardship, in the end, is the steady work of making an institution worth relying on.

What Trust Looks Like in Daily Operations

Trust becomes visible in ordinary work long before it appears in formal metrics. It shows up in whether people rely on the official process or keep private copies just in case. It shows up in whether they escalate early or wait because they are not sure how leadership will respond. It shows up in whether managers believe the numbers, whether users trust the workflow, and whether teams feel safe telling the truth before a small issue becomes a larger one. In my experience, organizations do not lose trust all at once. They lose it in small repeated moments where the system feels harder to rely on than it should.

That is why I have come to see trust as an operating asset, not a soft cultural idea. It affects the speed of decisions, the honesty of updates, the willingness to adopt change, and the degree to which the enterprise can move without protecting itself through hidden workarounds. When trust is high, the business becomes lighter. People waste less energy defending themselves from uncertainty. When trust is weak, even good systems feel heavier because people are quietly building private protection around them.

I have learned to read these behaviors as the leading indicators of trust, in the same way a careful operator reads the early signs of strain in a system before any alarm sounds. A rise in private spreadsheets is a trust signal. A pattern of late escalation is a trust signal. A meeting where people defend their version of a number rather than build from a shared one is a trust signal. None of these appear on a standard report, and that is precisely why they matter. By the time low trust becomes visible in delivery metrics or attrition, it has usually been shaping behavior for months. Leaders who learn to notice the quieter signals can respond while the cost is still small. Leaders who wait for the metric respond after the damage is already done.

Trust Runs in Every Direction

It is tempting to think of organizational trust as a single question, whether employees trust leadership. That matters, but it is only one direction of several, and a leader who attends to it alone will miss most of the picture. Trust runs upward, downward, and sideways at the same time, and the health of an enterprise depends on all three.

The downward direction is the one leaders most often overlook, which is whether leadership genuinely extends trust to the people doing the work. An organization that says it values its people but governs them through constant oversight, duplicate approvals, and a reluctance to delegate is sending a clearer message than any values statement. When leaders refuse to extend trust, they teach the enterprise to operate defensively, and they quietly signal that judgment lives only at the top. Extending trust is not the absence of accountability. It is the decision to give capable people real ownership and then hold them to it, which is how an institution grows leaders rather than dependents.

The sideways direction is whether functions trust one another, and whether the business trusts the technology organization. This is where a great deal of hidden cost accumulates. When finance does not trust operations data, when one plant does not trust a shared service, or when the business does not trust IT to deliver, people compensate with parallel work, side channels, and private reconciliation. The upward direction, whether people trust leadership, is real and important, but it is strengthened or weakened largely by the other two. People trust leaders who extend trust to them and who build an environment where they can trust their colleagues and their systems. In that sense, trust is less a feeling the organization has about its leaders and more a property of how the whole enterprise has learned to work together.

The Day I Realized Trust Was Part of the Operating Model

There was a point in my leadership journey when I realized trust was not simply a byproduct of good intentions. It was part of the operating model itself. People were not only asking whether the system worked. They were asking whether leadership would tell the truth early, whether ownership would remain visible, and whether the organization would support the responsible choice even when that choice was inconvenient. That lesson was reinforced across every major chapter of my career. The Y2K shift into ERP work taught me that business confidence and system confidence are inseparable. The outsourcing and layoff period at a global electronics components manufacturer taught me how quickly trust can become fragile when people feel that large decisions are happening around them instead of with them. Global consulting and broader ERP work showed me that clients will often tolerate bad news more easily than vague reassurance. International development project work added another layer by teaching me that trust has to be earned differently across cultures, but it still depends on clarity, respect, and follow-through everywhere.

By the time I reached my current role as CIO, that lesson had come full circle. Stable ERP operations, reliable payroll, clearer governance, stronger project delivery, and more disciplined communication all pointed to the same deeper reality. Trust was becoming easier for the business to justify because the enterprise was becoming easier to rely on. That is one of the reasons I value trust so highly. It is not only a leadership virtue. It is one of the conditions that allows an institution to function with less friction and more honesty.

That is why trust feels so practical to me. I have seen what happens when it is weakened through layoffs, through vague communication, through change that moves faster than explanation, and through systems that ask people to believe before leadership has done enough to make belief reasonable. I have also seen the opposite. I have seen trust rise when teams are developed, when expectations are clear, when leaders communicate early, and when modernization is managed with enough discipline that the business no longer needs as many private defenses to feel safe. In my experience, trust is one of the quiet currencies of executive leadership. You spend it when you are careless. You build it when the institution becomes easier to rely on.

How Trust Is Lost, and How It Returns

One of the hardest truths about trust is that it is asymmetric. It is built slowly, through many ordinary moments of reliability, and it can be lost quickly, through a few moments of carelessness. A single broken commitment can undo months of steady follow-through, because trust is a judgment about the future, and one vivid disappointment changes how people forecast what comes next. Leaders who understand this asymmetry treat their commitments carefully, because they know that the cost of a promise quietly abandoned is far higher than the cost of a promise never made.

Trust tends to erode through a recognizable set of patterns, and naming them helps leaders avoid them. It erodes through vague communication, which teaches people that the official story cannot be relied upon. It erodes through change that arrives faster than explanation, which leaves people feeling that things are happening to them rather than with them. It erodes through inconsistency, when the rules seem to bend for the influential and hold only for everyone else. And it erodes through blame, when telling the truth early turns out to be punished rather than valued, which trains people into the silence that lets small problems grow into large ones.

The encouraging part is that trust returns through the same channel it left, only more slowly. It returns through consistency, through systems that prove themselves reliable over time, through commitments that are kept even when keeping them is inconvenient, and through leaders who tell hard truths early and own their mistakes plainly. There is no shortcut. Trust cannot be restored through a campaign or a slogan, because it is not an opinion to be changed but a pattern to be re-earned. What I have seen work is patience and repetition. The enterprise watches, over many ordinary moments, whether the system and the people leading it can be counted on, and slowly it adjusts its forecast of the future. That slow rebuilding is unglamorous, but it is some of the most important work a steward of an institution ever does.

Enterprise Case Study: Trust Through Stability, Clarity, and Follow-Through

Context. In a large enterprise, trust does not grow only through speeches, values statements, or executive intention. It grows when people experience the system as more reliable over time. In the broader transformation materials, that reliability became visible through steadier project success, clearer governance, stable ERP separation, stronger HRIS stabilization, validated manufacturing execution, BI and Data-Lake improvements, and communication rhythms that made leadership intent easier to understand.

Tension. The tension was that trust can be weakened quietly long before failure becomes obvious. People create side files, delay escalation, recheck approved information, or rely on familiar individuals instead of official processes. None of those actions are irrational. They are often signs that the system still feels more fragile than leadership believes. The challenge was therefore not only to improve systems, but to reduce the hidden reasons people still felt they needed private protection.

Leadership Decision and Teaching Value. The leadership move was to build trust through steadier operations, visible ownership, clearer communication, stronger governance, and better follow-through. Project delivery improved. Service levels became more reliable. More of the business could work from governed information instead of local interpretation. This makes the case useful for graduate leadership programs, executive education, and CIO development because it reframes trust as a systems and leadership issue rather than a motivational slogan. It shows that trust becomes believable when the environment repeatedly proves itself easier to rely on.

I remember a point when one team quietly stopped keeping its own side file because the official process had finally become reliable enough to trust. No announcement was made. No celebration followed. The old file simply stopped appearing in meetings because people no longer felt they needed private protection to do responsible work. That small change mattered to me more than many visible milestones. It told me the environment had improved in a way people could actually feel. In my experience, that is one of the clearest signals that trust is becoming real. The organization is no longer depending on personal backup plans to compensate for a system it has not fully learned to believe in.

I also remember a moment when a team escalated a problem much earlier than they would have a year before. Nothing in the process forced them to do it. What had changed was their confidence that leadership would respond with clarity instead of blame. The issue itself was manageable, but the behavior around it told me something important. Trust had improved enough that people no longer felt they needed to protect themselves with silence. In my experience, that is another quiet sign that stewardship is working. The enterprise becomes safer for honesty before it becomes impressive in metrics.

Trust and the Arrival of AI

AI introduces a trust question the enterprise has not faced in quite this form before, and it does so on two fronts at once. The first is whether people can trust the output of a system whose reasoning they cannot fully see. Every earlier wave of technology asked people to trust a result they could, in principle, trace and check. AI often asks them to rely on an answer produced by a process that is genuinely opaque to them. That is a steeper trust requirement, and it cannot be met by enthusiasm or executive endorsement. It can only be met the way trust in any system is met, through consistency and verifiable reliability over time, which is exactly why the trust-transfer discipline from the chapter on quiet failure applies so directly here.

The second front is more human and, in my experience, more consequential. The way an organization introduces AI sends an unmistakable signal about whether it trusts its people. AI can be deployed as a tool that empowers capable people, giving them better leverage and freeing their judgment for higher work. Or it can be deployed in a way that quietly communicates surveillance and replacement, measuring people more than it helps them and treating their experience as a cost to be removed. Those two paths use similar technology and produce very different cultures. One strengthens the downward trust this chapter described, the trust leadership extends to its people. The other erodes it, and an organization that erodes trust in the name of efficiency will find that the efficiency is real and the erosion is more expensive.

This is why I believe trust is the precondition for healthy AI adoption, not a secondary consideration. In a high-trust environment, people will engage with AI honestly, tell leaders where it helps and where it falls short, and adopt it where it genuinely earns reliance. In a low-trust environment, they will treat it with quiet suspicion, maintain their private fallbacks indefinitely, and tell leaders what they think the metrics want to hear. The tool is the same. The outcome is decided by the trust that was, or was not, built long before the tool arrived. Stewardship in the age of AI therefore begins where stewardship always begins, with the patient work of making the institution worth relying on.

Why This Chapter Matters

The practical value of this chapter is that it moves trust from the category of culture, where it is admired but rarely managed, into the category of operations, where it can be observed, protected, and rebuilt. A leader who treats trust as an operating asset will watch its leading indicators, understand its asymmetry, and recognize that every commitment kept or broken is a deposit or a withdrawal. That is a more useful posture than hoping trust will follow from good intentions, because good intentions are invisible and behavior is not.

The lesson lands differently depending on the reader's seat. For the practicing CIO and the IT leader, the message is operational. Read the quiet signals of trust early, extend real ownership to capable people, and use stability and follow-through as the instruments that make trust easier to justify. For the consultant, the message is diagnostic. The private workarounds, late escalations, and parallel reconciliations in a client environment are a direct readout of where trust is weak, and they will tell you more than the engagement survey. And for the faculty member and the graduate student, the message is conceptual. This is a chance to study trust as a measurable operating condition with leading indicators and an asymmetric repair curve, rather than as a motivational theme.

Boardroom Perspective: Trust Lowers the Cost of Coordination

Boards should care about trust because trust lowers the cost of coordination across the enterprise. When trust is strong, functions argue less about basic truth, teams escalate sooner, and leadership spends less energy recovering clarity that should already exist. When trust is weak, the institution pays through hesitation, duplicated checks, slower decisions, and unnecessary defensive behavior. That is why trust should be treated as an operating issue, not only a cultural aspiration.

A mature board should therefore ask questions that surface the state of trust before it shows up in harder numbers. Where are people still maintaining private workarounds around official systems. How early do problems actually reach leadership, and what happens to the people who raise them. Where does the business still not trust its own data, its shared services, or its technology organization to deliver. What happens to institutional knowledge and confidence when a trusted leader departs. These are not soft questions. They are leading indicators of whether the enterprise can coordinate cheaply and act with confidence, or whether it will keep paying the quiet tax that low trust imposes on every decision.

From the CIO's Desk

One of the clearest leadership lessons of my career is that trust becomes believable through repetition. The organization watches whether leaders tell the truth early, whether systems become steadier, whether commitments are kept, and whether the environment becomes easier or harder to rely on over time. That is why I do not think of trust as something leaders can request on demand. In my experience, trust is earned when the business has enough repeated evidence that the system and the people leading it can still be counted on under pressure.

If I had to summarize my own view simply, it would be this. Stewardship makes trust easier to justify. It does not eliminate pressure or remove every disappointment, but it gives the organization stronger reasons to keep relying on the enterprise instead of building private protection around it. That is one of the most practical leadership outcomes I know.

Five Leadership Rules for Building Trust That Lasts

These are the rules I keep returning to. They are simple to state and demanding to live, which is usually the sign of a principle worth keeping.

First, make ownership visible. People trust systems and leaders more when it is clear who is responsible. Ambiguity about who owns a decision or a system is itself a quiet erosion of trust, because it leaves people unsure whom to rely on when something matters.

Second, reduce private workarounds. Hidden copies, shadow files, and repeated rechecking are often trust signals, not efficiency signals. Treat them as feedback about where the environment still feels fragile, and work to remove the reason for the workaround rather than simply discouraging the behavior.

Third, communicate early and clearly. Ambiguity weakens trust faster than hard truth. People can work constructively with a difficult reality they understand, but vague reassurance teaches them that the official story cannot be relied upon, which is far more corrosive over time.

Fourth, use stability to earn credibility. Steady operations, dependable support, and visible follow-through make trust easier to justify. Trust is a forecast about the future built from the evidence of the past, so every reliable cycle is a deposit and every broken commitment is a withdrawal.

Fifth, remember that trust compounds. Repeated evidence of reliability changes how the whole enterprise behaves. As trust grows, coordination gets cheaper, escalation gets earlier, and people stop building private defenses, which means the institution becomes both faster and more honest at the same time.

Leadership Lessons

- Trust is an operating asset, not a soft cultural idea, and it shapes the cost of nearly everything an enterprise does.
- Trust is asymmetric, built slowly through reliability and lost quickly through carelessness.
- The leading indicators of trust appear in behavior long before they appear in metrics, so leaders should learn to read them.
- Trust runs in every direction, and the downward trust leadership extends to its people is the one most often overlooked.
- Private workarounds and late escalations are honest signals about where the environment still feels fragile.
- AI raises the trust requirement, because people are asked to rely on output they cannot fully trace.
- Stewardship is the patient work of making an institution worth relying on, which is the same work that makes AI adoption healthy.

Discussion Questions

- Why should trust be treated as an operating asset rather than only a cultural virtue?
- What visible behaviors show that trust in an organization is either strengthening or weakening?
- How do reliability, governance, and communication make trust easier to justify?

- Why is trust asymmetric, and what does that asymmetry imply for how leaders treat their commitments?
- How does the way an organization introduces AI signal whether it trusts its people, and why does that matter for adoption?
- If you were teaching this chapter, what would you identify as the hidden cost of low trust inside a complex enterprise?

Application for Practice

- For the practicing leader: identify one place in your organization where people still create private workarounds. Determine what that reveals about trust, and what would have to change to remove the reason for it.
- For the IT leader: review one system, process, or team relationship that has become easier to rely on over time. Name the leadership behaviors that made that possible.
- For the consultant: in a client environment, catalog the private workarounds and late escalations you observe, and use them to map where trust is weakest across functions.
- For the faculty member or facilitator: design a short exercise in which students diagnose whether a described behavior is an efficiency problem or a trust signal, and choose the appropriate leadership response.
- For any reader: list three small signals that would tell you trust is weakening before the issue becomes obvious in formal metrics.
- For reflection: think of a time your trust in a system or a leader was rebuilt after it had been lost. What specifically restored it, and how long did it take?

Chapter 8: Governance as Accelerator

Opening

Governance rarely earns much affection when people experience it only as delay. But when it is designed well, it becomes one of the quiet ways an organization moves faster, decides more clearly, and protects itself from avoidable confusion.

There was a period when the organization was carrying more demand than it could reasonably execute. Every request made sense on its own. Each one reflected a real need somewhere in the business. But taken together, they created a system where too much was happening at once. Teams were stretched. Priorities competed. Delivery became inconsistent, not because people did not care, but because the organization was trying to move without enough shared clarity. What changed the situation was not less ambition. It was stronger governance. Once steering became more structured, capacity became visible, and trade-offs became explicit, the business stopped guessing what mattered most. Work became more deliberate. Delivery improved. What changed most was not process alone. It was confidence.

This chapter completes a pattern the earlier ones began. The book has argued that tools amplify what exists, that memory must be protected, that speed must be designed, that the enterprise must be integrated, that transformation is proven by behavior, and that trust is the substrate beneath all of it. Governance is the mechanism that holds those disciplines together in daily practice. It is how accountability becomes visible, how priorities become sequence, and how an enterprise learns to choose under pressure rather than drift. The first chapter offered five rules for AI accountability, and those rules were, in the end, a governance answer to a new kind of risk. This chapter widens the lens.

Governance, designed well, is not the opposite of speed. It is one of its most reliable sources, and it is one of the clearest expressions of stewardship a leader can practice.

Governance Became Useful When It Helped People Decide

My own view of governance changed over time. In the Y2K period, when I moved from accounting into ERP and enterprise systems, I saw early that systems are never only technical. They shape reporting, control, workflow, and the quality of decisions around them. Later, outsourcing and the offshore transition at a global electronics components manufacturer taught me how quickly structure and decision ownership can shift when operating models change. Global consulting and broader ERP work reinforced another lesson. Organizations often want faster outcomes while resisting the governance needed to make speed reliable. International development project work added the cultural dimension, showing me that governance must still make sense to the people living inside it or it becomes compliance theater. By the time I reached my current role as CIO, those lessons had come full circle. Governance mattered to me not because I liked process for its own sake, but because I had seen what happens when organizations expect disciplined execution without disciplined decision-making.

Governance, I came to see, is one of the clearest forms of stewardship. Across all of the work, the same point held. Governance becomes valuable when it improves decision clarity, demand management, and execution discipline. In our own environment, that meant standard project intake, clearer decision ownership, defined escalation paths, executive one-pagers, monthly steering committee reporting, and tighter visibility into scope, cost, resourcing, and trade-offs. It also meant telling the truth about capacity. Demand continued to outpace available resources, operational work still competed with project commitments, and stakeholder behavior could bypass governance unless leaders reinforced the discipline of prioritization. That is why I describe governance as an accelerator. It reduces confusion before confusion becomes rework and helps the enterprise move with confidence instead of optimism alone.

My respect for governance also grew because I had seen the alternatives in too many settings. In consulting, I saw programs slowed by weak decision rights and unclear ownership. In global project work, I saw how culture could make formal structure either meaningful or hollow depending on whether leaders connected it to daily reality. In enterprise leadership, I saw how overloaded teams suffered when executive ambiguity traveled downward as hidden work. Those experiences changed my relationship to governance permanently. I stopped seeing it as process overhead and started seeing it as one of the clearest ways leaders reduce unnecessary burden on everyone else.

Early in my career, I understood why so many people disliked governance. In many organizations, it was experienced as formality without help. More templates. More approvals. More conversations that seemed disconnected from the real work. That changed for me when I saw what good governance could do in a demanding environment. Good governance did not make people feel controlled. It made decisions easier to understand. It clarified who owned the next step, what mattered now, and what did not belong in the current sequence. Once governance started helping people decide, it stopped feeling administrative and started feeling useful.

That shift is important because most resistance to governance is not really resistance to discipline. It is resistance to wasted friction. Teams will embrace structure when they can see that it protects execution, reduces confusion, and keeps leadership from changing direction without explanation. In my own experience, governance became more accepted once it was clearly tied to delivery quality, team focus, and better use of capacity. People do not need more bureaucracy. They need decision paths that make the work feel more coherent. That is the version of governance worth defending.

That is why I have come to think of governance as a form of practical mercy in complex organizations. It reduces the amount of confusion people have to carry just to keep doing their work. When decision paths are visible, teams do not have to guess who will decide, which priority really comes first, or whether the latest request quietly changed the sequence without anyone saying so. Good governance does not remove pressure, but it prevents pressure from becoming disorder. In that sense, it is not only a management tool. It is one of the ways leaders make execution more humane and more reliable at the same time.

I have found that people rarely object to clarity when it truly reduces their burden. What they object to is performative governance that adds language without improving sequence. That distinction matters. Governance earns trust when teams can feel that a decision is clearer, the path is cleaner, and the next step is more believable than it was before the meeting began. In that sense, governance is one of the quiet ways leaders convert complexity into something the organization can actually carry.

The Meeting Where Governance Finally Made Sense

I can still remember the kind of meeting where governance finally stopped feeling theoretical to me. The room was full. Priorities were colliding. Different leaders were carrying different urgencies, and every request sounded reasonable when heard on its own. Without structure, that kind of meeting usually ends the same way. Everyone leaves with partial reassurance, no real sequence has been agreed, and the teams below inherit confusion disguised as momentum. What changed in the healthier version of that meeting was not the absence of pressure. It was the presence of clarity. The decision path was visible. The trade-offs were named. Demand was discussed against capacity rather than against hope. And because of that, the outcome became more durable than the energy in the room.

That experience stayed with me because it changed how I thought about governance in practice. Good governance does not exist to make leaders feel formal. It exists to protect teams from inheriting unresolved executive ambiguity. It turns priorities into sequence, sequence into execution, and execution into something the business can actually trust. In environments with many projects, sites, and competing demands, that discipline matters even more. The organization does not slow down because governance is present. It slows down because demand has outgrown clarity. Governance is one of the few mechanisms leaders have to close that gap before the cost shows up in rework, overload, and disappointment.

The hidden cost of unresolved ambiguity is that it does not stay in the conference room. It travels. It shows up in project teams preparing for multiple scenarios, managers hedging because the decision might still change, and support functions spending time on readiness for work that may never actually move. None of that effort looks dramatic on a dashboard, but it is real labor. Good governance reduces that waste by converting uncertainty into usable direction before it spreads through the system as rework, hesitation, and unnecessary caution.

I learned to appreciate this most when I saw what happened to teams in its absence. When executives leave a room with unresolved ambiguity, someone below still has to act. That means a project manager guesses at sequence, an analyst assumes a priority, a plant leader interprets intent locally, or a support team starts preparing for work that may never actually be approved. Governance matters because it stops that transfer of ambiguity from becoming normal. It gives the organization a cleaner handoff between decision and execution. And when that handoff is clear, the business moves with more confidence and less wasted effort.

What Good Governance Sounds Like

Over time, I learned that good governance has a recognizable sound to it. It is not defensive. It is not vague. It does not hide behind process language to avoid hard choices. Instead, it names the trade-offs clearly enough that people can understand why one priority is moving now and another is not. It explains sequence without sounding dismissive. It makes capacity visible without turning it into an excuse. When governance is healthy, people may still disagree, but they are less likely to leave the room confused about what was decided, why it was decided, and what happens next.

That matters because ambiguity often survives in the language leaders use with one another. If priorities are softened to avoid discomfort, teams below inherit uncertainty. If every request is described as strategic, the organization loses the ability to distinguish sequence from noise. Good governance does not eliminate pressure, but it reduces the amount of interpretation required to carry the work forward. In my experience, that is one of the most underrated leadership benefits of governance. It gives the enterprise clearer language for making difficult decisions before those decisions turn into operational confusion.

This is one reason governance is closely tied to trust in senior leadership. People may not always agree with a decision, but they can still work constructively when the reasoning is visible, the criteria are consistent, and the sequence makes sense. What weakens trust is not usually the existence of discipline. It is the suspicion that discipline will be applied unevenly, explained poorly, or changed quietly under pressure. Good governance helps prevent that. It makes the language of prioritization more stable, so the organization does not feel as though it is reinterpreting leadership intent every week.

That consistency matters most when pressure is rising. In those moments, people are watching for more than the decision itself. They are watching whether the criteria will still hold once an influential stakeholder pushes harder, once new urgency arrives, or once the room starts looking for reasons to reopen what was already settled. Governance builds trust when it proves that discipline survives pressure. That is one of the reasons the best governance cultures feel calmer than the weaker ones. People no longer have to spend so much energy guessing whether today's rules will still matter tomorrow.

The Room Before the Decision

There is a particular atmosphere in a room before an important governance decision is finally made. People are polite, but the tension is usually visible in what goes unsaid. One leader is worried about timing. Another is worried about cost. Someone else is thinking about what will happen if their team does not get what it needs this quarter. On the surface, everyone is discussing priorities. Underneath, they are also negotiating risk, trust, and credibility. I have sat in enough of those rooms to know that the quality of the decision depends as much on whether people can name the real trade-offs as on the content of the proposal itself. If the room cannot handle that honesty, governance turns into choreography. If it can, governance starts becoming leadership.

That is one reason I have never thought of governance as something separate from communication. The room before the decision tells you whether the organization is ready to choose with clarity or whether it is still trying to avoid the emotional cost of prioritizing honestly. In healthy environments, the conversation sharpens. People may disagree, but they leave with more understanding. In weaker ones, the discussion softens into vague reassurance, and the cost shows up later in teams that are forced to carry unresolved ambiguity. Over time, I learned that one of the best signs of mature governance is not the formality of the meeting. It is the degree to which the room can tolerate a clear decision without pretending that every good thing can happen at once.

I have also learned that governance helps contain the emotional spillover of executive tension. Every difficult decision carries some form of disappointment, constraint, or deferred ambition. If that tension is not processed clearly at the leadership level, it tends to leak downward into confusion, shifting priorities, and mixed signals. Good governance gives leaders a structured place to absorb that tension honestly before it becomes operational instability for everyone else. That is why a disciplined meeting matters. It protects the organization from carrying more emotional noise than the work itself already requires.

That kind of containment is not cold. It is caring. It protects the business from being asked to absorb leadership indecision indirectly. It protects project teams from whiplash. And it protects stakeholders from the false hope that everything can move at once if people just try harder. I have come to believe that one of the most humane things governance does is spare the organization from carrying unresolved tension farther than it has to.

The Agenda No One Could Prioritize

I remember one governance meeting where the agenda itself made the problem visible before anyone spoke. Every item looked legitimate. A plant need. A leadership request. A reporting dependency. A compliance concern. A project at risk. Each one could be defended. Each one mattered to someone. And that was exactly why the room was stuck. The challenge was not a lack of worthy work. It was the absence of an agreed way to decide which worthy work moved first. Without that discipline, the conversation kept circling the same point. If everything mattered, how was anyone supposed to act with confidence about what came next.

That meeting stayed with me because it captured the real burden of governance in modern organizations. The hardest part is rarely finding important work. The hardest part is creating enough clarity that important work does not compete in a way that weakens all of it at once. Once the room finally began naming trade-offs honestly, the energy changed. The decision was still difficult, but it became usable. That is the difference governance can make at its best. It turns a crowded agenda into a sequence the organization can actually carry.

I came to see this with unusual clarity. Demand continues to outpace available capacity. Operational work still competes with project commitments. Stakeholder behavior can bypass governance and create surprise work that disrupts sequence. That language matters because it turns vague frustration into governable reality. Decision checkpoints, re-baselining, defined roles, escalation paths, and quarterly review are not procedural decoration. They are what allow a crowded agenda to become an executable one. Without them, the organization keeps discovering the same limits too late.

That is why I now see demand management as one of the most honest forms of governance. It gives the organization a disciplined way to say what the system can currently carry, what it cannot, and what assumptions would have to change for the answer to be different. Without that truth-telling function, governance becomes ceremonial. With it, governance becomes design. It helps leaders shape a portfolio the enterprise can actually execute rather than merely admire on a slide.

Enterprise Case Study: Governance Through Separation and Cross Functional Execution

A graduate-level case that fits this chapter well is the governance required for a major separation effort I led. That work showed governance functioning as an execution accelerator rather than a compliance ritual. Multiple cross-functional workstreams moved in parallel: HRIS and payroll cutover readiness, productivity platform and infrastructure separation, ERP split planning, application changes, and plant-readiness dependencies. Risks, milestones, ownership, and executive focus areas were surfaced explicitly. That visibility reduced ambiguity across teams and allowed work to move with discipline during a period when business disruption would have been costly.

For a classroom, this is useful because students can study governance as a design problem. What information has to be visible. What belongs in steering review versus project management. How does governance create confidence without creating drag. The case matters because it demonstrates that in high-change environments, governance is not what slows work down. It is what prevents cross-functional execution from turning into confusion.

I saw the same lesson in our own governance rhythm. Ahead of one steering committee meeting, the focus was resource allocation and project prioritization driven by the demands of a major separation program. We laid out demand, current capacity by quarter, the near-term resource gap, downstream impacts, and recommended options to close the deficit. That is governance functioning exactly as it should. It makes constraints visible early enough that leadership can choose responsibly instead of discovering too late that execution has been overpromised.

That separation governance work made this especially concrete. We did not assume that good intentions would solve the resource problem. We forced ourselves to classify projects into critical, high-impact, and delay or pause categories, summarize current resource availability, and make the gap visible enough for executives to decide what had to wait. That is governance doing what it should do. It turns abstract overload into a visible choice. It also teaches the organization that pausing work is sometimes the most responsible way to protect what matters most.

Why Prioritization Is an Act of Respect

What made this lesson especially practical for me was realizing that governance does not only protect schedules and budgets. It protects the emotional quality of execution. When priorities are clear, people waste less energy trying to read executive intent from scattered signals. They can focus, finish, and communicate more honestly because the system is no longer asking them to guess what matters most. In my experience, that is one of the quiet reasons good governance feels lighter than weak governance. It reduces hidden labor before hidden labor turns into fatigue.

Over time, I came to see prioritization as more than a planning tool. It is a form of respect. It respects the finite capacity of teams. It respects the complexity of real work. It respects the fact that people cannot deliver their best effort when everything is presented as urgent and nothing is allowed to stabilize. Poor prioritization is not only inefficient. It is exhausting. It asks teams to carry ambiguity as if ambiguity were a normal operating condition. Good governance protects them from that by making clear what matters most now, what must wait, and what does not yet deserve the organization's full attention.

That is one reason I do not think of prioritization as a mechanical exercise. It is deeply human. Leaders set the emotional temperature of execution when they decide whether every request becomes a fire drill or whether the organization is allowed to work through a sequence with enough steadiness to succeed. In my experience, the strongest teams are not the ones carrying the most simultaneous urgency. They are the ones protected by leaders who are disciplined enough to say, with clarity and credibility, this matters, this waits, and this is how we will move.

That is why I believe prioritization must be taught as a moral as well as operational discipline. It tells the truth about limits before teams have to discover those limits through overload. It protects quality by refusing to pretend that everything urgent can move at once without consequence. And it reminds leaders that not choosing is still a choice. In governance settings, this kind of honesty matters because it turns prioritization from a private preference into a visible enterprise decision with shared accountability.

It also protects credibility. Teams can tolerate difficult prioritization more easily than they can tolerate a leadership culture that keeps promising everything and quietly delivering confusion. Over time, governance earns authority not because people enjoy hearing no, but because they begin to see that disciplined prioritization leads to fewer surprises, more stable commitments, and less wasted effort. That is how governance becomes an accelerator. It does not accelerate by pushing harder. It accelerates by removing the confusion that was slowing the organization down in the first place.

Governing AI Without Slowing It Down

AI is the clearest current test of whether an organization understands what governance is for. The instinctive reaction to a powerful, unfamiliar technology is one of two extremes. Some organizations govern AI so heavily, out of fear, that the capability is strangled before it can prove its value. Others govern it so little, out of excitement, that it spreads through the enterprise faster than anyone can answer for what it is doing. Both extremes come from the same misunderstanding, the belief that governance and speed are opposites. The argument of this chapter is that, designed well, governance is how an enterprise adopts AI quickly and safely at the same time, because it removes the confusion and risk that would otherwise force the organization to slow down later.

What governance for AI looks like is the same in spirit as the governance described throughout this chapter, applied to a new surface. It means clear decision rights about which use cases may proceed and who owns them. It means honest answers about what data the tools may touch and whether that data is governed well enough to trust. It means defined points where a human reviews and owns the output before it shapes a real decision. And it means evaluating each capability by the institutional value it creates rather than by how impressive it appears. Those are not brakes on AI. They are what allow leaders to say yes to more of it with confidence, because the path is visible and the accountability is clear. The first chapter's five rules for AI accountability were exactly this, governance written for a new kind of risk.

The deeper point is that AI does not change what governance is for. It raises the cost of not having it. An enterprise that already knows how to make trade-offs visible, assign ownership, and tell the truth about capacity will fold AI into that discipline naturally, governing it as one more category of demand and risk. An enterprise without that discipline will meet AI the way it met every other wave of overload, by starting more than it can absorb and discovering the consequences too late. Governance is what lets an organization move fast on AI precisely because it has decided, in advance, how it will choose.

Why This Chapter Matters

The enduring lesson is simple. Governance is not there to burden the enterprise with more process. It is there to reduce the cost of ambiguity before ambiguity becomes operational drag. For students, faculty, and practicing executives, that is what makes this a serious leadership chapter. Governance becomes an accelerator when it helps the organization choose clearly, sequence honestly, and move with less confusion than it otherwise would. That is not bureaucracy. That is stewardship expressed through disciplined decision-making.

The lesson reads differently depending on the reader's seat. For the practicing CIO and the IT leader, the message is operational.

Design governance around real decisions, tie it visibly to delivery and capacity, and judge it by whether teams inherit clarity or confusion. For the consultant, the message is diagnostic. The health of a client's governance is best read not in the existence of steering meetings but in whether decisions actually survive pressure and whether ambiguity is leaking downstream into hidden work. And for the faculty member and the graduate student, the message is conceptual. This is a chance to study governance as a design problem and prioritization as a moral discipline, and to examine why well-designed governance accelerates rather than delays.

Boardroom Perspective: Governance Is How the Enterprise Learns to Choose

Boards often say they want speed, but what they usually need is confidence that the enterprise knows how to choose under pressure. Governance creates that confidence. It makes priorities visible, trade-offs explicit, and ownership hard to confuse. Without it, the business can still appear active, but activity begins replacing decision quality. Projects move because no one wants to say no. Requests gain momentum because no one has converted demand into sequence. A mature board should therefore see governance not as a reporting ritual, but as one of the mechanisms that protects the institution from becoming governed by urgency alone.

That is why boards should ask where governance is creating genuine clarity and where ambiguity is still leaking into execution. Which priorities are truly agreed and which are being carried on momentum. Where does demand still outrun capacity because the enterprise has not yet become disciplined enough to make visible trade-offs. Which decisions are still being softened instead of settled. And as AI adoption accelerates, how is the enterprise governing which use cases proceed, who owns them, and what data they touch. These are not procedural questions. They are stewardship questions. They determine whether the organization can move with confidence or whether it will keep asking teams to absorb executive uncertainty downstream.

From the CIO's Desk

One of the most useful shifts in my own leadership was realizing that governance becomes trusted when it starts reducing hidden labor. Teams should not have to spend energy guessing which request really matters, preparing for multiple executive interpretations, or building private protection around the possibility that priorities may change without warning. Good governance lowers that burden. It gives people a cleaner line of sight between decision and execution. That is why I no longer think of governance as control language. I think of it as one of the ways leaders make the enterprise more livable under pressure.

If I had to summarize my own view simply, it would be this. Governance accelerates the enterprise when it turns ambiguity into sequence early enough that people can still do meaningful work once, rather than partial work twice. That is the standard I care about most. Governance should help the business feel more coherent, not more procedural. It should protect attention, preserve credibility, and make it easier for commitments to remain believable after the meeting ends. When it does that well, the organization moves with more confidence because clarity has become part of the operating model.

Five Leadership Rules for Governance That Accelerates

These are the rules I keep returning to. They are easy to state and demanding to live, which is usually the mark of a principle worth keeping.

First, design governance around real decisions. If the structure cannot help the enterprise choose clearly, it will become administration instead of acceleration. Every routine and report should exist to make a real decision easier, and anything that does not should be questioned.

Second, make trade-offs visible before commitment. Hidden constraints always return later as delay, overload, or rework. Surfacing the cost of a choice before it is made is what turns governance from a record of decisions into a tool for making better ones.

Third, align demand to capacity honestly. Governance earns trust when it tells the truth about what the system can currently carry. Demand will almost always outpace capacity, and the discipline is to make that gap visible early enough that leaders can choose rather than discover it through failure.

Fourth, use rhythm to reduce ambiguity. Regular steering, review, and escalation paths should make direction easier to follow, not harder to interpret. Predictable cadence is what lets people stop guessing whether today's priorities will still hold tomorrow.

Fifth, let governance protect people from executive uncertainty. The strongest governance cultures spare teams from doing hidden labor on behalf of unresolved priorities. When leaders resolve ambiguity at their level, they hand the organization a clean sequence instead of a confusing one, which is one of the most humane things governance does.

Leadership Lessons

- Governance and speed are not opposites, and designed well, governance is one of the most reliable sources of speed.
- Most resistance to governance is resistance to wasted friction, not to discipline itself.

- Unresolved ambiguity does not stay in the room, it travels downward and becomes hidden labor.
- Prioritization is a moral discipline as much as an operational one, because not choosing is still a choice.
- Governance builds trust when it proves that the criteria survive pressure and influence.
- AI raises the cost of weak governance, because it spreads faster than an undisciplined enterprise can answer for it.
- The best governance cultures feel calmer, because people no longer guess whether today's rules will hold tomorrow.

Discussion Questions

- Under what conditions does governance accelerate execution instead of slowing it down?
- How does prioritization function as a leadership discipline rather than simply a project-management technique?
- What are the warning signs that governance in an organization has become too weak or too complex?
- How should an enterprise govern AI so that it neither strangles the capability nor lets it spread faster than accountability can follow?
- As a consultant, how would you tell whether a client's governance produces real decisions or merely well-documented ambiguity?
- If every initiative is labeled urgent, how should leaders restore clarity and discipline?

Application for Practice

- For the practicing leader: map how one important decision currently moves through your organization. Identify where the process is clear and where ambiguity still slows execution.

- For the IT leader: identify one initiative that may be suffering from weak governance. Determine what would become clearer if priorities, ownership, or decision criteria were made more visible.
- For the consultant: in a client environment, assess whether decisions made in governance forums actually survive pressure, and where ambiguity is leaking downstream into hidden work.
- For the faculty member or facilitator: design a short exercise in which students must build a minimal governance model for an AI use case, defining decision rights, data boundaries, and human ownership.
- For any reader: review your current set of priorities. Identify where better prioritization would protect team capacity and improve delivery quality.
- For reflection: think of a time you inherited unresolved ambiguity from a decision made above you. What hidden labor did it create, and what clearer handoff would have prevented it?

Chapter 9: Calm Under Pressure

Opening

Pressure has a way of revealing what normal operations can conceal. It shows the quality of the operating model, the clarity of communication, and the steadiness of leadership all at once. Calm under pressure is often mistaken for temperament, but in leadership it is much more than that. It is a discipline. It is a way of protecting the room from becoming more chaotic than the facts require. It is one of the clearest ways a leader helps an institution keep thinking when conditions make it easier to react. In executive life, pressure is not rare. It comes through outages, security events, project failure risk, vendor problems, executive misalignment, delays, and moments when too many important things are happening at once. In those moments, the organization is not only watching what the leader decides. It is also absorbing how the leader behaves while deciding.

That is why this chapter matters for practicing CIOs, IT leaders, consultants, and graduate leadership programs alike. Calm is not simply a personal preference. It is an operating asset. It changes the quality of communication, the pace of escalation, the credibility of updates, and whether teams can still think clearly while the pressure is real. In my experience, a leader does not create calm by denying urgency. A leader creates calm by giving urgency enough structure that people can still work inside it without losing themselves.

Calm is also where the disciplines of the earlier chapters are tested most severely. Pressure is the moment when accountability cannot hide, when the strength of institutional memory is revealed, when designed speed either holds or collapses into reaction, when integration either keeps functions aligned or lets them fragment, and when trust either steadies the room or proves to have been thinner than anyone admitted. A calm season can disguise a great deal. A hard one cannot. I have come to treat calm under pressure as one of the purest expressions of stewardship. It is the discipline that keeps an enterprise behaving like itself precisely when circumstances are trying to pull it apart.

Pressure Reveals the Operating Model

My own understanding of this was shaped over many years and across very different environments. The Y2K period, when I shifted from accounting into ERP and enterprise systems, taught me early that systems are never only technical. When systems are unstable, the business feels exposed. The outsourcing and offshore transition at a global electronics components manufacturer taught me what uncertainty feels like when decisions reach people's livelihoods. Global consulting and broader ERP work taught me that clients do not only remember what went wrong. They remember whether the people leading the work made the situation easier or harder to carry. International development project work taught me that culture changes how people experience authority, escalation, and confidence under strain. By the time I reached my current role as CIO, those lessons had come full circle. Calm was no longer a personality trait in my mind. It was one of the most practical forms of stewardship available to a leader.

One reason pressure matters so much is that it reveals the truth of the operating model faster than ordinary conditions do. In calm seasons, weak communication can be hidden. Unclear ownership can be tolerated longer. Poor escalation discipline may not yet show its full cost. But when the environment tightens, those weaknesses stop hiding. Pressure reveals whether the organization knows how to communicate, whether it can distinguish signal from noise, whether people know who owns the next move, and whether the system around the work is strong enough to keep functioning while the facts are still moving.

That became especially clear in operational environments where uptime, stable systems, and issue response directly affected the confidence of the business. With my own teams, I often emphasized that if an outage affected the business, communication had to be immediate, clear, and repeated until recovery was complete. The point was never to dramatize the incident. The point was to keep the business from living inside avoidable ambiguity. People can tolerate disruption better than they can tolerate silence with no structure around it. Calm leadership does not eliminate the difficulty. It makes the difficulty more usable.

What Pressure Taught Me About Clarity

Over time, I learned that pressure does not simply test problem-solving. It tests clarity. In calm moments, organizations can hide behind incomplete alignment, informal assumptions, and half-defined ownership because the cost of confusion is spread out over time. Under pressure, all of that compresses. People want direction. Teams need facts. Leaders are expected to reduce uncertainty even before every answer is available. That is when I began to understand that one of the most valuable things a leader can provide in difficult moments is not immediate perfection. It is ordered thinking. It is the ability to separate what is known from what is suspected, what matters now from what can wait, and what the organization must do first to regain control.

That lesson stayed with me because pressure has a way of amplifying tone as much as action. If leadership becomes frantic, the organization absorbs that panic quickly. If leadership becomes vague, assumptions start multiplying in every direction. But if leadership remains steady and specific, even while the situation is still developing, people begin to settle into the work that matters. In my own experience, that steadiness does not come from personality alone. It comes from preparation, operating discipline, and the habit of thinking clearly before speaking loudly. That is one reason I believe calm leadership is not passive. It is active stewardship under strain.

What the First Update Feels Like

One of the moments that reveals a leader most clearly is the first update after something has gone wrong or might be about to. The facts are incomplete. The room is restless. People want certainty that does not yet exist. In those moments, the pressure to sound complete can be stronger than the discipline to be precise. But I learned that the first update does not need to be perfect to be useful. It needs to be honest, structured, and calm enough that people can orient themselves. What do we know. What are we confirming. What matters now. Who owns the next step. That rhythm does more than move information. It helps stop emotion from writing the narrative before leadership has found the facts.

I came to respect this more deeply in environments where go-lives, cutovers, payroll, and plant operations left very little room for drama. When the business is depending on a stable outcome, the emotional quality of communication matters almost as much as the technical quality of the response. A rushed, vague, or theatrical update can make an issue feel larger than it is. A calm and specific update can keep the organization thinking clearly long enough for the right people to do the right work. That is one reason I do not separate communication from execution in moments of pressure. The first update is part of the operating model. It either reinforces trust or quietly weakens it.

That is why I have come to believe that clarity under pressure is one of the purest expressions of leadership maturity. In steady times, many organizations can appear composed because the environment is forgiving. Under strain, composition has to be created on purpose. The leader must help people distinguish signal from noise, sequence from speculation, and responsibility from emotional spillover. When that happens, pressure does not disappear, but it becomes more workable. The organization can keep thinking.

Why Tone Is a Leadership Tool

I have come to believe that tone is one of the most underestimated tools in executive leadership. Not because leaders should perform calm for appearance, but because tone becomes part of the operating model the moment pressure rises. If the leader sounds scattered, people begin guessing. If the leader sounds dramatic, the issue often feels larger than the facts require. If the leader sounds falsely relaxed, teams may feel unseen and start compensating with their own anxiety. But when the leader sounds grounded, clear, and visibly engaged, people begin to trust that the problem is still being carried inside a system of thought rather than a system of panic.

Calm as an Enterprise Asset

I no longer think of calm as an individual virtue alone. I think of it as an enterprise asset. Calm reduces waste. It keeps teams from spending too much energy interpreting the emotional climate instead of solving the problem. It makes updates more useful. It helps stakeholders hear what matters instead of what sounds loudest. It reduces the chance that reactive communication will create a second problem layered on top of the original one. In our own environment, strong uptime and steady service performance were not only signs of technical discipline. They were signs that the organization could work in an environment that was becoming more trustworthy over time.

Calm Is Communicated Before It Is Felt

One reason calm leadership matters so much is that people often decide how worried to become by listening to the first credible signal they receive. In operational moments, that signal is frequently the leader's tone. Before the system is fully stabilized, before the root cause is fully understood, and before the full sequence of response is visible, people are already listening for cues. Is the message steady. Is it precise. Does it sound grounded enough to trust. Calm is often communicated before it is personally felt, which means leaders sometimes have to lend the organization emotional stability before the room has fully found its own.

That is not performance. It is stewardship. It does not require pretending everything is fine when it is not. It requires enough internal discipline to communicate uncertainty without spreading disorder. In my experience, some of the most trusted leaders are not the ones who always have the answer first. They are the ones who help the organization stay thinkable long enough for the answer to emerge. That is a very practical form of calm. It protects attention, reduces rumor, and gives the people closest to the issue a better chance to work the problem without fighting unnecessary emotional turbulence at the same time.

I sometimes think of this as borrowed stability. Before the room has fully settled, the leader lends steadiness through structure, tone, and sequence. That is not manipulation. It is service. People do better work when they do not have to guess whether leadership is still thinking clearly. They do better work when the atmosphere gives them enough order to focus on the problem instead of on the emotion around it. In that sense, calm leadership is not only reassuring. It is operationally productive.

The First Five Minutes Matter

The first five minutes of a high-pressure moment often shape everything that follows. People are watching more closely than they realize. They are listening for confidence, but also for order. If the initial response is scattered, the organization becomes scattered with it. If the early signals suggest blame, people begin protecting themselves before they begin solving. But if the first five minutes create enough structure for people to understand what is happening, who is leading, and what matters first, the situation becomes more manageable almost immediately. I have learned that the opening moments of pressure are not only technical. They are behavioral. They determine whether the organization enters the issue as a team or as a collection of anxious individuals.

That is why calm has to become operational before it becomes emotional. The facts may still be developing. The risk may still be real. But the system benefits immediately when leadership creates a path for attention to follow. What do we know. Who owns the next step. What will be updated next. In my experience, those simple anchors change the quality of response more than dramatic language ever could. They help the organization move from fear toward function. And once that happens, the technical work has a better chance to succeed because it is no longer carrying the full weight of the room's uncertainty by itself.

Those first minutes also protect the technical team from carrying too much unnecessary emotional weight. If the room becomes chaotic, the people solving the issue are forced to manage both the problem and everyone else's reaction to it. Strong leadership prevents that. It creates enough order that the specialists closest to the issue can stay close to the issue. In my experience, that is one of the most practical ways leaders help pressure remain manageable. They keep the response from multiplying the problem.

I was reminded of this vividly during a plant network event that could easily have turned into a very different kind of night. The issue itself mattered, but the deeper lesson came from the response. A team member stepped forward calmly, took first response ownership, and told me to stay out of the weeds unless I was needed. I listened. The system had done what it was designed to do, and the team had grown strong enough to lead without waiting for the title in the room to rescue them. That moment stayed with me because it captured a core truth of stewardship. A scalable organization does not pause to wait for the CIO when the people and systems are ready to act.

That moment also reminded me that calm under pressure is a system quality, not only a personal one. A mature team does not need the CIO to perform calm on its behalf if the ownership, confidence, and preparation have already been distributed well. In fact, one of the best signs of real leadership maturity is that the right people can lead the moment without waiting for the highest title to take over. That is not absence. It is stewardship succeeding at scale.

That lesson matters to me because it captures the kind of leadership I most want institutions to grow. Not leadership that centralizes every answer in one title, but leadership that develops people deeply enough that sound judgment is distributed across the system. Calm under pressure becomes more scalable when the team has been developed, trusted, and prepared well enough to act without waiting for rescue. In my experience, that is one of the clearest signs that stewardship is working. The enterprise can keep functioning with confidence because leadership has become larger than one person's immediate presence.

Enterprise Case Study: Calm Under Pressure During Stable Go Lives and Live Support

This chapter can be strengthened with a case drawn from my own enterprise. Several major go-lives and transitions came through stable: an ERP separation go-live with smooth plant operations, validated manufacturing execution after go-live, a manufacturing time-entry launch with no process disruption, a payroll stabilization period completed with stable results, and a separation phase executed with no reported issues. These outcomes did not happen because pressure was absent. They happened because pressure was anticipated. Planning, testing, ownership, and communication were structured in advance. That is what made calm leadership visible in the outcome, even when the work itself was complex and time-sensitive.

This is useful for graduate programs because it lets students examine pressure without waiting for failure. They can ask what conditions make stable execution possible, how leaders communicate risk without spreading anxiety, and how preparedness changes the emotional temperature of a major transition. It is a case about pressure management through design, not through heroics.

I saw this reinforced again and again. Stable ERP operations, validated manufacturing execution, a clean time-entry launch, and a successful payroll stabilization are not only examples of technical readiness. They are evidence that pressure had been absorbed upstream through preparation, testing, ownership, and communication discipline. The business felt less turbulence because the operating model had already done more of the emotional work in advance. That is one of the quiet gifts of preparedness. It allows the organization to experience complex change without having to feel every internal strain directly.

Preparedness Changes the Emotional Temperature

One of the most underappreciated effects of preparedness is emotional. When an organization has rehearsed its response paths, clarified ownership, tested key transitions, and built communication habits before the critical moment arrives, people do not just respond better. They feel different while responding. The room is less frantic. Escalations are more purposeful. Updates carry more signal and less noise. That does not mean the work becomes easy. It means the organization is less likely to create secondary chaos on top of the original issue. I have come to see that as a major leadership responsibility. Strong leaders do not only prepare systems. They prepare the emotional conditions for clearer action.

That matters because people remember how an organization felt during a critical moment. They remember whether information moved clearly, whether leaders were visible without becoming theatrical, and whether the team seemed organized enough to carry the situation without turning every issue into a spectacle. In that sense, preparedness is more than operational discipline. It is cultural reassurance. It gives people evidence that the environment around them can hold when something important is under stress. For a CIO, that kind of stability is not incidental. It is part of the trust contract with the business.

That is why I do not treat preparedness as an operational checklist alone. It is also a cultural message. It tells the business that the organization expects pressure and has chosen not to wait for pressure to teach it how to behave. Testing, rehearsal, communication paths, stabilization planning, fallback options, and clear ownership all say the same thing in different forms. We are taking your stability seriously. In high-pressure environments, that message matters as much as the technical plan because it lowers the fear that the enterprise is improvising under conditions where improvisation will be too expensive.

The Week the Team Could Have Burned Out

There was a week in one of our most demanding operating seasons when I could see the team approaching the edge of what sustained pressure would allow. The issue was not a single crisis. It was the accumulation of many legitimate demands arriving without enough recovery in between them. People were still performing. Updates were still moving. The work was still getting done. But the signs were there: shorter patience, thinner margins for error, less emotional reserve, and the kind of fatigue that makes even capable people begin to lose confidence in their own judgment. Moments like that taught me that pressure is not only something leaders manage for the business. It is something they must manage for the people carrying the business through it.

What mattered in that week was not simply helping the team endure. It was helping them avoid paying a long-term price for a short-term push. We had to simplify decisions, protect focus, and be honest about what could wait without pretending the pressure was smaller than it was. I learned then that one of the leader's responsibilities in hard seasons is to keep the work from consuming the people more deeply than the situation truly requires. Calm leadership is not only about projecting steadiness outward. It is also about noticing when the people inside the response need protection from becoming collateral damage of the urgency around them.

I have become more convinced over time that pressure should never be allowed to become theatrical if it can be made truthful instead. Teams can endure a hard season more sustainably when leaders reduce secondary burden: fewer unnecessary meetings, fewer mixed messages, fewer avoidable escalations, and fewer promises that everything will be fine when the better answer is that the work is hard but manageable. Calm leadership does not deny the strain. It protects people from carrying more strain than the reality already requires.

Another lesson I learned in those seasons is that calm leadership protects more than the immediate response. It protects memory. Teams remember whether the leader helped the room stay thinkable or made the pressure feel larger than it already was. They remember whether updates were clear, whether ownership stayed visible, and whether people were allowed to focus on solving the issue rather than defending themselves from confusion. That memory matters because it shapes how the organization enters the next hard moment. Calm under pressure is not only useful in the event itself. It becomes part of the enterprise's confidence about what kind of place this is when things get difficult.

Calm in an Accelerated, AI-Saturated World

AI changes the conditions in which calm has to be created, and mostly it raises the premium on it. A modern incident no longer unfolds at human speed. Alerts multiply, dashboards refresh constantly, automated systems generate volumes of signal, and external commentary can move faster than the facts. In that environment, the scarce resource is not information. It is ordered thinking. The discipline this chapter describes, separating what is known from what is suspected, what matters now from what can wait, becomes more valuable precisely because everything around the leader is accelerating. The faster the information environment moves, the more an enterprise needs a human capable of slowing the room to the speed of good judgment.

There is also a specific temptation worth naming. In the pressure of a first update, it is tempting to let an AI tool generate the communication, because it is fast and fluent. But a crisis update is exactly the kind of moment where fluency without grounded honesty is dangerous, as the earlier chapters argued. A tool can help a leader organize facts or draft a structure, but the leader still owns the tone, the truth, and the accountability for what the message claims. People under pressure can tell the difference between a leader who is present and a message that merely sounds composed. Calm cannot be generated. It has to be carried by someone who is willing to stand behind the words.

AI also introduces a new category of pressure. Sometimes the incident itself will involve an AI system, a model behaving unexpectedly, a recommendation that caused harm, an automated process that moved faster than its oversight. Those moments will test calm in an unfamiliar way, because the failure mode is less intuitive and the explanations are harder to reach quickly. The response, though, is the same one this chapter has described throughout. Create order before reassurance, keep updates honest and proportional, protect the people closest to the problem, and refuse to let the novelty of the technology make the room more frantic than the facts require. Calm is the human discipline that does not become obsolete no matter how capable the tools become. If anything, it becomes rarer and more valuable.

Why This Chapter Matters

For students, faculty, and practicing executives, the deeper lesson of this chapter is that calm is not the absence of urgency. It is the discipline that keeps urgency from becoming disorder. Calm under pressure helps the organization think, communicate, and act with enough clarity that the response remains proportional to the issue. That is why this chapter belongs in leadership education. It teaches that steadiness is not a personality trait reserved for a few people. It is a leadership discipline that can be designed, practiced, and reinforced through the operating model itself.

The lesson reads differently depending on the reader's seat. For the practicing CIO and the IT leader, the message is operational.

Build calm into the operating model through rehearsed communication, clear escalation, and distributed ownership, so that steadiness does not depend on one person's presence. For the consultant, the message is diagnostic. The way an organization behaves in its first thirty minutes of pressure reveals more about the health of its operating model than any steady-state review, so watch how the room metabolizes a hard moment. And for the faculty member and the graduate student, the message is conceptual. This is a chance to study calm as a designed system quality rather than a personal temperament, and to examine the difference between urgency and confusion.

Boardroom Perspective: Calm Turns Pressure Into Usable Direction

Boards rarely need a leader to sound louder during pressure. They need a leader who can help the enterprise keep thinking. In difficult moments, calm does not reduce seriousness. It increases usability. It helps the board distinguish signal from noise, short-term reaction from structured response, and emotional urgency from the facts that should actually govern the next decision. That is why calm is not a personality preference in executive leadership. It is an operating asset. It protects the institution from making the situation harder than it already is.

A mature board should therefore ask not only what happened, but how the organization is metabolizing the pressure. Are updates becoming clearer or more reactive. Is the operating model reducing fear or multiplying it. Are teams being given enough structure to act or being left to absorb uncertainty on behalf of leadership. These questions matter because pressure always reveals more than the issue itself. It reveals the quality of the leadership system surrounding the issue. Calm is valuable at board level because it keeps the institution from spending its strength on noise when that strength is needed for decision and recovery.

From the CIO's Desk

One of the most practical lessons of my career is that people often remember how leadership felt during pressure longer than they remember the technical details of what happened. They remember whether the room became safer to think in, whether updates made the next step clearer, and whether the leader helped the issue feel containable enough to work. That is why I pay so much attention to tone, sequence, and the discipline of not making the problem emotionally larger than the facts already make it. Calm is not silence. It is structured steadiness in service of action.

If I had to summarize my own view simply, it would be this. Calm under pressure is one of the clearest ways a leader protects everyone else's ability to do their work well. It protects attention. It protects judgment. It protects the response from becoming more chaotic than the issue requires. In my experience, that is what mature leadership looks like in demanding moments. Not pretending the strain is small, but refusing to let strain take over the operating rhythm of the enterprise.

Five Leadership Rules for Calm Under Pressure

These are the rules I keep returning to. They are simple to state and demanding to live, which is usually the mark of a principle worth keeping.

First, create order before you create reassurance. People do better work when they know what is known, what is next, and who owns it. Structure calms a room faster than comfort does, because it gives anxiety somewhere useful to go.

Second, let updates reduce noise. Communication during pressure should narrow uncertainty, not dramatize it. The goal of the first update is not to sound complete but to help people orient, so honesty and structure matter more than polish.

Third, protect the technical team from emotional spillover. The people closest to the issue should not also have to carry the room's unmanaged anxiety. One of the leader's jobs in a hard moment is to absorb the turbulence so the specialists can stay close to the problem.

Fourth, pace the response with visible rhythm. Clear checkpoints and predictable updates help the organization keep thinking. When people know when the next update will come, they stop refreshing for rumors and return to the work.

Fifth, remember that calm is contagious, and so is confusion. Leadership tone becomes part of the operating model the moment pressure arrives. Whichever the leader transmits will spread, which is why steadiness under strain is a responsibility rather than a mood.

Leadership Lessons

- Calm is an operating asset, not a temperament, and it can be designed and rehearsed.
- Pressure reveals the operating model faster than calm seasons ever do.
- Under pressure, ordered thinking is more valuable than immediate perfection.
- Calm is often communicated before it is felt, so leaders sometimes lend the room stability first.
- A scalable organization does not wait for the CIO when its people and systems are ready to act.
- AI accelerates the information environment, which raises the premium on the human discipline of calm.
- People remember how leadership felt under pressure, and that memory shapes how they enter the next hard moment.

Discussion Questions

- What does calm leadership look like in practice during a high-pressure operational event?
- How do governance, preparation, and communication affect an organization's ability to respond under pressure?
- Why is early clarity often more valuable than delayed perfection in a crisis or disruption?
- How does an accelerated, AI-saturated information environment change what calm leadership requires?
- As a consultant, what would you observe in an organization's first response to a disruption to judge the health of its operating model?
- If you were teaching this chapter in a graduate leadership class, what would you identify as the difference between urgency and confusion?

Application for Practice

- For the practicing leader: think of a recent high-pressure event in your organization. Identify what helped create clarity and what added confusion.
- For the IT leader: map the first thirty minutes of response to a likely disruption in your environment. Decide who needs to know what and who owns the first decisions.
- For the consultant: design a short observation rubric for a client's incident response that distinguishes structured calm from theatrical urgency.
- For the faculty member or facilitator: run a brief tabletop exercise in which students must deliver a first update with incomplete facts, then critique whether it created order or noise.

- For any reader: identify one way your team could improve preparedness so that pressure creates less noise and more orderly action.
- For reflection: write a short note on how you want your communication to feel to others during pressure, and recall a moment when your tone either steadied a room or unsettled it.

Chapter 10: What Great CIOs Say No To

Opening

Demand for technology is constant, and without discipline, organizations eventually ask more of their teams than those teams can sustain. That is where execution begins to weaken, even when intentions are good. One of the most underestimated leadership disciplines in technology is the ability to say no without becoming careless, defensive, or small. Many organizations celebrate responsiveness, but mature leadership eventually learns that saying yes to everything is not service. It is often a way of weakening the system. Great CIOs understand that every yes has a cost. It draws time, attention, funding, sequencing, and emotional energy away from something else already underway. In that sense, the question is rarely whether a request is valid. The deeper question is whether the organization can carry that request now without quietly undermining commitments it has already made.

That is why this chapter matters for practicing CIOs, IT leaders, consultants, and graduate leadership programs alike. The discipline of saying no is not mostly about personality. It is about stewardship. It protects execution quality. It protects trust. It protects the business from accepting more work than the current operating model can responsibly absorb. In my experience, some of the best leadership decisions are not the ones that create the biggest excitement in the room. They are the ones that protect the integrity of the work already in motion.

This chapter is the natural companion to the ones on speed, governance, and indecision. Designed speed asks what order work should move in. Governance asks how the enterprise chooses. Indecision warns against leaving questions open too long. Saying no is the discipline that makes all of them possible, because an enterprise that cannot decline anything cannot sequence, cannot govern, and cannot protect what it has already committed to. Restraint is not the absence of ambition. It is the discipline that keeps ambition believable. In that sense, a well-placed no is one of the clearest acts of stewardship a leader performs, because it protects the people and the promises already carrying the weight of the enterprise.

Why Strategic Restraint Matters

My own understanding of this developed over many years and across very different settings. The Y2K shift from accounting into ERP work taught me early that systems are never only technical. The outsourcing and offshore transition at a global electronics components manufacturer taught me that leadership decisions reach people's stability as much as their workflow. Global consulting and broader ERP work taught me that clients often ask for more because the pressure is real, but leaders still have to decide what the system can absorb honestly. International development project work added the cultural lesson that saying no or not now must still be communicated in ways people can trust. By the time I reached my current role as CIO, those lessons had come full circle. Prioritization was no longer a project-management technique in my mind. It was one of the clearest ways leadership protects the enterprise from its own accumulation of good ideas.

That became especially visible when demand started outpacing available capacity. Across the work, the pattern was clear. Operational work still competed with project commitments, stakeholder behaviors could bypass governance, and some of the most important delivery risks came not from technical difficulty alone but from trying to carry too much at once. In one capacity review, the organization faced a significant near-term gap between required effort and available hours, especially across applications,

BI, AI, and site work. The response options made the leadership lesson plain. Bring in targeted external help, stop non-critical work, or reduce scope and accept the trade-offs visibly. That is what disciplined no looks like in executive life. It is not indifference. It is choosing which realities the enterprise can carry without pretending that all of them can be solved simultaneously.

That lesson became even more practical for me because some of the most important restraints in executive life are not about rejecting an idea. They are about protecting the institution from mistaking appetite for readiness. In consulting years, it was common to see clients ask for acceleration before process maturity, ownership clarity, or cross-functional readiness had caught up. In manufacturing and coatings environments, I learned the same lesson from the other direction. Even a good request can become destructive when it lands in an already stretched environment where ERP work, BI demand, HRIS stabilization, service issues, and operational support are all competing for the same leadership and technical capacity. That is why saying no well belongs in graduate leadership education. It forces leaders to study the discipline of preserving trust in execution, not just enthusiasm in planning.

Capacity, Credibility, and Execution

One of the clearest ways leaders lose credibility is by promising more than the system can deliver and then asking teams to absorb the gap through effort alone. That may work briefly, but over time it damages trust. Teams learn that every yes may cost them more ambiguity than leadership is admitting. Stakeholders learn that visible approval is not always the same thing as executable commitment. And the operating model becomes noisier because too many partially valid priorities are being carried at once. Strong CIOs learn that saying no or not now is sometimes the most respectful form of support available to the business because it keeps the current portfolio from quietly becoming less believable every week.

Enterprise Case Study: Prioritization, Capacity, and the Discipline of Saying Not Now

Context. In a growing enterprise, demand almost always exceeds available capacity. The issue is rarely a lack of important work. It is the accumulation of too many worthwhile requests arriving at the same time. Our project and steering discipline made this visible in practical ways through project intake, resource balancing, quarterly review, and the movement from activity-based reporting toward value, risk, and throughput. Over time, stronger governance and execution discipline helped project success rise from the mid-fifties to above ninety-five percent while maintaining stronger budget and scope performance.

Tension. The tension was not whether the requests were valid. Many were. The tension was whether the enterprise could continue saying yes without weakening execution quality, exhausting teams, and reducing confidence in what had already been approved. Our own demand planning kept reinforcing the same leadership burden. Projects cannot begin without confirming resources and technical capability, and prioritization must account for impact, dependencies, sequencing, and current constraints. In practical terms, the system needed leaders willing to protect focus rather than merely reward urgency.

Leadership Decision and Teaching Value. The leadership move was to make capacity visible enough that trade-offs could be faced honestly. That meant stronger intake discipline, visible prioritization, PMO governance, and willingness to defer, re-sequence, or augment only where the business impact truly justified it. This is a useful case for graduate leadership programs and executive education because it reframes saying no as a system-protection act, not a lack of commitment. It allows discussion of responsiveness versus discipline, capacity truth-telling, and how mature leaders preserve the credibility of existing commitments by refusing to overload the operating model with every new idea at once.

Why Protecting Capacity Became a Leadership Imperative

There was a stage in my leadership journey when I realized that protecting capacity was not a project-management concern. It was an executive responsibility. Up to that point, many organizations I had seen were still treating capacity as if it were elastic. If a request mattered enough, people assumed the team would find a way. If a leader asked with enough urgency, the work would somehow expand to absorb the new commitment. But that is not how sustainable execution works. Capacity is not a motivational problem. It is a design reality. Teams can stretch for short periods, but if leadership keeps treating every stretch as normal, quality weakens, predictability falls, and trust begins to erode.

That is why saying no became more important to me over time, not less. It was not about control. It was about stewardship. The enterprise was better served by fewer clear commitments delivered well than by a long list of half-protected promises. In practice, this meant learning to evaluate requests against sequence, readiness, available talent, business impact, and the real cost of interrupting work already underway. Once I began looking at demand through that lens, the question changed. It was no longer, can we technically do this. The better question was, what will this decision do to the health of the system that has to carry it.

That shift was reinforced whenever I saw what happened after leaders said yes too quickly. The issue was rarely laziness or lack of care. The issue was that every additional commitment changed the quality of the commitments already in motion. It introduced more context switching, thinner ownership, and less recovery space for the people carrying the work. Over time, I stopped treating yes as the collaborative answer by default. I began treating it as a decision that had to earn its place against the cost it would create elsewhere in the system.

Why Every Yes Has a Cost

One of the hardest lessons in leadership is that every yes has a cost, even when that cost is not immediately visible. A new request rarely arrives alone. It arrives attached to a timeline, a stakeholder expectation, a hidden set of dependencies, and an opportunity cost that will be paid somewhere else in the system. Early in my career, I understood the political appeal of saying yes. It sounded collaborative. It sounded responsive. It avoided friction in the moment. But over time I saw the downstream reality more clearly. Each additional yes shapes the quality of the promises already in motion. It changes what teams can finish well, what they must rush, and what begins to slip quietly without anyone naming it yet.

That is why capacity discipline became more than an operational concern for me. It became a way of telling the truth about the system. Leaders do not serve the business well by pretending teams can absorb unlimited work if they just care hard enough. They serve it by making choices that preserve the credibility of delivery, the health of the people doing the work, and the trust that commitments still mean something. Every serious organization eventually has to learn this lesson. The question is whether it learns it through disciplined prioritization or through accumulated disappointment. In my experience, the healthier path is to make the cost of yes visible early enough that better decisions are still possible.

One reason those trade-offs stay hidden is that the first cost of yes is often paid by the team, not the person making the request. It appears as a tighter schedule, a deferred improvement, a rushed handoff, or a quiet drop in attention on work that was already promised. No single compromise looks dramatic enough to become a crisis immediately. But they accumulate. And when they do, the organization begins experiencing slippage, thinner communication, and lower confidence without always connecting those symptoms back to the earlier decisions that overloaded the system. Great CIOs therefore learn to make the cost of yes visible before the cost becomes cultural.

The Promise Hidden Inside a No

A well-timed no often contains a promise that is easy to miss in the moment. It promises that the work already underway still matters. It promises that the team's current commitments will not be quietly devalued by whatever arrived five minutes later. It promises that leaders are paying attention to sequence, not just pressure. In environments where everything feels urgent, that kind of protection is more than an operational preference. It is one of the ways leaders signal that quality, focus, and credibility still have meaning. A no can feel uncomfortable in the meeting, but over time it can become one of the most trustworthy things a leader says.

I came to understand this more clearly once I had seen what happened when leaders avoided that discomfort for too long. Work became crowded. Timelines lost credibility. Good people spent more time recovering from overload than delivering thoughtful execution. A disciplined no does not reduce ambition. It protects the conditions under which ambition can still succeed. That is why saying no, deferring, or resequencing work should never be mistaken for a lack of commitment. Sometimes it is the clearest evidence that a leader is committed enough to protect the integrity of the system carrying the work.

I also learned that a disciplined no is often best heard as a structured not now. Timing matters. Sequence matters. The organization may eventually need the idea, but not at the expense of destabilizing what is already underway. Saying no well, then, requires explanation, not just refusal. Leaders have to show what current commitments are being protected, what conditions would need to change for the answer to be different, and how the decision supports the enterprise rather than merely shutting down the request. When people understand that, even a disappointing answer can strengthen trust instead of weakening it. Work then becomes possible to categorize honestly. Some initiatives move immediately. Others are delayed deliberately. In many cases, the answer is not no, but not now.

The Request That Sounded Reasonable

Many of the hardest requests to decline are not unreasonable. In fact, they often sound completely justified. A leader wants a report before a board meeting. A plant needs support for a timing issue that could affect output. A manager is trying to solve a real problem for their team and believes the request is small. I have heard all of these, and in isolation many of them make perfect sense. What makes them difficult is not the logic of the request. It is the condition of the system receiving it. By the time a reasonable request reaches an already stretched team, it becomes part of a larger pattern. The leader now has to judge not only the merit of the idea, but the cost of adding it to a system already carrying more than it can responsibly absorb.

That is why saying no often requires more empathy than saying yes. It requires understanding that the request is real, the need may be valid, and the pressure behind it is often genuine. But it also requires protecting the work already in motion from becoming quietly disposable. In my experience, some of the best leadership decisions happen when someone is willing to say, this matters, but not at the expense of everything already committed. That is not resistance. It is clarity with consequences in mind. And when leaders do that consistently, teams learn that capacity is not a vague complaint. It is a real condition of delivery that deserves to be respected.

That is one reason I have come to see prioritization as a form of kindness, not only discipline. Teams cannot do their best work when every request arrives carrying the same level of urgency. They need leaders willing to protect focus, tell the truth about timing, and make it acceptable for some things to wait. In practical terms, that means choosing clarity over false reassurance. It means helping people understand that protecting current commitments is not indifference to new needs. It is one of the clearest ways to respect the people doing the work and the outcomes the business is already counting on.

That is one reason saying no is not the opposite of service. Sometimes it is the strongest expression of service available. It keeps leaders from trading long-term credibility for short-term relief. It prevents the enterprise from teaching teams that current commitments can always be weakened by the next persuasive interruption. And it gives the business a clearer picture of what the system can actually carry responsibly. In my experience, people may resist that discipline at first, but they come to respect it when it produces steadier execution and fewer surprises.

Saying No to the AI Everyone Is Excited About

AI will test this discipline more than almost anything else a CIO faces, because the pressure to say yes to it is unusually strong and comes from every direction at once. The board reads about it. Competitors announce it. Every vendor attaches it to their product. Inside the enterprise, enthusiasm produces a steady stream of proposals, each one plausible, each one urgent, each one promising transformation. An organization without the discipline of restraint will say yes to far too many of them, scatter its limited capacity across a dozen half-resourced experiments, and discover months later that it has a great deal of activity and very little institutional value. The ability to say not now to an exciting AI proposal is, right now, one of the most valuable disciplines a technology leader can have.

The principle is the same one this chapter has argued throughout, applied to a louder temptation. The question is not whether an AI use case is interesting. Almost all of them are. The question is whether it creates real institutional value, whether the enterprise has the data and the governance to support it, and whether the organization can carry it now without weakening commitments already underway. That echoes the fifth rule from the opening chapter, to evaluate AI by institutional value rather than novelty, and it requires a leader willing to disappoint a room full of excitement. Saying no to a weak AI idea is not being behind. It is protecting the capacity and the credibility the enterprise will need for the AI work that genuinely matters.

There is a quieter version of this restraint as well. Even where AI genuinely helps, a leader has to decide where it does not belong, which decisions must remain fully human, and where automating something would trade away judgment, accountability, or trust for speed the business does not actually need. That is restraint of a higher order, declining not because the enterprise cannot do something but because it should not. In an era that will reward enthusiasm with applause, the leaders who protect their organizations best will often be the ones disciplined enough to say, this is impressive, and we are still not going to do it yet.

From the CIO's Desk

One of the clearest leadership lessons of my career is that a rushed yes often feels generous in the meeting and expensive in the months that follow. Teams absorb the cost first. They carry thinner focus, more interruptions, and a higher chance that current commitments will quietly weaken. That is why I no longer hear every request as a test of support. Sometimes the most supportive thing a leader can do is protect the work already underway from being diluted by the next reasonable idea that arrives without enough room to carry it well.

I have also found that the quality of a no often determines whether the relationship grows or weakens afterward. People can usually handle a disciplined answer if they believe the leader has understood the request, respected the need behind it, and explained the sequence honestly. What undermines trust is not restraint by itself. It is careless restraint, vague restraint, or political restraint that leaves people feeling unheard. So the best

CIOs do more than say no. They translate no into enterprise logic. They explain what is being protected, what would need to change, and why stewardship sometimes requires choosing fewer promises so the promises already made remain worthy of belief.

If I had to summarize my own view simply, it would be this. Saying no well is one of the ways a leader keeps yes meaningful. It protects execution from becoming wishful, protects teams from carrying avoidable overload, and protects the enterprise from mistaking motion for disciplined progress. In my experience, restraint is not the opposite of ambition. It is one of the ways ambition becomes believable enough to last. I have also learned that a disciplined no protects the leader from performing optimism they no longer believe. There is a quiet relief that comes when the room no longer expects you to promise what the system cannot responsibly carry. That relief matters because it makes honesty sustainable, and teams trust leaders more when restraint sounds clear and calm than when enthusiasm sounds generous but leaves everyone paying for it later.

Five Leadership Rules for Saying No Well

These are the rules I keep returning to. They are simple to state and demanding to live, which is usually the mark of a principle worth keeping.

First, explain what the current yeses are protecting. People accept restraint more readily when they can see which existing commitments would be weakened by a new demand. A no that names what it protects feels like stewardship rather than refusal.

Second, make not now a disciplined answer, not a vague escape. Sequencing builds trust when leaders are clear about what would need to change for the answer to be different. A precise not now respects the request while protecting the system, where a vague maybe simply prolongs the ambiguity.

Third, evaluate requests by system impact, not only local merit. A reasonable idea can still create unreasonable drag when it enters an overloaded portfolio. The question is never only whether the request is worthy, but what it will cost the work already underway.

Fourth, let prioritization protect team integrity. Capacity is not just a planning number. It is one of the conditions under which people can still do credible work. Protecting it is a way of respecting both the people and the outcomes the business is counting on.

Fifth, treat restraint as part of stewardship. The enterprise grows stronger when leaders protect execution quality before they expand promise volume. Saying no well is one of the ways a leader keeps every yes worth believing.

Leadership Lessons

- Saying yes to everything is not service, it is a way of weakening the system.
- Every yes has a cost, and the first cost is usually paid by the team, not the requester.
- Capacity is a design reality, not a motivational problem, and treating it as elastic erodes trust.
- A disciplined no often contains a promise that current commitments still matter.
- Saying no well requires more empathy than saying yes, because the need behind the request is usually real.
- AI raises the pressure to say yes, which makes the discipline of restraint more valuable, not less.

- Restraint is not the opposite of ambition, it is what keeps ambition believable enough to last.

Discussion Questions

- Why is the ability to say no a core leadership discipline rather than simply a personality trait?
- How does disciplined prioritization protect team capacity, delivery quality, and organizational trust?
- What is the practical difference between saying no and saying not now?
- Why does AI intensify the pressure to say yes, and how should a leader decide which AI proposals to decline?
- As a consultant, how would you help a client distinguish AI initiatives that create institutional value from those that are mostly novelty?
- If every stakeholder believes their initiative is urgent, how should a leadership team restore focus without damaging relationships?

Application for Practice

- For the practicing leader: list the major initiatives currently competing for your team's attention. Identify which are truly aligned to business priorities and which are diluting capacity.
- For the IT leader: identify one request your team should have deferred, sequenced differently, or declined. Determine what would have improved if that decision had been made earlier.
- For the consultant: review a client's active portfolio and propose which initiatives should be paused or resequenced to protect execution quality, with the reasoning made visible.
- For the faculty member or facilitator: design a short exercise in which students must decline three reasonable-sounding

requests in an overloaded environment and defend each decision in enterprise terms.

- For any reader: review how your organization currently distinguishes between urgent work and important work, and note where that distinction is weak or inconsistent.
- For reflection: think of a rushed yes you later regretted. What did it cost the work already underway, and what would a disciplined not now have protected?

Chapter 11: The Cost of Indecision

Opening

Most leaders think of indecision as hesitation. In my experience, the greater danger is drift. Work continues, meetings continue, updates continue, but the questions that should have been resolved remain unresolved long enough to become everyone else's hidden burden. That is the real cost of indecision. It is not only that a decision was late. It is that uncertainty stayed in the system long enough to create rework, weaken confidence, and force teams to keep moving without the clarity they should have had much earlier.

That is why this chapter matters for practicing CIOs, IT leaders, consultants, and graduate leadership programs alike. Decision quality is not measured only by the intelligence of the final answer. It is also measured by whether the organization received that clarity soon enough to work responsibly. In a complex enterprise, delayed clarity is expensive. It asks people to improvise around missing decisions, to hold too many assumptions at once, and to absorb uncertainty that leadership should have processed before it reached the team.

This chapter is the mirror image of the one before it. The discipline of saying no protects the enterprise from too many decisions made too quickly. The cost of indecision is the opposite failure, too few decisions made in time. Both are failures of stewardship, because both leave the organization carrying a burden that leadership should have carried first. The connecting idea runs through the whole book. Whether the problem is overcommitment, weak governance, or prolonged ambiguity, the people with the least authority usually end up absorbing the consequences of decisions the people with the most authority did not make cleanly. Timely clarity is one of the most practical ways a leader keeps that from happening.

When Uncertainty Starts Making Decisions for the Organization

One of the hardest truths I learned in leadership is that indecision does not create a neutral environment. When leaders delay too long, uncertainty starts making decisions on the organization's behalf. People fill the silence with assumptions. Managers create local workarounds. Teams interpret priorities through whatever partial signals they have. Meetings continue. Work continues. Activity even increases. But direction becomes less coherent with each passing day. That is why indecision is so costly. It rarely looks like stillness. It looks like movement without agreement, effort without alignment, and progress that later has to be unwound.

In my own experience, this became especially clear in environments where ownership was not yet visible. The longer important decisions remained suspended, the more the organization learned to improvise around them. At first, that can look adaptive. Teams appear resourceful. Work keeps moving. But improvisation is not the same as alignment. Eventually, somebody has to reconcile the competing decisions that were made in the absence of clarity. That reconciliation is expensive. It costs time, trust, and momentum. Over time I came to see timely direction not as a sign of certainty, but as a form of stewardship. Leaders owe the organization enough clarity to keep uncertainty from becoming the hidden operating model.

When Delay Becomes a Decision

I learned this lesson gradually across very different chapters of my career. The Y2K shift from accounting into ERP work taught me that systems are never only technical. Unclear decisions about process, reporting, or control do not stay inside IT. They show up as friction in the business. The outsourcing and offshore transition at a global electronics components manufacturer taught me that delayed clarity affects people's trust and sense of security as much as their workflow. Global consulting and broader ERP work taught me how often clients could tolerate a hard answer more easily than they could tolerate prolonged ambiguity. International development project work reinforced that culture changes how people experience authority and delay. By the time I reached my current role as CIO, those lessons had come full circle. I had seen enough to know that organizations usually recover more quickly from a difficult decision than from a long season of avoidable uncertainty.

That is why I have come to see indecision less as a personal weakness and more as an organizational design issue. When ownership is vague, priorities are unstable, and decision rights are unclear, the enterprise does not pause. It drifts. People keep trying to move. They solve around the gap. They make local assumptions. They preserve optionality because no one has made the call that would let the work settle. That drift is costly because it rarely looks dramatic at first. It simply becomes part of the emotional and operational tax people carry every week.

What makes delay so dangerous in leadership is that the organization rarely experiences it as simple waiting. It experiences it as drift. Calendar time passes, but the real cost shows up in the decisions people begin making in the silence. A manager creates a workaround because the issue cannot stay unresolved forever. A team interprets a half-signal as direction. A stakeholder assumes the absence of objection means quiet approval. None of that is irrational. It is what organizations do when they are trying to keep moving. But the longer that pattern continues, the harder it becomes to distinguish intentional direction from accumulated improvisation.

I learned this in especially vivid ways across my own arc from ERP work into executive leadership. In early systems environments, unclear decisions around process, reporting, or ownership always traveled farther than leaders expected. In consulting, delayed clarity often pushed teams into expensive parallel preparation. In global work, indecision could become even more costly because distance, cultural rhythm, and limited local capacity left less room for vague guidance to be interpreted safely. Later, as a CIO, the same pattern appeared in a more mature form. If steering paths were unclear, if roles were blurred, or if priorities remained unresolved too long, the organization did not pause politely. It started protecting itself with local assumptions. That is why timely clarity matters so much to me. It reduces the amount of private interpretation the enterprise has to keep carrying just to keep moving.

I came to see this as one of the hidden forms of systems damage in leadership. Indecision does not only postpone action. It redistributes decision-making into the wrong places. It forces people lower in the system to make judgments without the context, authority, or cross-functional visibility that the original decision required. By the time leadership eventually returns to the issue, the organization is no longer choosing from a clean set of options. It is now choosing among the consequences of delay. All of it points back to why timely clarity matters so much. It protects the organization from living too long inside a decision vacuum.

That is one reason indecision can feel deceptively responsible in executive environments. It sounds careful. It sounds thoughtful. It sounds as though leadership is protecting the business from premature judgment. Sometimes that is true. But not always.

There is a point when more waiting no longer produces better insight. It only enlarges the area in which the organization must keep guessing. That is the moment leaders have to recognize. Otherwise caution begins masquerading as wisdom while uncertainty quietly becomes the stronger operating force.

The Hidden Cost of Unclosed Questions

The hidden cost of indecision is that the question does not disappear simply because it was not answered. It moves downward. It becomes a burden on teams that now have to keep working without knowing which assumption will hold. It becomes a source of repeated escalation because no one is sure what was actually decided. It becomes rework because the work moved in one direction while the unresolved decision was still waiting somewhere else. In PMO and steering work, I saw this repeatedly. Questions left unresolved long enough eventually return as schedule pressure, stakeholder frustration, and work that no longer trusts the path it is on.

That is why visible decision paths matter so much. In stronger environments, people know how decisions move, who owns what, when an issue is ready for resolution, and where uncertainty should be surfaced rather than buried. I saw this clearly in our own turnaround. Projects were no longer unmanaged or informal. Roles, escalation paths, and decision ownership were defined. Leadership had stronger visibility into capacity constraints, competing priorities, and delivery trade-offs. That may sound procedural, but it is actually one of the clearest ways to reduce the cost of indecision. It gives the organization a stronger path from uncertainty to direction before drift becomes embedded in the work.

What Ambiguity Costs the People Doing the Work

One of the less visible costs of indecision is the burden it places on the people still trying to do good work inside the uncertainty. They spend time preparing for multiple possibilities because none of them can be ruled out. They hesitate before committing effort because they are not sure whether the direction will hold. They revisit the same question in different meetings because the answer never fully lands. That kind of ambiguity creates real labor, even when it does not show up on a project plan. It drains confidence, slows execution, and teaches teams to conserve effort until clarity feels more reliable.

That is why delayed clarity can damage morale even when leaders believe they are protecting optionality. People do not experience optionality the same way executives do. What leaders experience as more time to think, teams often experience as more time to wait, recheck, and hold back. The work becomes heavier because every step must now account for multiple possible futures. In that kind of environment, initiative narrows. People conserve energy instead of investing it. That is one of the least visible, but most expensive, costs of indecision.

The Meeting That Ended Without an Answer

I remember a meeting where everyone in the room understood the issue, but no one was ready to decide. The facts were familiar. The risks were known. The options had been discussed before. And still the conversation drifted toward one more review, one more conversation, one more round of confirmation. When the meeting ended, there was no explosion, no visible failure, and no dramatic conflict. But what left the room with us was heavier than it looked. Teams would now go back to their work carrying the same uncertainty, making private assumptions about what leadership probably meant, and quietly spending energy on possibilities that might never become real.

That meeting stayed with me because it clarified something important. Indecision is not only a gap in direction. It is a transfer of burden. The people with the least authority often end up carrying the most uncertainty because the people with the authority to decide have not yet closed the question. Over time, that pattern teaches an organization to live cautiously. It weakens initiative without anyone announcing that initiative has become risky. And it reminds me why clarity matters so much. A timely decision does more than move the work. It frees people to stop defending themselves against ambiguity and start doing the work that matters.

The longer I have led, the more convinced I have become that disciplined leadership is not mainly about appearing decisive. It is about reducing the amount of unnecessary burden the organization has to carry because leaders were unwilling to create clarity in time. When ambiguity lingers too long, people do not feel empowered. They feel exposed. That is one reason I believe leadership has to be measured not only by the quality of the decision, but by whether the system around the decision leaves people steadier, clearer, and more able to move together.

It is also why visible ownership matters so much. The organization can tolerate a difficult decision more easily than a leaderless one. When people know where the decision belongs, what criteria will guide it, and when clarity is expected, waiting feels structured rather than arbitrary. But when ownership is diffuse, the silence itself becomes destabilizing. People begin acting as though the question is already decided, even though it never was. Over time, those informal assumptions harden into parallel operating realities that become much harder to reconcile later.

Enterprise Case Study: Decision Clarity and the Hidden Cost of Delay

Context. In the early phases of the IT turnaround, weak governance, inconsistent priorities, and poor project success did not only create execution problems. They created decision problems. Too much work depended on informal interpretation, unclear ownership, or questions that stayed open too long. That meant the operating model itself was carrying unresolved choices deeper into delivery than it should have.

Tension. The tension was not that leaders lacked intelligence or intent. It was that unclear decision environments allowed drift to become normal. When ownership is vague and priorities remain unstable, organizations do not stop. They keep moving with too many assumptions at once. Teams begin solving around the uncertainty. Confidence weakens because people are no longer sure whether the current path will still be the path next week. That hidden burden shows up later as slower execution, more rework, and lower trust in commitments.

Leadership Decision and Teaching Value. The leadership move was to build visible decision paths through stronger governance, defined escalation, clearer ownership, and regular steering review. In practice, that meant fewer unmanaged projects, tighter PMO rhythm, more explicit trade-offs, and a decision structure the organization could actually trust. The turnaround journey later showed the effect in measurable form, with project success rising above ninety-five percent and decision quality improving because the work was no longer depending on informal interpretation to keep moving. This makes the case useful for graduate leadership programs, CIO development, and executive education because it reframes indecision as an operating-model issue rather than only a personality issue.

For graduate classrooms, this case helps students see indecision as an organizational design issue rather than only a personal hesitation issue. They can discuss how leaders create decision paths, what makes ownership visible, and how better governance reduces the hidden operational cost of delayed clarity. The deeper pattern matters for leadership education because it shows that timely clarity does not only help one decision. It changes the environment in which future decisions are made, because people begin trusting that questions will not be left unresolved long enough to become someone else's hidden burden.

Why Visible Decision Paths Matter

Over time, I learned that organizations make better decisions when the path to a decision is visible. People do not need every issue escalated to the same level, but they do need to understand how decisions move, who owns what, when an issue is ready to be resolved, and where ambiguity should be surfaced rather than buried. Once those paths are visible, something important changes. Teams stop treating every hard issue as a negotiation with no end point. They begin to trust that unresolved questions will move toward clarity instead of simply circling. That trust reduces the emotional drag of uncertainty.

This is one reason governance matters so much in decision-heavy environments. Good governance does not only define priorities. It defines how uncertainty gets processed before it turns into operational drift. In my own work, clearer decision paths helped teams move with more confidence even when not every answer was immediate. They knew where questions belonged. They knew who had authority. And they knew that waiting had a structure rather than a fog. That difference may sound administrative, but in practice it protects momentum.

Explainable direction matters because people can work through disappointment more easily than through uncertainty. A delayed initiative, a constrained budget, or a difficult trade-off can still be carried constructively when leaders explain the logic clearly enough that the organization sees the choice as disciplined rather than arbitrary. In that sense, visible decision paths do more than improve efficiency. They preserve dignity. They help people understand that leadership is taking the burden seriously enough to close the question rather than leaving the system to absorb it in fragments.

The same point showed up in our performance. Strong project success in the mid-nineties did not emerge from a culture of waiting. It emerged from clearer governance, more visible trade-offs, and stronger decision discipline around scope, budget, schedule, and benefits. That matters in this chapter because it shows what the alternative to indecision looks like in practice. When leaders create clearer decision paths, the organization does not only move faster. It starts trusting that important questions will not be left open long enough to become hidden burdens for everyone else.

When Indecision Meets AI

AI introduces a particularly seductive new form of indecision, and leaders should learn to recognize it. It is the decision to wait. Faced with a fast-moving, unfamiliar technology, many organizations adopt a posture that sounds prudent, we will wait until the technology matures, we will watch and see, we will revisit this next year. Sometimes patience genuinely is wise. But often this is drift wearing the costume of caution, a way of avoiding the harder governance decisions about where AI belongs, who owns it, and what data it may touch. And while leadership waits, the same thing happens that this chapter has described throughout. The silence does not stay empty. People fill it.

What fills the silence, in the case of AI, is ungoverned adoption. When the enterprise will not decide where AI is and is not allowed, employees decide for themselves, quietly, one tool at a time. They paste sensitive information into systems no one has reviewed. They rely on outputs no one has validated. They build personal workflows around capabilities the organization never formally adopted. This is the indecision pattern exactly, the question left open long enough that people lower in the system answer it through local improvisation, except that here the stakes include data exposure and decisions made on unverified output. Not deciding about AI is itself a decision. It decides that the enterprise will be shaped by whatever its people adopt in the absence of direction.

There is a second trap as well, the temptation to use AI as a reason to keep deferring. It is easy to ask for one more analysis, one more model run, one more synthesis before committing, and AI makes producing those almost effortless. But more analysis only improves a decision up to a point, and beyond it, the tool simply becomes a more sophisticated way to postpone the discomfort of choosing. The discipline this chapter argues for does not change in the age of AI. Leaders still owe the organization timely clarity, including timely clarity about AI itself. Deciding where these tools belong, with whatever certainty is honestly available, protects the enterprise far better than waiting for a certainty that will never quite arrive.

Why This Chapter Matters

For students, faculty, and practicing executives, the deeper lesson of this chapter is that indecision is rarely neutral. It alters the operating model even while leaders are still telling themselves they are only waiting. It redistributes authority downward, increases hidden labor, and teaches teams to survive through interpretation instead of alignment. The enduring lesson is simple. A hard decision made in time can still be improved. A question left open too long begins making its own decisions through drift, assumption, and hidden labor.

The lesson reads differently depending on the reader's seat. For the practicing CIO and the IT leader, the message is operational. Build visible decision paths and close questions before ambiguity hardens into drift, treating timely clarity as a deliverable rather than a courtesy. For the consultant, the message is diagnostic. The private assumptions, parallel preparation, and repeated escalations in a client environment are direct evidence of decisions that were never cleanly made, and they will point you to the real bottleneck faster than any org chart. And for the faculty member and the graduate student, the message is conceptual. This is a chance to study indecision as an organizational design issue with measurable downstream cost, rather than as a personal failing, and to examine the difference between thoughtful analysis and avoidable delay.

Boardroom Perspective: Indecision Is Still a Decision

Boards sometimes treat delayed choice as prudence, especially when the trade-off is uncomfortable and the desire for more certainty sounds responsible. But indecision is still a decision. It decides that ambiguity may continue spreading through the enterprise. It decides that lower levels of the organization will keep carrying interpretation, local workaround behavior, and hidden waiting costs in the absence of formal direction. That is why mature boards should not only ask whether leadership is gathering enough information. They should also ask what the organization is already paying while clarity remains deferred.

A mature board should therefore look for the signals that indecision has already become operational cost. Where are teams still making private assumptions because leadership has not fully closed the question. Which priorities remain blurred because no one has yet turned debate into direction. What work is being duplicated or slowed because the decision path is not visible enough for the enterprise to trust it. And where is the enterprise deferring a decision about AI while ungoverned adoption quietly spreads in the silence. These are not only governance questions. They are stewardship questions, because they reveal whether the institution is being protected from drift or quietly being taught to live inside it.

From the CIO's Desk

One of the clearest lessons of my career is that people can carry a hard decision better than they can carry endless uncertainty. Unresolved questions rarely stay still. They migrate into the operating model. Teams begin compensating. Managers create local interpretations. Good people spend energy preparing for possibilities that may never become necessary. That is why I no longer think of indecision as a harmless pause. In many environments, it becomes a quiet tax on confidence, attention, and momentum, and that tax is paid first by the people who feel the burden long before leaders see it in a formal report.

I have also learned that delayed clarity changes a leader internally before it changes the room externally. The longer a decision stays open without good reason, the more leadership energy gets spent carrying unfinished tension instead of giving direction. In my experience, that is one of the quiet reasons timely decisions matter so much. They do not only move the work. They release the organization, and often the leader, from carrying uncertainty longer than stewardship requires.

If I had to summarize my own view simply, it would be this. The cost of indecision is rarely paid by the person who delayed the answer. It is paid by the people who now have to keep moving without it. Leaders do not need perfect certainty to be responsible. They need enough signal, enough ownership, and enough willingness to close the question before ambiguity becomes more expensive than the risk of acting. That is one of the most practical forms of stewardship I know. It protects trust, protects execution, and gives the enterprise back its ability to move together.

Five Leadership Rules for Avoiding the Cost of Indecision

These are the rules I keep returning to. They are simple to state and demanding to live, which is usually the mark of a principle worth keeping.

First, make ownership and decision paths visible. Questions drift longest when no one can clearly see who has both the authority and responsibility to close them, or how an issue is supposed to move toward resolution. Visible ownership turns waiting from a fog into a structure.

Second, distinguish analysis from delay. More information is useful only if it can materially improve the decision rather than simply postpone discomfort. Difficulty does not justify drift, and at some point more waiting only enlarges the area in which the organization has to keep guessing.

Third, do not let unresolved questions drift downward. If leadership has not decided, the work below should not be forced to absorb the ambiguity indefinitely. Indecision at the top becomes hidden labor at the bottom, carried by the people with the least authority to resolve it.

Fourth, use governance to process uncertainty early. Steering, escalation, and clear ownership exist to convert waiting into process and process into direction before drift becomes embedded in the work. Good governance does not only set priorities, it creates pathways out of uncertainty.

Fifth, remember that timely clarity is a form of care. The organization works better when leaders close questions before ambiguity hardens into drift. A decision made in time can still be improved, but a question left open too long begins making its own decisions, and rarely good ones.

Leadership Lessons

- Indecision is rarely stillness, it is drift, which looks like movement without agreement.
- When leaders delay too long, uncertainty starts making decisions on the organization's behalf.
- The cost of indecision is paid by the people who must keep moving without the answer, not by the person who delayed it.
- Indecision redistributes authority downward, forcing judgments to be made without the needed context.
- Visible decision paths preserve dignity, because people can work through disappointment more easily than uncertainty.
- Not deciding about AI is still a decision, and the silence is filled by ungoverned adoption.
- A hard decision made in time can still be improved, but few decisions improve by remaining open indefinitely.

Discussion Questions

- Why can indecision be more damaging to an organization than a wrong decision made in time?
- How does uncertainty spread through an organization when decision ownership is unclear?
- What leadership mechanisms help reduce the hidden cost of indecision?
- Why is deferring a decision about AI itself a decision, and what fills the silence while leadership waits?
- As a consultant, what downstream signals would tell you that a client's real problem is a decision that was never cleanly made?
- How should leaders distinguish between decisions that require deeper analysis and decisions that require timely direction?

Application for Practice

- For the practicing leader: identify one recurring issue in your organization that may be getting worse because a decision keeps being delayed. Name the hidden cost of waiting.
- For the IT leader: map one important decision path in your environment. Identify who owns the decision, what information is needed, and where ambiguity still creates drag.
- For the consultant: in a client environment, trace one area of rework or parallel preparation back to the decision that was never cleanly closed, and propose how to surface it.
- For the faculty member or facilitator: design a short exercise in which students must decide whether a described delay is genuine prudence or disguised drift, and justify the distinction.
- For any reader: think about a time when uncertainty led different teams to make different assumptions. Identify what governance or communication mechanism would have prevented that drift.
- For reflection: write a short note on the difference between thoughtful analysis and avoidable delay in your own leadership context, and a decision you are currently holding open.

Chapter 12: Institutional Resilience

Opening

Resilience is often misunderstood as toughness or endurance, but in enterprise leadership it means something more disciplined than simply surviving strain. Resilience is the institution's ability to keep its shape under pressure, to continue deciding, communicating, and operating without becoming dependent on improvisation every time something difficult happens. That is why this chapter matters for practicing CIOs, IT leaders, consultants, and graduate leadership programs alike. In my experience, resilient organizations are not the ones that never face disruption. They are the ones that have already invested enough clarity, ownership, governance, and preparation that disruption does not have to become chaos.

My own understanding of resilience was shaped slowly across very different chapters of my career. The Y2K shift from accounting into ERP work taught me early that systems are never only technical. When they fail, the business feels exposed. The outsourcing and offshore transition at a global electronics components manufacturer taught me that continuity is also about people's confidence in the institution when conditions become uncertain. Global consulting and broader ERP work taught me that organizations often depend too heavily on individual heroics because the system itself has not been designed to recover well. International development project work reinforced that resilience must travel across culture, timing, and local realities if it is going to hold under pressure. By the time I reached my current role as CIO, those lessons had come full circle. I no longer thought of resilience as a technical recovery plan alone. I thought of it as one of the clearest expressions of stewardship available to leadership.

Some of the clearest lessons about resilience came during periods of intense operational activity when multiple major initiatives were moving at once. Core systems were being separated, new capabilities were being introduced, and critical processes such as payroll and manufacturing time entry were changing in parallel. Any one of those could have produced disruption. Together, they could easily have become unstable. They did not. The reason was not that pressure was absent. It was that the pressure had been absorbed earlier through preparation. Ownership was clear. Testing was thorough. Communication paths were defined. Teams understood not only what they were responsible for, but how their work connected to the larger system. The business experienced these changes with far less disruption than the underlying complexity would suggest. That is what resilience looks like in practice. It does not remove difficulty. It prevents difficulty from turning into instability.

This chapter and the one on calm under pressure are close companions, but they are not the same. Calm is how a leader carries the room through a hard moment. Resilience is what makes the hard moment less likely to scatter the institution in the first place. One is a discipline of presence, the other a discipline of design. Both express the same conviction that runs through this book and through much of what I have come to believe about leadership: the strongest organizations are not built on heroes. They are built on clarity, discipline, and continuity that can survive the absence of any single person. Resilience is that conviction made operational. It is the steady, often invisible work of ensuring the enterprise can keep its shape when people change, pressure rises, or something important goes wrong.

Why I Stopped Admiring Repeated Heroics

There was a time earlier in my career when repeated heroics still looked impressive to me. The person who could always fix the issue, carry the hidden knowledge, or rescue the project at the last minute seemed indispensable. And to be fair, many of those people were carrying extraordinary weight. But over time I started to see the cost more clearly. Every repeated rescue was also evidence of something the system had not yet learned to hold on its own. Documentation was missing. Redundancy was weak. Standards were incomplete. Knowledge remained concentrated. The hero deserved appreciation. The pattern deserved scrutiny.

That shift changed how I thought about leadership. I became less impressed by environments that celebrated recovery every week and more interested in environments where recovery was needed less often because the system itself had grown stronger. That does not diminish the people who carry difficult moments. It puts the responsibility back where it belongs. Leaders must ask why the same person keeps having to save the day, why the same risks keep returning, and what the enterprise still has not institutionalized. Resilience begins when gratitude for the hero is matched by discipline about the design.

The Cost of Depending on One Hero

Every organization has at least one area where too much success still depends on one person knowing exactly what to do. Sometimes that person is brilliant. Sometimes they are simply the only one who has been close to the process long enough to understand its history. Either way, the pattern creates a kind of fragile comfort. People feel reassured because they know who to call. But that reassurance comes at a cost. It delays documentation. It discourages cross-training. It reduces the urgency to standardize. Over time, the organization begins treating dependence as if it were expertise, when in fact it is a warning about design.

I learned that the real danger is not only what happens if that person leaves. It is what happens while they stay. The system never fully matures because it never has to. Knowledge remains concentrated. Improvement is harder to scale. Leaders begin confusing heroic consistency with resilience. But resilience is something else. It is the moment when the same good outcome can still happen even if the hero is unavailable. That is why I no longer measure strength by how impressive the rescue looks. I measure it by how little rescue is needed in the first place.

Continuity Beyond Heroics

One of the most dangerous mistakes organizations make is confusing heroics with resilience. A major issue occurs. Talented people work extraordinary hours. The problem gets solved. The business recovers. Everyone feels relieved. But relief is not the same thing as resilience. Heroics depend on exceptional individuals. Resilience depends on repeatable systems. Heroics are hard to sustain. Resilience is designed so the organization does not have to keep demanding the same emergency effort every time something breaks. In my experience, that distinction matters deeply because many institutions survive through commitment long before they mature through design.

That is why documentation, backup paths, runbooks, monitoring, tested recovery procedures, and visible ownership matter so much. They reduce dependence on memory by personality. They make continuity less fragile during transitions. They also strengthen trust because the business no longer has to wonder whether the system will still work if one key person is unavailable. In leadership terms, resilience becomes one of the clearest ways a CIO protects both the institution and the people carrying it.

Resilience Is a Design Decision

One reason resilience matters so much is that it reveals the truth of the operating model faster than most performance metrics do. In stable seasons, weak handoffs, poor documentation, unclear ownership, and thin backup paths can remain partially hidden. But when pressure arrives, those weaknesses stop hiding. The organization either has a path from disruption to direction, or it quietly falls back on a few people to hold everything together. That is why I have come to think of resilience as business shape. It describes whether the institution can absorb strain without deforming every time conditions become difficult.

I saw this in a practical way. Stable ERP separation execution, validated manufacturing execution after go-live, manufacturing time-entry stability, payroll stabilization in one region with steady performance, strong uptime, and continued movement toward cleaner service operations all point to the same deeper leadership lesson. Resilience becomes visible when the enterprise can absorb complexity without translating that complexity into daily instability for the business. These outcomes do not suggest the absence of pressure. They suggest that pressure was already being managed through design, governance, and prepared execution before the business had to feel it directly.

The more I worked in complex environments, the more convinced I became that resilience is not an accidental trait of good teams. It is a design decision. Leaders decide whether ownership is visible, whether dependencies are understood, whether documentation is current, whether backup paths exist, and whether response routines have been practiced before the pressure arrives. These choices are easy to postpone because the system may appear to be functioning without them. But when a disruption comes, the absence of that design work becomes visible immediately. What people often call resilience in the moment is usually the delayed result of many quiet decisions that were made long before the issue appeared.

That is why I think resilience belongs in the language of leadership design, not only crisis response. A resilient environment is one in which people know what to do next, where to escalate, how to communicate, and what conditions must be protected first. It does not depend on inspiration arriving at the right moment. It depends on structure that has already been built. In that sense, resilience is one of the clearest forms of stewardship because it protects the institution from having to rediscover its own weaknesses every time something important is under strain.

For that reason, I no longer think of resilience as something you discover only in a crisis. You discover its absence there. Real resilience is built much earlier, in the quieter decisions about documentation, redundancy, ownership, cross-training, monitoring, and whether teams are being developed broadly enough that the work can keep moving when one familiar person is unavailable. In my experience, resilient organizations do not wait for disruption to learn how dependent they have become. They keep asking that question while the environment still feels normal enough to answer it honestly.

The Handover No One Had Practiced

I remember a moment when a routine handover suddenly became more complicated than it should have been. Nothing dramatic had failed. The issue was simpler and more revealing. The usual person was unavailable, and the people stepping in realized how much of the process still lived in habit rather than in a resilient design. Important details were known, but not documented clearly enough. Escalation paths existed, but only in people's heads. The work still got done, but the room felt the strain immediately. What should have been a smooth transfer exposed the hidden places where the system was still leaning too hard on memory, familiarity, and the quiet heroics of people who usually made things look easy.

That moment mattered because it revealed something more useful than a crisis would have. It showed the organization where resilience had not yet been fully built. No one needed to panic, but everyone could see what still depended on continuity of personnel rather than continuity of design. I have come to value those moments because they tell the truth without waiting for a larger failure to make the point. They show leaders what still needs to be documented, trained, standardized, and rehearsed if the institution is going to become stronger than the people currently holding it together.

That is one reason I have come to respect practiced backup paths so much. A resilient handover is not only about having notes available. It is about whether the backup person has enough context, confidence, and decision support to lead without turning the absence of one individual into a new operational event. When that capability exists, the institution feels steadier. People can trust that continuity is real, not only assumed. And that is exactly what resilience should do. It should reduce the number of moments in which the business suddenly remembers how much depends on one person.

What Resilience Cost Me and Taught Me

Some of the deepest lessons I learned about resilience came long before my current CIO chapter, during a period when I was managing internationally funded development projects for public-sector clients, including a national government and a national port authority in different parts of Africa. At times I was overseas for more than four months at a stretch, away from my family, working inside a culture that was not my own, under conditions that tested every assumption I had about planning, pace, and personal endurance. Resources were limited. Schedules were difficult to stabilize. The environment required more patience, more adaptability, and more emotional control than I had ever needed before. Even the daily rhythm of work was shaped by realities that many outside the context would not fully understand, including a broader culture that did not always move according to the kind of linear, planned schedule many project leaders are trained to expect. It was exhausting. At times it felt almost unbelievable. And yet it was one of the most formative leadership classrooms of my life.

What made that experience even harder was that the pressure was not only technical. It was human. Several foreign resources quit and left at different times, which meant the people who remained had to absorb the load and keep the work moving under already difficult conditions. There were moments when the strain felt larger than the plan itself. But that is exactly why the experience mattered. It taught me that resilience is not the ability to keep pretending conditions are normal. It is the ability to keep leading when conditions are clearly not normal, without losing respect for the people, the context, or the purpose of the work. It taught me that leadership in hard places depends less on ideal process than on humility, patience, cultural respect, and the willingness to stay steady when the environment is asking much more of you than the plan ever anticipated.

Another defining lesson in resilience came years later when I was leading the launch of a brand new state of the art chemical coatings plant while the technical team was stationed offshore. We were not simply implementing a system. We were launching an entire division. During the launch, there were stretches when my team and I worked fifteen hour days for weeks at a time. Staffing was limited. The pressure was real. I even remember seeing our finance lead on a lift truck in the warehouse because the launch demanded all hands wherever help was needed. That is not something I look back on with pride, because no leader should confuse extraordinary strain with an ideal operating model. But I do look back on it with respect. The team stayed with me. We pushed through together. And on the other side of that experience, we carried forward lessons that served us well in future projects. Resilience, I learned, is not only about surviving the impossible week. It is about extracting enough learning from the impossible week that the next one does not have to cost quite as much.

I have also come to believe that resilient teams are built the same way resilient systems are built, through trust, development, and repetition. Organizations do not become durable because one strong person keeps absorbing the shock. They become durable when many people know enough, care enough, and feel supported enough to carry responsibility together. That is why I no longer think of resilience as a heroic trait. I think of it as the visible result of disciplined leadership, intentional people development, and systems designed to keep holding even when no single person is at the center of the response.

That conviction did not come from theory. It came from watching what hard environments reveal. International development work taught me that resilience must survive distance, imperfect conditions, and the loss of familiar assumptions. Plant launch work taught me that endurance without learning is too expensive to celebrate for long. And the broader modernization journey taught me that resilience is strongest when it becomes developmental, when teams are coached deeply enough that confidence, judgment, and operating knowledge begin spreading across the system instead of collecting in one overused corner of it. For me, that is one of the clearest marks of stewardship. The institution becomes less brittle because leaders have chosen to grow people, not only projects.

That is why resilience and development belong together. Leaders strengthen resilience every time they explain more than they need to, train beyond the immediate requirement, rotate responsibility thoughtfully, and make the reasoning behind the work more visible to the broader team. Those investments may feel slower in the moment, especially when the current expert can simply do it faster. But the long-term result is profound. The organization becomes less brittle. The next difficult season has more capable hands available to carry it. And the leader is no longer building a function around personal indispensability, but around shared institutional strength.

Enterprise Case Study: Resilience Through Stable Execution, Redundancy, and Preparedness

A compelling enterprise case for this chapter comes from a cluster of stable execution outcomes I lived through alongside the broader transformation story. An ERP separation go-live was successful with stable operations. Manufacturing execution was validated after go-live. Manufacturing time entry went live without process disruption. A payroll stabilization period concluded with stable results. Security and network operations were strengthened through mature monitoring and response capabilities. These are not isolated wins. They are signs of a system that has been made less dependent on improvisation and more capable of absorbing complexity without visible breakdown.

Tension. These transitions could easily have produced disruption. In weaker environments, payroll errors, cutover confusion, unclear ownership, or unstable access would have shifted the burden back onto people improvising under strain. The leadership challenge was not simply to keep projects moving. It was to create enough preparation, documentation, support, and governance that the business would not have to feel every internal seam. This is exactly the kind of case graduate leadership programs can use to move beyond abstract resilience language. Students can examine what has to be true operationally for resilience to show up in results, how leaders decide where redundancy matters most, and why a stable outcome is often the clearest evidence of invisible leadership discipline.

Leadership Decision and Teaching Value. The leadership move was to build resilience before the strain arrived. That meant strong planning, clear ownership, post-launch support, monitoring, communication standards, and practical backup paths. It also meant reinforcing that resilience is a leadership and operating-model issue, not only a technical recovery issue. For graduate leadership programs, CIO development, and executive education, this case is useful because it helps learners distinguish resilience from heroics and shows how institutional strength becomes visible through stable, uneventful execution. I saw this reinforced in practical ways. Stable operations, validated manufacturing execution, a clean time-entry launch, payroll stabilization, identity and access standardization across major applications, and movement toward a service management platform all point to the same deeper lesson. Resilience becomes visible when the enterprise can absorb complexity without translating that complexity into daily instability for the business.

What Stability Revealed About the Operating Model

One of the most useful signals in any operating environment is not dramatic recovery. It is stable execution over time. When major transitions land cleanly, when payroll runs without disruption, when a separation or go-live happens without the business feeling every internal complexity, leaders learn something important about the operating model underneath. They learn that planning is stronger, ownership is clearer, and critical dependencies are being managed earlier. Stability is not boring when you understand what it represents. It is proof that leadership discipline has become embedded in the system.

That is why I pay attention to quiet outcomes. Stable operations reveal maturity in a way that heroic storytelling never can. They suggest that the organization is beginning to carry its own weight through governance, documentation, repeatable processes, monitoring, and practiced communication. In my experience, that is one of the clearest signs that stewardship is working. The environment becomes less dependent on individual memory and more capable of sustaining performance as a system. That is the kind of resilience worth building because it strengthens the enterprise without needing constant applause.

That is one reason resilience is easy to undervalue in leadership conversations. Its best evidence often looks ordinary. A service is available. A handoff works. A payroll closes. A go-live feels uneventful to people outside the team. But behind that ordinariness is invisible labor that deserves respect: knowledge transfer, rehearsal, architecture discipline, vendor coordination, monitoring, fallback planning, and people who have been developed well enough to respond without unnecessary escalation. Resilience is not glamorous because it is one of the ways leadership removes drama from the life of the institution. That, in my view, is one of its highest forms of value.

Another reason I care so much about resilience is that the absence of it rarely stays technical for long. A weak handover becomes a business delay. A hidden single point of failure becomes a leadership distraction. An under-documented process becomes a trust issue the moment something changes and people realize the continuity they assumed was never actually built. That is why I have come to see resilience as a business continuity discipline, not only an IT concern. The system either carries the institution through change, or it quietly forces the institution back into dependence on improvisation.

That is one reason mature operations matter so much in this chapter. Continuous monitoring, co-managed network and security operations, stronger runbooks, better recovery planning, and more disciplined service transition work all reduce the amount of risk the enterprise has to carry consciously every day. Those investments do not eliminate pressure, but they make continuity less dependent on reaction time alone. In practical terms, resilience grows when detection improves, handoffs are cleaner, fallback paths are real, and the business is no longer learning about fragility only after a disruption has already begun.

I also believe resilience strengthens confidence in a way that endurance alone never can. Endurance asks people to survive the season. Resilience helps them believe the institution is learning how not to demand the same emergency from them every time. That shift matters for morale, retention, and the quality of future leadership. People stay steadier when they believe the organization is building beyond the current pressure instead of merely absorbing it. In that sense, resilience is one of the clearest ways a leader communicates respect for the future of both the people and the institution.

When Resilience Has to Survive AI Dependence

AI introduces a new version of the oldest problem in this chapter, the single point of dependence, and leaders should see it coming. For years the fragility I learned to watch for took the shape of one indispensable person. Increasingly it will take the shape of one indispensable tool. As enterprises hand more work to AI systems, a quiet risk grows alongside the benefit. The organization can become so reliant on a model, a vendor, or an automated process that it slowly forgets how to operate without it. That is the hero problem wearing new clothing. It feels like capability while it works, and it reveals itself as fragility the moment the tool is unavailable, degraded, or wrong.

Resilience in the age of AI therefore asks a question that is easy to defer and expensive to ignore. If this AI capability went down tomorrow, or produced output the business could no longer trust, could the enterprise still function. Could people still make the decision, run the process, or serve the customer without it. An organization that cannot answer yes has not gained a capability. It has acquired a dependency it does not yet understand. The discipline is the same one this chapter has argued for throughout: maintain the human knowledge, the documented process, and the fallback path so that the tool augments the institution rather than becoming a load-bearing wall no one can inspect.

There is a more hopeful side as well, because AI can genuinely strengthen resilience when it is designed as augmentation rather than sole dependence. It can improve detection, help generate and maintain runbooks, surface risks earlier, and distribute knowledge more widely than a single expert ever could. The deciding factor is the same one that has always separated resilience from fragility. Is the capability building shared institutional strength, or is it concentrating critical function in a place the enterprise cannot survive without and cannot fully see into. Used well, AI can make an organization steadier. Used carelessly, it simply makes the next single point of failure faster and harder to notice.

Why This Chapter Matters

For students, faculty, and practicing executives, the deeper lesson of this chapter is that resilience should not be mistaken for endurance alone. Endurance gets through the week. Resilience changes what the next week will require. It reduces dependence on heroics, distributes knowledge more intelligently, and gives the enterprise a better chance to remain stable when people change, pressure rises, or something critical goes wrong. That is why resilience belongs in leadership education. It teaches leaders to ask not only who can save the day, but what kind of institution they are building that may need saving less often over time.

The lesson reads differently depending on the reader's seat. For the practicing CIO and the IT leader, the message is operational. Treat resilience as a design decision made in quiet times through documentation, redundancy, cross-training, and rehearsed transitions, not as something discovered during a crisis. For the consultant, the message is diagnostic. The clearest signs of fragility in a client are the indispensable people and the unpracticed handovers, so look for where success still depends on one person rather than one trusted system. And for the faculty member and the graduate student, the message is conceptual. This is a chance to study resilience as repeatable institutional design rather than heroic endurance, and to examine why stable, uneventful execution is often the strongest evidence of leadership discipline.

Boardroom Perspective: Resilience Is the Business's Ability to Keep Its Shape

Boards often discuss resilience in terms of recovery plans, cyber readiness, and continuity protocols. Those matter, but they do not fully capture the deeper question. Can the institution keep its shape when pressure arrives. Can it still make decisions clearly, communicate credibly, and carry essential work without leaning too heavily on one person, one workaround, or one emergency exception. That is why resilience should be treated as a business capability, not only a technical one. It determines whether the enterprise can absorb strain without quietly becoming less coherent every time something difficult happens.

A mature board should therefore ask where resilience still depends too much on familiarity rather than design. Which critical processes are still being stabilized by a few trusted people instead of by a trusted system. Where are transitions likely to create uncertainty because knowledge remains concentrated. Which parts of the operating model still recover because people care deeply, but would struggle if that same level of personal heroics were unavailable. And as AI adoption grows, where is the enterprise becoming dependent on a tool it could not operate without. These are not only risk questions. They are stewardship questions, because they show whether the institution is becoming stronger in a repeatable way or merely surviving through effort.

From the CIO's Desk

One of the clearest leadership lessons of my career is that resilience becomes visible long before a crisis if leaders are willing to look for the right signs. It appears in whether a handover feels calm or fragile, whether a team can still operate well when one familiar expert is away, and whether a major change can land without making the business feel as unstable as the internal effort required to support it. Resilience, I learned, is rarely something dramatic. I think of it as disciplined continuity that has been designed carefully enough to look ordinary when it works.

If I had to summarize my own view simply, it would be this. Resilience is the discipline of helping the enterprise become less surprised by stress. It does not eliminate hard seasons, transitions, or disruption. It makes them less likely to scatter the institution when they arrive. In my experience, that is one of the deepest forms of stewardship. Leaders leave the business stronger when they stop designing around the hope that pressure will be rare and begin designing around the truth that pressure will come.

I also came to see that resilience changes how leaders carry responsibility personally. When the system is stronger, the leader can stay steadier because every issue does not feel like a private test of whether they alone can hold the enterprise together. That is one reason I care so much about building resilience into the operating model. It protects the organization, but it also protects leaders from confusing indispensable effort with mature leadership.

Five Leadership Rules for Building Institutional Resilience

These are the rules I keep returning to. They are simple to state and demanding to live, which is usually the mark of a principle worth keeping.

First, design for continuity before disruption tests it. The most expensive time to discover fragility is during the moment that needs stability most. Resilience is built in quiet seasons through choices that feel optional until the day they are not.

Second, reduce dependence on individual memory. Documentation, cross-training, and visible ownership make continuity more repeatable. Gratitude for an indispensable expert should always be paired with the discipline of making the expertise survivable without them.

Third, treat stable execution as evidence, not as something to ignore. Uneventful outcomes usually reflect design discipline that deserves to be protected and repeated. Quiet stability is not luck. It is the visible result of invisible preparation.

Fourth, rehearse transitions as seriously as incidents. Many resilience gaps are exposed not by crisis, but by ordinary change in people, roles, or systems. A practiced handover reveals fragility while it is still cheap to fix.

Fifth, build resilience into the operating model, not into one heroic person or one indispensable tool. The institution becomes stronger when continuity can survive absence, growth, and pressure without losing its shape, whether the dependency is a person or a system.

Leadership Lessons

- Resilience is keeping the institution's shape under pressure, not simply enduring strain.
- Repeated heroics are usually evidence of fragility, because the system never matured enough to need rescue less often.
- The danger of an indispensable person is not only that they might leave, but that the system never grows while they stay.

- Resilience is a design decision made in quiet times, not a trait discovered in a crisis.
- Stable, uneventful execution is often the clearest evidence of invisible leadership discipline.
- AI introduces a new single point of dependence, so resilience now means the enterprise can still function if the tool cannot.
- Endurance gets through the week, but resilience changes what the next week will require.

Discussion Questions

- Why are repeated heroics usually a sign of fragility rather than resilience?
- How do documentation, redundancy, ownership, and monitoring strengthen institutional resilience?
- What is the difference between a resilient system and a system that merely survives through individual effort?
- How does heavy dependence on an AI tool create a new kind of single point of failure, and how should leaders guard against it?
- As a consultant, how would you identify the indispensable people and unpracticed handovers that reveal fragility in a client organization?
- If one person in an organization seems indispensable during every crisis, what leadership problem does that reveal?

Application for Practice

- For the practicing leader: identify one area in your organization where success still depends too heavily on one person's knowledge or intervention. Name the risk that creates.
- For the IT leader: review a recent operational success that appeared uneventful. Identify the planning, documentation,

governance, or redundancy that likely made that stability possible.

- For the consultant: in a client environment, map the top single points of failure, whether people or tools, and propose practical steps to reduce dependence on each.
- For the faculty member or facilitator: design a short exercise in which students must build a continuity plan for a critical process whose only expert has suddenly become unavailable.
- For any reader: list the top three single points of failure in your environment, and identify one practical step that would reduce dependence on each.
- For reflection: think of a handover that exposed how much depended on one person. What did it reveal that a crisis would have revealed more expensively?

Chapter 13: Organizational Memory

Opening

Organizations do not only need information. They need memory. Information answers a question in the moment. Memory preserves understanding across time. It helps future leaders know why a decision was made, what condition shaped a standard, and what lesson cost the organization too much to have to pay for again. That is why this chapter matters for practicing CIOs, IT leaders, consultants, and graduate leadership programs alike. When organizational memory is weak, institutions keep rediscovering what they should already know. When it is strong, they begin from a wiser position than the one they started from before.

This chapter is a deliberate companion to the earlier one on data as institutional memory, but it reaches for something broader and harder to store. That chapter was about whether the enterprise can trust what its numbers mean, the definitions, the sources, the reporting truth. This chapter is about the memory that rarely fits in a database at all. It is the reasoning behind decisions, the context that lives in experienced people, the judgment about why a path was chosen, and the lessons that fade when the people who learned them move on. Data memory protects what the organization knows. Decision memory protects why the organization knows it, and that why is usually the first thing to disappear.

My own understanding of this was shaped slowly across very different chapters of my career. The Y2K shift from accounting into ERP work taught me early that systems are never only technical. They either preserve clarity or they lose it. The outsourcing and offshore transition at a global electronics components manufacturer taught me that when people leave, institutions lose more than labor. They lose context, history, and judgment if memory has never been transferred well. Global consulting and broader ERP work taught me how often organizations cannot explain why an older configuration, process, or exception still exists. International development project work reinforced that culture, experience, and local knowledge must also be preserved or future leaders will keep relearning the same difficult truths. By the time I reached my current role as CIO, those lessons had come full circle. I no longer thought of memory as documentation alone. I thought of it as a stewardship responsibility.

Organizations forget faster than they realize. People transition. Roles evolve. Projects complete. Priorities shift. Over time, important context fades unless it is intentionally preserved. That is why memory is not just about history. It is about continuity. It protects the enterprise from paying again for lessons it has already learned and helps future leaders begin with more clarity than the last team had to build for itself.

Why Institutions Relearn the Same Lesson

Institutions often relearn the same lesson not because the lesson was unclear, but because it was never preserved in a form the organization could keep using. A difficult implementation ends, and everyone involved knows what went wrong and what should change next time. But if that insight stays mostly in conversation, it fades as people move, roles change, and the urgency of the moment disappears. Then, months or years later, the organization finds itself debating the same issue again as if it were new. That repetition is expensive. It consumes time, weakens confidence, and makes the business look less mature than it really could be.

I came to see that pattern as one of the great hidden costs of weak organizational memory. The enterprise pays once when the lesson is learned through friction, delay, or failure. It pays a second time when that lesson is not preserved well enough to guide future action. That is why handoffs, decision records, notes, standards, and lessons-learned discipline matter so much. They are not administrative leftovers. They are how an institution keeps earning the benefit of what it has already lived through.

That is why I do not think of memory as an administrative concern. I think of it as a leadership responsibility. Institutions become stronger when they do not have to rely on charisma, memory, or proximity to carry wisdom forward. They become stronger when lessons are preserved in ways that ordinary people can keep using. In that sense, good memory is one of the quiet ways leaders honor the people who come after them. It says the future should not have to start from confusion just because the past was never written down clearly enough to remain useful.

This is one reason I connect organizational memory so closely to my own path from ERP work into broader CIO leadership. In every stage of that journey, from early systems roles to consulting, from coatings and manufacturing to global project work and enterprise modernization, the same question kept returning. Could the organization preserve enough meaning to act intelligently after the people, pressure, or project stage had changed. In weaker environments, memory stayed trapped in experienced individuals, local files, or verbal history. In stronger environments, standards, governed definitions, runbooks, governance routines, and decision records gave the institution a better chance to keep learning across time. This, more than anything, is why memory matters so much to me. It is one of the quiet ways leaders prevent the future from having to start over.

The hidden cost of relearning is not only time. It is credibility. Every time an institution has to rediscover what it already paid to learn, people begin to doubt whether the organization can hold onto its own progress. Meetings become slower because history has become harder to trust. New leaders are asked to solve old problems as though they were arriving for the first time. And teams become more dependent on personalities and memory by proximity instead of on standards the institution itself can carry. Organizational memory, seen this way, is one of the clearest signs of maturity. It shows whether the business knows how to keep wisdom, not just create it once.

What I Learned When Knowledge Walked Out the Door

Some of the clearest lessons about organizational memory did not come from dashboards or architecture diagrams. They came from transitions. A key employee left. A leader moved on. A long-running process changed hands. And suddenly, work that had once seemed routine became harder to explain. Reports were delayed because no one could remember why a field had been defined a certain way. Exceptions kept appearing because the original decision had never been written down. Teams were forced to reconstruct reasoning that had once lived comfortably inside one person's experience. Those moments reinforced something important for me. Knowledge is not institutional just because the organization has used it for a long time. It only becomes institutional when it can survive the absence of the person who used to carry it.

That lesson changed the way I think about stewardship. Stewardship is not only about making good decisions. It is also about making decisions legible to the people who come after you. In practice, that means documenting reasoning, making ownership explicit, preserving context, and building systems that remember more than the meeting in which the idea was first agreed. The older I get in leadership, the more I respect this quiet work. Organizations rarely praise it in the moment. But they pay dearly when it is missing.

Memory Is Built in the Small Decisions

Organizational memory is rarely built through one grand act of documentation. It is built in the small decisions leaders make every day about whether something should be written down, standardized, named clearly, or left to informal understanding. A report title. A documented handoff. A note explaining why an exception exists. A short record of why one path was chosen over another. None of these choices seem large when they happen. But over time they accumulate into either clarity or confusion. That is why memory is not only a systems issue. It is an attention issue. Leaders decide, often without realizing it, whether the organization will remember by what they choose to formalize and what they allow to remain implied.

The longer I have led, the more I have come to respect those small acts of preservation. They make it easier for teams to inherit work without inheriting avoidable uncertainty. They reduce the friction of transition. They make better judgment possible because the reasoning behind past choices stays more stable. And they protect the enterprise from paying again for lessons it has already bought once through experience. In that sense, memory is not passive storage. It is one of the ways leadership shows care for the future of the institution.

That is why memory is about more than documentation volume. It is about preserving meaning in a form the organization can still use when the original voices are no longer in the room. A folder full of files is not yet memory if no one knows what is authoritative, what was superseded, or why the decision mattered in the first place. Leaders have to care about traceability, not just storage. They have to make it easier for the next team to understand not only what was done, but what was being protected, measured, or decided when the work was first shaped.

The Reasoning Behind the Decision

If there is one form of memory that organizations lose most reliably, it is the reasoning behind their own decisions. The outcome usually survives. The configuration remains in the system. The policy stays in the handbook. The exception keeps running. But the why behind each of them evaporates, often within a year, because the reasoning lived in a conversation that was never captured. Later, a new team inherits the outcome with no access to the thinking that produced it, and they face an unwelcome choice. They can leave the decision in place without understanding it, which preserves a constraint no one can justify, or they can overturn it without knowing what it was protecting, which sometimes reintroduces the very problem the original decision was designed to prevent.

This is why I have come to value decision records far more than I did earlier in my career. A decision record does not need to be elaborate. It needs to capture what was decided, what alternatives were considered, what the decision was protecting or optimizing for, and what conditions might justify revisiting it later. That small discipline changes the position of every future leader. Instead of inheriting a museum of unexplained choices, they inherit a reasoning trail they can actually build on. They can tell the difference between a decision that still holds and one whose original conditions have passed, which is exactly the judgment the earlier chapter on legacy thinking depends on.

The deeper point is that preserving reasoning is an act of respect across time. It treats the future leaders of the enterprise as colleagues who deserve context rather than as inheritors who must reconstruct it through guesswork. In my experience, the organizations that do this well are noticeably calmer during transitions, because a role change transfers understanding and not only tasks. The ones that do it poorly experience every departure as a small loss of institutional intelligence, and over enough departures, the enterprise quietly forgets why it works the way it does.

Memory by Personality vs Memory by Institution

A great deal of organizational memory lives inside people long before it ever reaches formal documentation. Experienced employees know why a process evolved, what workaround once protected the business, and which relationship matters when things become difficult. There is great value in that. But there is also risk. If memory lives only inside individuals, then continuity becomes fragile. The business feels strong while those people remain in place, but one transition can expose how much of the institution was being carried privately instead of institutionally. I have seen that repeatedly over the years, and it is one reason I take knowledge transfer, documentation, runbooks, and standards more seriously now than I did earlier in my career.

My own experience reinforced that lesson. Stronger operating models consistently show up where runbooks, standards, accountability policies, communication expectations, and governance rhythms are visible enough that the institution does not depend on one person remembering everything in order to function. That is why organizational memory is not nostalgia. It is design. It is one of the ways leaders reduce fragility, preserve context, and make future decisions more intelligent than they otherwise would have been.

The Meeting Where No One Could Explain the Decision

There is a particular kind of meeting that stays with you because everyone in the room knows something is wrong before anyone says it out loud. A long-standing rule, exception, or configuration comes up. It is important enough to shape the decision that follows. But when the questions begin, no one can explain why it exists. One person remembers part of the history. Another offers a guess. A third assumes there must have been a good reason but cannot name it. The meeting continues, but the confidence has already gone out of it. What was supposed to guide a decision has instead become a reminder that the organization is now negotiating with a past it no longer understands.

I have seen moments like that often enough to know they are never about one rule alone. They are about memory, ownership, and discipline. They reveal whether the enterprise has preserved its own reasoning well enough to act with confidence. When no one can explain why something exists, the organization is not only missing a note. It is missing a piece of itself. That is why I believe organizational memory becomes most visible at the moment it fails. The cost is not only analytical. It is strategic, cultural, and deeply practical, because it slows the very decisions leaders need to make well under pressure.

That kind of failure rarely begins at the meeting itself. It usually begins much earlier, when the organization decides not to record the reasoning behind a choice, not to preserve the rationale behind an exception, or not to build a more durable decision trail because the people closest to the issue still remember it well enough for now. But for now is not a stewardship strategy. Over time, unrecorded reasoning becomes organizational amnesia. What should have been inherited as clarity is experienced later as confusion, and the institution is forced to negotiate with its own forgotten past in real time.

Enterprise Case Study: Knowledge Transfer, Turnover, and the Cost of Forgotten Lessons

Context. In many organizations, expertise accumulates inside people faster than it is institutionalized. That expertise may support systems, relationships, reporting, escalations, plant knowledge, or decision context that rarely appears fully in formal artifacts. The problem usually remains partly hidden until someone changes roles, retires, or leaves unexpectedly. Then the institution discovers that it preserved output, but not understanding.

Tension. The tension is that organizations often appreciate expertise while underestimating dependency. Teams assume experience will somehow transfer, documentation will somehow stay current, and future leaders will somehow reconstruct the context if needed. In reality, meaning disappears gradually. A process remains, but the reason fades. A system setting survives, but the business logic behind it is gone. Questions reappear that the organization had already answered years earlier. That is when turnover becomes more than a staffing event. It becomes a memory event.

Leadership Decision and Teaching Value. The leadership move is to preserve knowledge intentionally through documentation, standards, runbooks, role clarity, shared decision records, succession readiness, and cultural storytelling that keeps meaning attached to information. This makes the case useful for graduate leadership programs, executive education, and CIO development because it reframes continuity as a knowledge problem as much as a staffing problem. Leaders can discuss what should be documented, what should be taught, what should be standardized, and how an enterprise decides which lessons are too expensive to lose.

I remember one transition when a report everyone depended on kept arriving late, not because the data was unavailable, but because no one could fully explain the reasoning behind one critical part of it after the original owner had moved on. The work still got done, but the confidence around it changed. Meetings became slower. People started checking the output more defensively. What looked like a minor documentation gap was really a memory gap, and the organization felt it immediately. That moment stayed with me because it showed how quickly institutional confidence can weaken when reasoning was never made durable enough to outlast the person who carried it.

How AI Changes What We Can Remember

AI changes the mechanics of organizational memory more than almost any tool before it, and that is both an opportunity and a trap. On the opportunity side, AI is genuinely good at the work that human memory does poorly. It can capture and summarize discussions, make years of documents searchable in plain language, surface a relevant past decision the moment a similar question arises, and help a departing expert externalize knowledge that would otherwise leave with them. For the first time, an enterprise has tools that could make its own history far more retrievable than it has ever been. Used well, AI could meaningfully reduce the relearning tax this chapter has described.

The trap is subtle, and it is the same one that runs through this chapter. AI is excellent at preserving and retrieving what was done. It is far weaker at preserving why it was done, because the reasoning often was never written down for the tool to learn in the first place. An AI system can tell you that a decision was made and summarize the document that recorded it. It cannot reconstruct the judgment, the trade-off, and the context that lived only in the room, if no one ever captured them. There is a real risk that organizations will mistake powerful retrieval for genuine memory, assuming the tool remembers the reasoning when in fact it is only retrieving the residue. Confusing access to documents with understanding of decisions is a modern form of the same amnesia.

So the discipline does not change in the age of AI. It becomes more worth doing, because the tools to preserve and surface reasoning are finally strong enough to repay the effort. Leaders still have to capture the why, not only the what. They still have to record what a decision was protecting and what conditions might justify revisiting it. AI can then make that reasoning searchable, connectable, and usable in a way that was never possible before. But it can only preserve the understanding the organization was disciplined enough to record. The tool extends institutional memory. It does not excuse the institution from building it.

Why This Chapter Matters

For students, faculty, and practicing executives, the deeper lesson of this chapter is that organizational memory must be intentionally designed rather than assumed to emerge on its own. The outcome of a decision survives by default. The reasoning behind it survives only if someone preserves it. That asymmetry is the whole challenge, because the reasoning is exactly what future leaders need most and lose first. A leader who understands this builds memory deliberately, treating the why behind decisions as an asset worth capturing rather than a conversation that can safely evaporate.

The lesson reads differently depending on the reader's seat. For the practicing CIO and the IT leader, the message is operational. Preserve reasoning through decision records and knowledge transfer, treat every role change as a memory event, and reduce the work that lives only in one person's head. For the consultant, the message is diagnostic. When a client cannot explain why its own rules, exceptions, and configurations exist, you have found both a fragility and a relearning cost that will keep recurring until the reasoning is captured. And for the faculty member and the graduate student, the message is conceptual. This is a chance to study organizational memory as the preservation of reasoning across time, distinct from data alone, and to examine why institutions so reliably forget the why behind their own choices.

Boardroom Perspective: Memory Determines Whether Learning Compounds

One of the clearest differences between a growing institution and a merely aging one is whether learning compounds. In weaker environments, the same lessons return repeatedly under slightly different names. A reporting problem comes back. A control weakness returns. A project stumbles over a dependency the previous team had already discovered. The business keeps moving, but it is paying again for what it should already understand. That is why I have come to think of organizational memory as a multiplier on leadership. It determines whether each year makes the institution wiser or simply busier.

This matters especially in technology leadership because the environment changes quickly. Systems evolve. Platforms are upgraded. Teams transition. Roles shift. If the reasoning behind key choices is not preserved, future leaders inherit outcomes without context. A configuration remains, but no one remembers why it was chosen. A customization survives, but its original justification is gone. Documentation may still exist somewhere, yet the meaning around it has faded. In those moments, organizations usually do not realize they have lost memory until the cost of relearning becomes operationally visible.

A mature board should therefore ask where memory is still concentrated rather than shared. Which processes become fragile when one experienced person is unavailable. Where are decisions still poorly traceable after six or twelve months. What parts of the operating model still depend on historical explanation rather than visible documentation, standards, or system design. These are not only knowledge-management questions. They are stewardship questions, because they reveal whether the institution is becoming wiser over time or simply older.

From the CIO's Desk

One of the most practical lessons of leadership for me is that organizations become calmer when they no longer have to depend on memory by personality. Work feels steadier when context survives the meeting, the role change, and the handoff. People make better decisions when they do not have to keep reconstructing why something exists or what a number was meant to mean. The longer I serve, the more aware I become that titles are temporary, but institutional consequences are not. Success becomes less about personal contribution and more about what the enterprise will still know, still trust, and still be able to do when the people in the current room are no longer there.

I have also seen how easily good people are forced into defensive work when context is missing. They begin checking what should already be explainable, rebuilding what should already be reusable, and approaching familiar work as if it were newly uncertain. That is discouraging for teams and expensive for institutions. In my experience, preserving memory well is one of the quiet ways a leader helps future effort begin with confidence instead of reconstruction.

If I had to summarize my own view simply, it would be this. Organizations grow wiser when they stop depending on memory by personality and begin building memory by institution. That means preserving reasoning, not only results. It means transferring context, not only tasks. And it means helping future leaders begin from a stronger position than the one you inherited. To me, that is one of the clearest responsibilities of enterprise leadership. It is not only building systems. It is preserving understanding.

Five Leadership Rules for Preserving Organizational Memory

These are the rules I keep returning to. They are simple to state and demanding to live, which is usually the mark of a principle worth keeping.

First, preserve reasoning, not only outcomes. The decision record matters most when future leaders need to understand why the current path exists. An outcome without its reasoning is a constraint no one can evaluate, and it is the why that fades first.

Second, reduce memory by personality. If one person still carries too much context alone, the institution remains fragile no matter how capable that person is. The goal is for understanding to survive any single departure.

Third, make handoffs and transitions part of the design. Knowledge transfer should not begin only when someone is already leaving. Treat every role change as a memory event, and capture the context before it walks out the door.

Fourth, document and standardize what is too expensive to relearn. The most critical lessons, definitions, and decisions should not remain trapped in private memory or verbal history. Standards and runbooks let continuity survive turnover without heroic reconstruction.

Fifth, treat memory as an operating asset and an act of stewardship. The organization gets stronger when what it learns can still be found, trusted, and used after the room has changed. Preserving understanding is one of the ways leaders make the future less fragile than the past.

Leadership Lessons

- Information answers a question in the moment, but memory preserves understanding across time.
- The outcome of a decision survives by default, while the reasoning behind it survives only if someone preserves it.
- Knowledge becomes institutional only when it can survive the absence of the person who carried it.
- Institutions relearn the same lesson when insight stays in conversation instead of being preserved in a usable form.
- Decision records protect future leaders from inheriting a museum of choices no one can explain.
- AI can make an organization's history far more retrievable, but it cannot remember reasoning that was never recorded.
- Preserving memory is an act of respect across time, treating future leaders as colleagues who deserve context.

Discussion Questions

- Why must organizational memory be intentionally designed rather than assumed to emerge naturally?
- How does the memory of reasoning differ from the memory of data, and why does the reasoning fade first?
- What risks emerge when important context remains concentrated in a few individuals instead of becoming part of the enterprise?
- How can AI strengthen organizational memory, and where might it create a false sense that the reasoning has been preserved?
- As a consultant, how would you help a client distinguish rules and configurations that still hold from those whose original reasoning has been lost?

- Why do institutions so often relearn the same lesson, and what leadership disciplines can reduce that repetition?

Application for Practice

- For the practicing leader: identify one important form of knowledge in your organization that is still carried more by people than by the enterprise. Determine what would make that knowledge more durable.
- For the IT leader: choose one long-standing rule, exception, or configuration in your environment and try to reconstruct the reasoning behind it. Note how easily, or not, the why can still be found.
- For the consultant: in a client environment, review a recent role transition and identify what reasoning or context should have been easier to find, explain, or reuse.
- For the faculty member or facilitator: design a short exercise in which students must write a decision record for a significant choice, capturing alternatives, intent, and the conditions that would justify revisiting it.
- For any reader: create a short plan to strengthen one part of institutional memory in your organization through better decision records, documentation, ownership, or knowledge transfer.
- For reflection: think of a time you inherited a decision whose reasoning no one could explain. What did that cost you, and what record would have changed it?

Chapter 14: Choosing Durability Over Novelty

Opening

Technology loves novelty. There is always a new platform, a new promise, and a new demonstration that makes the future look easier than it usually is in real business life. I understand the attraction. Innovation matters. Curiosity matters. The willingness to improve matters. But leadership matures when it learns that novelty and durability are not the same thing. A new tool may impress the room quickly. A durable capability serves the institution long after the excitement has faded. That is why this chapter matters for practicing CIOs, IT leaders, consultants, and graduate leadership programs alike. In my experience, the enterprise becomes stronger not only through what it adopts, but through what it can still trust and sustain after the first wave of enthusiasm has moved on.

My own view of this was shaped slowly across many chapters of my career. The Y2K shift from accounting into ERP work taught me early that systems are never only technical. They become part of how an enterprise thinks, reports, and trusts itself. The outsourcing and offshore transition at a global electronics components manufacturer taught me that decisions made for efficiency can still weaken continuity if leaders do not understand what they are trading away. Global consulting and broader ERP work reinforced how often organizations overvalue what is new while underinvesting in what makes the new environment durable. The coatings world introduced me to another industrial context where process discipline mattered as much as innovation. International development project work taught me that durability has to survive across culture, geography, and leadership turnover if it is going to matter. By the time I reached my current role as CIO, those lessons had come full circle. I no longer admired motion by itself. I admired what could still hold once ordinary work returned and the room stopped talking about the launch.

I have learned that the most durable choices often feel less exciting in the room than the more fashionable alternative. They usually ask for more discipline up front, more integration thinking, and more patience from the people making the decision. But over time, those choices reduce friction, lower support burden, and make the next change easier to absorb. In my experience, that is one of the clearest signs of stewardship in leadership. It is the willingness to choose what will still serve the enterprise well after the launch energy is gone.

There is also a quieter reason durability matters, which is trust. People come to trust an environment that behaves predictably, where the tools they rely on keep working and the ground does not shift under them every quarter. Every fashionable choice that later becomes a burden teaches the organization to brace itself against the next one. Every durable choice teaches the opposite, that the enterprise can be relied upon. In that sense, choosing durability is not only an architectural decision. It is one of the ways a leader keeps the institution worth trusting, which is the same thread that runs through every chapter of this book.

Some of the most expensive decisions in enterprise leadership are the ones that look impressive too early. A tool arrives with a strong demo. A platform promises faster insight, smoother adoption, or broader automation. A leader sees the possibility of momentum and wants the organization to benefit. I understand that instinct. Innovation matters. But over time, I learned that what looks impressive at the beginning is not always what proves durable once the business has to live with it. That is why this chapter is not anti-innovation. It is pro-endurance. It is about the discipline of choosing what will still serve the enterprise well after the excitement fades and the operating realities become visible. It belongs beside the chapters on legacy thinking and resilience, because all three describe the same stewardship instinct from different angles: build what the institution can still trust and sustain when the applause is gone.

What Architecture Teaches You About Character

Architecture taught me something I did not fully appreciate early in my career. Technology choices reveal leadership character over time. They reveal whether a leader is disciplined enough to think beyond immediate appeal, patient enough to value coherence over novelty, and honest enough to admit that every shortcut eventually becomes part of the operating burden. Good architecture is not glamorous in the moment. It rarely earns applause the way visible launches do. But it shapes the organization's future more deeply than many leaders realize. It determines how easily systems can scale, how reliably information can move, how resilient integrations will be, and how much complexity the business will keep paying for long after the original decision makers have moved on.

That lesson became even more practical for me as the enterprise matured across multiple brands, regions, and operating realities. A CIO can be tempted to admire a capability because it is modern, but mature stewardship asks a harder question. Will this choice still make the enterprise easier to run a year from now. Will it reduce support burden. Will it simplify handoffs. Will it improve trust in data, ownership, and execution. Those are the questions that matter when you are accountable not only for introducing change, but for living with the full cost of it afterward. In that sense, durability is not caution. It is disciplined ambition.

I learned this in real operating environments, not in abstract strategy sessions. In manufacturing and distribution settings, novelty often enters the conversation dressed as speed. People want faster dashboards, smarter automation, cleaner user experiences, and new capabilities that promise better insight or easier work. Some of those promises are real. But real executive discipline begins when leaders ask what must also be true underneath the promise. Does the data model hold. Are process definitions stable enough to support scale. Is change management strong enough that adoption will last. Is the service model ready to support the capability after the project team has moved on. A new capability may be attractive on the front end and quietly expensive on the back end. Durable leaders learn to see both sides of that equation.

The Demo That Won the Room

I still remember moments when a demonstration won the room quickly. The visuals were strong. The workflow looked smoother than the current state. The possibility of improvement felt immediate. In those moments, leaders can feel pressure to move from excitement to approval without pausing long enough to examine the longer arc. I understand that pressure because part of the CIO role is helping the business remain open to progress. But I have learned that the most important work often begins after the demo ends. How will this connect to the existing operating model. What discipline will be required to govern it. What process variation will it reduce, and what complexity might it quietly introduce if adoption is uneven. A strong demonstration can open a door, but it does not answer the stewardship question by itself.

That is one reason I teach durability as a decision discipline rather than as a technical preference. The issue is not whether a tool is new. The issue is whether the institution will become clearer, steadier, and more capable because it adopted it. Graduate students, consultants, and practicing CIOs all need to study that distinction because executive life is full of choices that sound progressive in the room while creating a larger support burden over time. Durable leadership asks leaders to evaluate novelty against standards such as maintainability, integration, security posture, user trust, training load, governance fit, and long-term business value. Those are not anti-innovation criteria. They are the conditions that keep innovation from becoming another source of hidden drag.

The Capability We Chose Not to Adopt

Some of the decisions I am most grateful for in hindsight were the ones where we chose not to adopt something impressive. I remember a capability that demonstrated beautifully and generated real enthusiasm. It promised to solve a visible pain point, and the temptation to move quickly was strong. But when we looked underneath the demonstration, the harder truths appeared. It would have added another integration to maintain, another set of definitions to reconcile, another tool for users to learn, and another dependency the support team would carry long after the excitement faded. The pain point it solved was real, but smaller than the complexity it would have introduced. We chose not to adopt it, and we strengthened the capability we already had instead.

That decision was not popular in the moment, because saying no to something modern can look like a lack of ambition. But a year later, the wisdom of it was clear. The environment stayed simpler. The support burden stayed lower. The team kept its attention on the work that mattered rather than on maintaining a capability that mostly impressed. I have come to believe that some of the most valuable leadership decisions are invisible precisely because they prevented complexity that never arrived. No one celebrates the drag that was avoided, but the institution is steadier for it. That is the quiet arithmetic of durability. The cost of novelty is usually paid later, and the benefit of restraint usually shows up as an absence of problems.

The Real Cost of Novelty

It helps to be precise about where the cost of novelty actually lands, because it rarely appears in the decision that approves it. A new capability is usually evaluated on its front-end promise, the demo, the feature list, the projected improvement. But the real cost accumulates on the back end, in places that are easy to discount in the moment. Every new tool adds integration surface that someone must maintain. Every new platform adds a set of definitions and conventions that must be reconciled with everything around it. Every novel capability adds training load, because people have to learn it, and support load, because someone has to keep it running when it breaks. None of these costs is dramatic on its own. Together, across many enthusiastic adoptions, they become the quiet drag that leaders later mistake for the natural weight of a complex business.

There is also a subtler cost, which is fragmentation. Each tool adopted for a local reason makes the overall environment a little less coherent, a little harder to reason about as one system. The user experience splinters across more interfaces. Ownership becomes harder to trace. The seams multiply. This is the same complexity tax described in the chapter on legacy thinking, except that here it is being created in real time rather than inherited. An organization can accumulate technical debt just as easily through too much novelty as through too little renewal, and the version created by chasing the new is harder to question because it still looks modern.

Seeing both sides of the equation is the discipline this chapter asks for. It does not ask leaders to reject the new. It asks them to price it honestly, to weigh the front-end promise against the full back-end cost, and to remember that the institution will live with the second long after it has forgotten the first. A capability earns its place not by being impressive but by leaving the enterprise clearer, steadier, and more capable once ordinary work resumes. Anything that fails that test is not progress. It is motion that the support team will pay for quietly for years.

Durability Is Built Through Lifecycle Discipline

Durability is not built only in the moment of approval. It is built afterward through lifecycle discipline. Leaders have to decide what should be standardized, what should be retired, what should be simplified, and what no longer deserves permanent space in the environment. In my experience, enterprises grow more fragile when they keep adding but struggle to remove. Complexity accumulates quietly. A temporary workaround survives too long. A local variation becomes normal. A one-time exception hardens into another support obligation the institution now has to carry. Durable leadership interrupts that pattern. It asks whether the environment is becoming easier to trust and support, or merely more crowded with the residue of earlier decisions.

That is why I have come to see standardization as one of the most generous acts a CIO can perform for the future of the enterprise. Standardization lowers the amount of unnecessary thinking required to keep ordinary work moving. It reduces the number of seams people must remember, the number of local exceptions they must interpret, and the number of hidden dependencies support teams must quietly carry. In multi-site environments, this matters even more. What feels like a harmless difference in one place multiplies into cost, confusion, and delay across the wider system. Durable leaders are willing to make some things simpler so the business can become more capable. That is not a loss of flexibility. It is a form of operational kindness.

Lifecycle discipline also means having the courage to retire what the enterprise has outgrown. Adding a capability is easy and visible. Removing one is harder and rarely celebrated, which is exactly why so few organizations do it well. But an environment that only ever grows eventually collapses under its own accumulated weight. The leaders who keep an enterprise durable are the ones willing to sunset the tool that no longer earns its keep, consolidate the overlapping capabilities, and protect the environment from becoming a graveyard of decisions no one was willing to reverse. Durability is as much about disciplined subtraction as it is about careful selection.

Durability in the Age of AI

There has never been a more powerful test of this chapter than AI, because AI is the most compelling novelty most of us will encounter in our careers. The demonstrations are genuinely astonishing. The pressure to adopt is intense and comes from every direction. And the gap between what dazzles in a demo and what proves durable in daily operation is wider here than almost anywhere else. Everything this chapter argues applies to AI with unusual force. A capability that impresses the room is not the same as a capability the enterprise can trust, sustain, and support a year from now, and the excitement around AI makes that distinction easy to forget exactly when it matters most.

The durable questions are the same ones, asked with more discipline. Will this AI capability still make the enterprise easier to run once the novelty fades. Does the data underneath it hold. Is the governance strong enough that adoption will last and stay trustworthy. Who will support it, own its output, and answer for it after the launch energy is gone. Is it solving a real institutional problem or mostly demonstrating that the organization is modern. Many AI initiatives will pass these tests and genuinely deserve to be built. Many others will not, and the discipline to tell the difference, to choose the durable AI capability over the impressive one, will separate the enterprises that are strengthened by this era from the ones that merely accumulate expensive experiments.

There is also a durability concern specific to how quickly this field moves. Tools, models, and vendors in the AI space are changing faster than almost any technology category before them. A capability that looks leading-edge today may be unsupported or surpassed within a short time, which makes architectural discipline more important, not less. Durable leadership in this moment means favoring choices that keep the enterprise flexible rather than locked to a single fast-moving dependency, preserving the ability to adopt what proves lasting and to walk away from what does not. The goal is not to resist AI. It is to adopt it the way a steward adopts anything, by asking what will still serve the institution well after the excitement has moved on to the next astonishing thing.

Why This Chapter Matters

The practical value of this chapter is that it gives leaders a second question to ask after the one everyone else is asking. The room asks whether a capability is impressive. The steward asks whether it will still be serving the enterprise well a year from now, once ordinary work has resumed and the support burden has become visible. Holding both questions at once is what keeps an organization open to genuine progress without becoming a collection of expensive enthusiasms. Durability is not the enemy of innovation. It is the discipline that lets innovation accumulate into capability rather than into drag.

The lesson reads differently depending on the reader's seat. For the practicing CIO and the IT leader, the message is operational. Evaluate every new capability against its full lifecycle cost, and treat standardization and disciplined retirement as ongoing responsibilities rather than occasional projects. For the consultant, the message is diagnostic. A client's environment tells you whether it has confused novelty with durability, because the back-end residue of impressive decisions shows up as fragmentation, support burden, and tools that mostly demonstrate. And for the faculty member and the graduate student, the message is conceptual. This is a chance to study technology decisions as expressions of leadership character over time, and to examine why the cost of novelty so reliably arrives after the decision that approved it.

Boardroom Perspective: Durable Choices Compound

Boards often hear innovation in the language of opportunity. That is understandable. Innovation can improve productivity, visibility, customer experience, and strategic flexibility. But durable board-level leadership also asks how a new choice will age inside the institution. Will it simplify the landscape or fragment it further. Will it strengthen operating discipline or create another dependency that only a few people understand. Will it reduce the cost of future change or increase it. These are not technical questions alone. They are stewardship questions because they determine whether the enterprise is building capability or merely accumulating motion. When boards learn to ask those questions well, technology decisions become more connected to institutional strength and less vulnerable to hype.

A mature board should therefore press past the excitement of any single capability and ask how the environment is aging as a whole. Is the technology landscape becoming simpler or more fragmented over time. Where is the enterprise adopting faster than it is retiring, so that complexity is quietly accumulating. Which recent adoptions have actually reduced support burden, and which have increased it. And in the case of AI especially, are decisions being made for durable institutional value or for the appearance of being current. These questions protect the institution from a pattern that is easy to fall into and expensive to reverse, where each individually reasonable adoption combines into an environment no one can fully sustain.

From the CIO's Desk

One of the clearest lessons of my career is that the cost of a technology decision is usually paid in a different season than the one in which it was made. The excitement arrives at approval. The burden arrives at support. That gap is why durability is so easy to undervalue, because the people celebrating the launch are rarely the ones who will carry the complexity a year later. I have learned to keep both seasons in view at once, to ask not only whether a capability will impress us now but whether it will still be serving us, simply and reliably, when it has become ordinary.

I have also come to believe that some of the most important leadership decisions are the ones that prevent problems no one will ever see. A capability not adopted, a complexity not introduced, a dependency not created. None of those earn applause, because the drag they would have produced never arrives. But the institution is steadier for them, and over time that steadiness compounds into something a flashier approach rarely achieves. Durability is quiet by nature. Its reward is the absence of trouble, which is one of the hardest forms of value for an organization to notice and one of the most important for a leader to protect.

If I had to summarize my own view simply, it would be this. Innovation opens doors, but durability is what the enterprise actually lives in. A leader serves the institution best by choosing what will still hold, still scale, and still be trusted after the launch energy is gone. That is not a rejection of the new. It is a commitment to making sure the new becomes lasting capability rather than another layer of complexity the business will quietly carry for years.

Five Leadership Rules for Choosing Durability Over Novelty

These are the rules I keep returning to. They are simple to state and demanding to live, which is usually the mark of a principle worth keeping.

First, judge a capability by its full lifecycle, not its demonstration. The demo shows the front-end promise. Durability lives in the back-end reality of integration, support, training, and governance that the enterprise will carry long after the excitement fades.

Second, ask what must be true underneath the promise. A new capability is only as durable as the data model, process discipline, change management, and service model beneath it. If the foundation is weak, the novelty becomes drag.

Third, price the cost of novelty honestly. Every adoption adds integration surface, definitions to reconcile, and support burden. Weigh that full cost against the benefit, and remember the institution lives with the cost long after it forgets the promise.

Fourth, practice disciplined subtraction. Durability depends as much on what you retire as on what you select. Sunset what no longer earns its keep, consolidate the overlapping, and protect the environment from becoming a graveyard of decisions no one would reverse.

Fifth, treat durability as disciplined ambition, not caution. Choosing what will still serve the enterprise after the applause is gone is not a rejection of progress. It is how a steward makes sure progress compounds into capability rather than into hidden complexity.

Leadership Lessons

- Novelty and durability are not the same thing, and mature leadership learns to tell them apart.
- Technology choices reveal leadership character over time, in how they age rather than how they launch.
- The cost of a capability is usually paid in a different season than the one in which it was approved.
- Some of the most valuable decisions are the ones that prevent complexity that never arrives.
- An enterprise can accumulate technical debt through too much novelty as easily as through too little renewal.
- Durability depends as much on disciplined retirement as on careful selection.
- AI is the strongest test of this discipline, because the gap between what dazzles and what endures is unusually wide.

Discussion Questions

- What is the difference between novelty and durability in technology leadership, and why does it matter for institutional strength?
- Why does the cost of a new capability so often arrive after the decision that approved it, and where does that cost land?
- How does disciplined retirement of old capabilities contribute to durability, and why do organizations do it so rarely?
- Why is AI an especially demanding test of durability over novelty, and how should leaders evaluate AI capabilities accordingly?
- As a consultant, what signs in a client's environment would tell you it has confused novelty with durable capability?

- If you were teaching this chapter, what would you identify as the hidden long-term cost of an organization that adopts faster than it retires?

Application for Practice

- For the practicing leader: choose one recent technology adoption and assess its full lifecycle cost, including integration, support, training, and governance, against the benefit it has actually delivered.
- For the IT leader: identify one capability in your environment that no longer earns its keep, and outline what it would take to retire or consolidate it.
- For the consultant: review a client's technology landscape and identify where it is adopting faster than it is retiring, with a recommendation for restoring coherence.
- For the faculty member or facilitator: design a short exercise in which students evaluate an impressive AI demonstration against durability criteria and decide whether to recommend adoption.
- For any reader: write a short evaluation rubric that distinguishes a capability worth adopting from one that mostly impresses, using criteria such as maintainability, integration, support, and long-term value.
- For reflection: think of a time you or your organization adopted something impressive that became a burden, or declined something impressive and were glad later. What did the experience teach you about durability?

Chapter 15: Leaving the Enterprise Better

Opening

One of the questions that has mattered more to me as the years have gone on is not whether a leader was visible, but whether the institution became stronger because that leader served there. Titles come and go. Projects finish. Roadmaps change. Vendors change. Technologies certainly change. But the deeper question remains. Is the enterprise easier to trust, easier to run, and easier to change well because of the leadership it received. That is the question at the heart of this chapter. For practicing CIOs, IT leaders, consultants, and graduate leadership programs alike, the issue is not legacy in the flattering sense. It is stewardship in the practical sense. What exactly is left behind when the meeting ends, the initiative closes, or the leader eventually moves on.

This chapter is closely related to the one before it, but it asks a different question. The chapter on durability was about the technology choices that last. This chapter is about the leadership inheritance that lasts, the people, habits, standards, and institutional capability a leader hands to whoever comes next. A durable platform is part of a good legacy, but it is not the heart of one. The heart of a leadership legacy is whether the enterprise can keep thinking clearly, deciding responsibly, and operating with trust after the leader is no longer the one in the room. That conviction sits at the center of how I have come to understand leadership, and it echoes a belief I return to often: the strongest organizations are not built on heroes. They are built to remain steady when any single person, including the leader, is gone.

What Stronger Really Means

Stronger does not only mean bigger budgets, more platforms, or more visible transformation. Sometimes stronger looks quieter than that. It looks like clearer ownership. It looks like steadier governance. It looks like project work that no longer depends on heroic recovery. It looks like data people can trust without debate. It looks like teams that can lead without waiting for the most senior title in the room. In my experience, that is the kind of strength that matters most because it remains useful after attention moves elsewhere. A leader has truly added value when the organization becomes less dependent on improvisation and more capable of carrying its own responsibilities with clarity.

That is why I have learned to be suspicious of strength that depends on me. An enterprise that runs well only because one leader is personally holding it together is not strong. It is exposed. It feels capable while that person is present and reveals its fragility the moment they are not. Real strength is the opposite. It is the capability that stays in the building after the leader leaves it. The clearest measure of whether I made an organization stronger is not how much depended on me while I was there. It is how little needs to depend on me once I am gone.

What Leaders Actually Leave Behind

Leaders usually leave behind more than the visible achievements listed in annual updates. They leave habits. They leave standards. They leave communication rhythms, decision paths, and beliefs about what good work looks like here. They leave systems that either make the next team steadier or force the next team to spend its first year cleaning up avoidable residue. They leave people who were either developed or merely used. They leave an environment that either depends less on personality or still waits for one central figure to rescue every difficult week. The longer I have served, the more I have realized that these quieter legacies matter more than recognition ever could. They shape the future character of the enterprise long after the applause is gone.

The uncomfortable part of this truth is that a leader does not get to choose whether to leave a legacy. They only get to choose what kind. Every leader leaves the next team an inheritance, and that inheritance is either an asset or a liability. A leader who hoarded knowledge leaves confusion. A leader who tolerated unclear ownership leaves ambiguity. A leader who chased visibility leaves a function organized around a personality that is no longer there. None of these leaders intended to harm the institution, but intention is not the same as inheritance. What you build into the operating model, and what you fail to build, is what the next team receives whether you meant it or not.

Developing People Is the Most Durable Legacy

Of everything a leader leaves behind, developed people are the most durable. Systems age. Standards eventually need revision. Even good governance has to be refreshed as the enterprise changes. But a person who grew in judgment, confidence, and capability under your leadership carries that growth forward into every room they enter for the rest of their career, including rooms you will never see. That is why I have come to believe that developing people is not a soft complement to the real work of leadership. Over a long enough horizon, it is the most consequential work a leader does, because it compounds in places and times far beyond the leader's own tenure.

There is a line in this distinction that I take seriously. Leaders leave behind people who were either developed or merely used. A leader who only uses people extracts their effort to deliver the current result and leaves them no stronger than they were before. A leader who develops people delivers the result and grows the person at the same time, so the institution gains both the outcome and a more capable contributor. The difference rarely shows up in this quarter's metrics. It shows up years later, in whether the organization is full of people who learned to lead well or merely people who learned to survive being managed.

This is also where legacy becomes genuinely unselfish, because the leader who develops people is building value they will not be present to enjoy. The colleague who becomes a stronger leader, the analyst who grows into an owner, the manager who learns to lead with steadiness rather than noise, these are gifts to a future the developing leader has already left. In my experience, that is one of the clearest signs that someone is leading for the institution rather than for themselves. They are investing in capability that will mostly pay off after they are gone, which is exactly what stewardship means.

I have come to believe that this is also the most honest test of how a leader treated power while they held it. A leader who used their position mainly to remain central tends to leave people who learned to wait for direction. A leader who used their position to grow others tends to leave people who learned to lead. Years later, you can often read the character of a past leader simply by looking at the people they developed, because capable, confident people who think for themselves are rarely an accident. They are usually the evidence that someone chose, over and over, to build others up rather than to keep importance for themselves.

The Leader Who Was Hard to Replace

I have watched leadership transitions go in very different directions, and the contrast taught me a great deal about what legacy really is. I have seen a respected leader depart and leave a kind of crater behind, not because they were incompetent, but because too much had lived in them personally. The relationships were theirs. The context was theirs. The judgment that held everything together was theirs, and largely undocumented. The organization had felt strong while they were present, and discovered only at their departure how much of that strength had been borrowed from one person. The transition was painful, the relearning was expensive, and the institution spent a long time recovering capability it had assumed it owned but had only been renting.

I have also seen the opposite, a leader whose departure was almost uneventful, in the best possible way. The work continued. The team kept its rhythm. Decisions still got made well because the criteria were shared, not personal. People who had been developed simply stepped up, because they had been carrying real responsibility all along. That leader was, in a narrow sense, easy to replace, and I have come to see that as one of the highest compliments a steward can earn. They had built something that did not depend on them, which meant they had built something that would last.

The lesson I drew is uncomfortable for the ego but clarifying for the work. Being hard to replace can feel like a sign of importance, but it is often a sign of a stewardship failure. The leader who is genuinely indispensable has, usually without meaning to, built an institution that is fragile in exactly the place it can least afford to be. The deeper aim is to become, over time, less necessary, because the strength has been transferred into people and systems that no longer need the leader to hold them together.

Legacy Is Built in What the System Can Do Without You

The longer I have served in leadership, the more convinced I have become that legacy is rarely built in the visible moments people remember first. It is built in what the institution can still do well when the leader is not present, when the original project team has moved on, and when the energy of the launch has long faded into ordinary work. That is why I no longer measure leadership mainly by how much depended on me while I was in the seat. I measure it by whether the organization became steadier, clearer, and more capable because of my time there. If the system still needs the leader to explain everything, to rescue everything, or to personally reconnect every important thread, then the deeper work of stewardship is not yet finished.

Over the years I have become more committed to leadership that scales through people, habits, governance, and institutional memory than leadership that depends on one powerful figure. Titles matter less over time than systems, values, and developed people. Sustainable success follows disciplined leadership, humble stewardship, and intentional people development. Legacy is not what one leader accomplishes alone. Legacy is what continues because the institution no longer depends on one leader's constant presence to remain steady.

That is also why I have become more careful about the difference between strategic modernization and decorative modernization, because the two leave very different inheritances. Strategic modernization strengthens the institution. It improves integration, reduces friction, protects data integrity, clarifies ownership, and creates a stronger base for future change. Decorative modernization may look current, but it leaves the organization carrying many of the same old burdens in a slightly newer wrapper. Over time, I learned to ask harder questions. Will this choice reduce the number of seams the business has to manage. Will it become easier to support at scale. Will it preserve continuity when people change roles. Will it still make sense when the enterprise is tired, busy, and no longer talking about the project every day. Those questions do not kill innovation. They purify it, and they make sure the modernization a leader leaves behind is an asset rather than a more fashionable version of the same drag.

Planning Your Own Succession

If leaving the enterprise better is the goal, then planning your own succession is not an afterthought to be handled near the end. It is a discipline to practice throughout your tenure. The leaders who hand off well are rarely the ones who started thinking about it in their final months. They are the ones who treated succession as an ongoing responsibility from early on, by developing people deliberately, distributing real ownership rather than hoarding it, documenting reasoning, and resisting the quiet temptation to make themselves the indispensable center of everything important. Succession, done well, is less an event than a habit of building capability into others while you still have the time and standing to do it.

This asks something genuinely difficult of a leader, because it runs against a natural instinct. It is satisfying to be the one who solves the hard problem, who carries the key relationship, who is needed in every important room. Building your own replaceability means deliberately giving away some of that centrality, letting others carry what you could carry faster, and accepting that the institution growing less dependent on you is a success rather than a loss. In my experience, that is one of the truest tests of whether a leader is serving the enterprise or serving their own sense of importance. The steward chooses the institution's long-term strength over their own short-term indispensability.

The reward for this discipline is an institution that can outlast any single leader, including the one who built it. That is the quiet aim beneath all of it. Not to be remembered as irreplaceable, but to leave behind an enterprise so capable that it does not need to remember you in order to keep thriving. A leader who achieves that has given the organization the most durable gift available, the ability to continue well without them, which is the clearest evidence that they led for something larger than themselves.

What Kind of Enterprise We Leave Behind in the Age of AI

The arrival of AI gives this chapter a new and serious dimension, because today's leaders are deciding what kind of AI-era enterprise they will hand to those who come next. That inheritance is being shaped right now, in choices that will outlast every current leader. A steward has to think carefully about what those choices leave behind. The most important question is not which AI tools a leader adopts. It is whether they leave behind an institution that can govern, judge, and adapt its use of AI wisely after they are gone, or one that has become dependent on tools it does not understand and cannot sustain.

There is a real risk worth naming. A leader who races to adopt AI without building the surrounding judgment can leave a successor a difficult inheritance, an enterprise reliant on capabilities no one fully understands, governed by no one in particular, and fragile in ways that will only become visible later. That is the opposite of leaving the enterprise better. The durable legacy in the age of AI is not a collection of impressive tools. It is an organization that has learned how to think about AI well, that has the governance to adopt it responsibly, the data foundation to use it safely, and the developed people to apply judgment to what it produces. Those capabilities will outlast any specific model or vendor.

This is where the threads of this book come together in the context of the most disruptive technology of our moment. The accountability, trusted data, governance, restraint, and developed people that earlier chapters described are exactly what a leader needs to leave behind so the enterprise can meet AI wisely without them. The tools will keep changing, faster here than almost anywhere. What endures is the institution's capacity to adopt them with judgment. Leaving that capacity behind, rather than just leaving behind the tools themselves, is what stewardship in the age of AI finally requires.

Why This Chapter Matters

The practical value of this chapter is that it offers a leader a different scoreboard. The usual measures, budgets, launches, visible transformation, all reward presence and activity. This chapter proposes a harder and more honest measure: what would remain strong here if you left tomorrow. That question reframes the daily work. It turns developing people, distributing ownership, and building durable systems from optional virtues into the central project, because they are the only things that survive a leader's departure. A leader who internalizes this scoreboard makes different choices, and those choices compound into an institution that is genuinely stronger rather than merely busier.

The lesson reads differently depending on the reader's seat. For the practicing CIO and the IT leader, the message is operational. Treat succession and people development as ongoing responsibilities from the start, and measure your leadership by how little needs to depend on you rather than how much. For the consultant, the message is diagnostic. The clearest sign of a leader's true legacy is what happens at the handoff, so look at how dependent a client's function is on its current leader, because that dependence is a risk hiding inside apparent strength. And for the faculty member and the graduate student, the message is conceptual. This is a chance to study legacy as institutional capability rather than personal achievement, and to wrestle with the uncomfortable but clarifying question of what an organization would retain if its leader were suddenly gone.

Boardroom Perspective: Succession Is a Stewardship Question

Boards often treat succession as a contingency to be addressed when a transition is imminent. But succession is better understood as an ongoing measure of institutional health, not a plan to be dusted off in an emergency. The real question a board should ask is not only who would replace a given leader, but how much the enterprise currently depends on that leader to function at all. An organization that runs well only because of one person's presence carries a hidden risk that no strategy deck will reveal. A mature board treats the depth of leadership capability beneath the top role as a core indicator of whether the institution is genuinely strong or merely well-led for the moment.

A mature board should therefore ask the questions that surface this. Where does the enterprise still depend too heavily on a single leader's relationships, knowledge, or judgment. How deliberately is the organization developing the people who would carry it forward. What would remain healthy, and what would become fragile, if a key leader were suddenly unavailable. And in the case of AI especially, is the enterprise building the durable judgment to govern these tools after current leaders are gone, or merely accumulating capabilities that will become someone else's problem. These are not contingency questions. They are stewardship questions, because they determine whether the institution has been built to outlast the people who currently lead it.

From the CIO's Desk

One of the clearest lessons of my career is that the ego and the institution often want different things, and a leader has to keep choosing the institution. The ego wants to be needed, to be central, to be the one without whom things would fall apart. The institution needs the opposite. It needs a leader secure enough to build capability in others, distribute ownership, and become, over time, less necessary. I have come to believe that the willingness to make yourself replaceable is one of the truest signs of leadership maturity, precisely because it asks you to value the organization's strength over your own sense of importance.

I have also learned that the most meaningful parts of a legacy are usually invisible at the moment they are created. The colleague developed, the ownership handed over, the system built to run without you, the reasoning documented so the next team does not have to guess. None of these earn applause in the moment, because their value only becomes clear later, often after the leader has moved on. But they are what actually remain. The visible achievements fade into history. What endures is the strengthened capability of the people and the institution, quietly continuing to do good work because someone chose to build for their benefit rather than for recognition.

If I had to summarize my own view simply, it would be this. The goal is not to be remembered as irreplaceable. The goal is to leave behind an enterprise so capable that it does not need you in order to thrive. A leader who manages that has given the institution the most durable gift there is, the ability to continue well without them. That, to me, is what it means to leave the enterprise better, and it is the deepest expression of stewardship I know.

Five Leadership Rules for Leaving the Enterprise Better

These are the rules I keep returning to. They are simple to state and demanding to live, which is usually the mark of a principle worth keeping.

First, measure your leadership by what survives your absence. If the enterprise still needs your constant presence to stay coherent, the work of stewardship is not yet finished. The clearest measure of strength is how little needs to depend on you once you are gone.

Second, develop people rather than merely using them. Developed people are the most durable legacy a leader leaves, because their growth compounds in rooms and years far beyond your tenure. Delivering the result and growing the person are not in tension. They are the same work done well.

Third, treat succession as an ongoing habit, not an end-of-tenure event. Distribute real ownership, document reasoning, and resist becoming the indispensable center while you still have the time and standing to build capability in others.

Fourth, choose strategic modernization over decorative modernization. Leave behind systems that strengthen the institution rather than ones that merely look current, because the next team inherits the operating reality, not the launch announcement.

Fifth, leave behind judgment, not only tools, especially with AI. The durable legacy in a fast-moving era is an institution that can govern and adapt its technology wisely after you are gone, not a collection of impressive capabilities no one fully understands.

Leadership Lessons

- The real measure of leadership is not how much depended on you while present, but how little needs to once you are gone.
- Every leader leaves an inheritance, and the only choice is whether it is an asset or a liability.
- Developed people are the most durable legacy, because their growth compounds far beyond a leader's tenure.
- Being hard to replace can feel like importance, but it is often a sign of a stewardship failure.
- Strategic modernization strengthens the institution, while decorative modernization leaves old burdens in a newer wrapper.
- In the age of AI, the durable legacy is the judgment to govern the tools, not the tools themselves.
- The goal is not to be remembered as irreplaceable, but to leave an enterprise capable of thriving without you.

Discussion Questions

- What is the difference between a legacy of durable capability and a legacy of personal visibility, and why does it matter?
- Why might a leader who seems indispensable actually represent a stewardship failure rather than a strength?
- How does developing people create a more durable legacy than building systems alone?
- Why is planning your own succession best understood as an ongoing habit rather than an end-of-tenure event?
- In the age of AI, what does it mean to leave behind judgment rather than only tools, and why does that distinction matter for a successor?

- If you were teaching this chapter, what would you identify as the hardest part of leading in a way that makes yourself less necessary over time?

Application for Practice

- For the practicing leader: ask honestly what would remain strong, and what would become fragile, if you left your role tomorrow. Identify the single greatest dependence on you personally.
- For the IT leader: choose one area where too much currently depends on you, and outline how you would transfer that capability into people and systems over the next year.
- For the consultant: in a client engagement, assess how dependent a function is on its current leader, and identify the succession and development gaps that represent hidden risk.
- For the faculty member or facilitator: design a short exercise in which students must build a one-year plan to make a hypothetical leader less indispensable while keeping the function strong.
- For any reader: identify one person you could develop more deliberately, and one responsibility you could hand to them, as an investment in capability beyond your own tenure.
- For reflection: write a short statement describing what you want your leadership to leave behind in people, systems, and the institution's capacity to thrive without you.

Chapter 16: What Endures

Opening

Technology will keep changing. Platforms will change. Architecture patterns will change. Security threats will change. The language of innovation will change. But some things endure because they are not tied to the fashion of a given era. Trust endures. Accountability endures. Governance endures. Clarity endures. The responsibility to leave the enterprise more capable than you found it endures. That is what this culminating chapter is meant to hold together. After all the systems, initiatives, pressures, and transitions, what remains meaningful is not whether a leader kept pace with every trend. It is whether the institution became steadier, wiser, and stronger because of the way that leader chose to serve it.

By the time a leader has spent enough years inside real organizational work, some of the usual measures of success begin to feel incomplete. Delivered projects matter. Stability matters. Results matter. But eventually a quieter question begins to matter more. What will still be true here after the visible work is over. That is the question that stays with me now. Not what looked impressive in the moment, but what actually endured. Not what won approval in a meeting, but what kept serving the institution after the meeting ended and attention moved on.

This chapter draws the threads of the book together. Each earlier chapter examined one discipline, accountability, data truth, speed, integration, transformation, legacy thinking, trust, governance, calm, restraint, indecision, resilience, memory, durability, and the work of leaving the enterprise better. This chapter asks what remains when all of those disciplines have done their work and the visible effort has passed. The answer, I have come to believe, is not any single achievement. It is the strengthened life of the institution itself.

What Remains After the Work Is Done

The reason this matters so much to me is that I have watched too many organizations confuse novelty with endurance. They invest heavily in what is current, but underinvest in what gives that investment a chance to hold. A stronger operating model, visible ownership, disciplined governance, trusted information, and people who know how to lead without constant rescue often outlast the platform that first brought those lessons into focus. In other words, the deepest contribution of leadership is rarely the tool itself. It is the capability, maturity, and confidence the institution still has after the tool is no longer the center of attention.

What remains after the work is done is rarely the slide deck, the milestone, or the applause. What remains is the condition of the system, the confidence of the people, the clarity of the operating model, and the trust the organization now has in its own ability to keep moving. Over time, I have come to respect those outcomes more than the visible markers that often accompany them. A cleaner decision rhythm remains. A stronger standard remains. A more trusted platform remains. A calmer organization remains. These things do not always look dramatic, but they shape the daily life of the enterprise long after the original work has disappeared from view.

That is why I believe stewardship is one of the deepest forms of leadership. It asks leaders to care not only about the outcome they can claim, but about the conditions they are creating for people they may never lead directly. It asks them to think beyond the visible cycle of pressure and performance and to consider the longer life of the institution. In the end, what endures is not only what was built. It is what was strengthened. It is what became clearer, steadier, and more trustworthy because someone chose to lead with discipline, humility, and continuity in mind. That, to me, is what makes leadership worth remembering.

The Leadership That Stays Behind

When urgency fades, the institution reveals what leadership really built. Did the systems become more understandable. Did decision paths become more coherent. Did people become stronger and more capable of carrying responsibility without a constant need for escalation. Did the organization retain what it learned. These are the quieter questions that endure after go-live celebrations, executive updates, and transformation milestones have passed. In my experience, they are also the most honest ones. They show whether leadership created temporary movement or lasting strength.

In the end, the leadership that stays behind is not mainly remembered through titles or formal authority. It remains in the standards people still trust, the clarity they inherit, the confidence they feel when the system behaves as expected, and the way the culture responds when something difficult appears. It remains in the people who now lead with more steadiness because someone once led them that way. It remains in the routines that feel ordinary only because they were built carefully enough to become normal. These are not small things. They are the evidence that leadership entered the life of the institution deeply enough to outlast personality.

That is the kind of standard I hope this book leaves with the reader. Not a dramatic conclusion, but a steadier one. Leadership is worth remembering when it leaves people, systems, and institutions more capable of carrying what matters. Stewardship is worth practicing because it asks leaders to care about that deeper outcome even when the visible reward is small. And what endures, in the end, is not only the work itself. It is the strengthened life of the organization that continues after the work has passed into memory.

The Seasons That Leave a Mark

When I think about what endures in leadership, I do not only think about the systems, standards, or governance structures that remain after the visible work is done. I also think about the seasons that leave a mark on the leader. There were periods in my journey when the work was physically exhausting, emotionally demanding, and impossible to explain fully to people who were not inside it. Long stretches away from family. Launches that required more from the team than any of us would have called sustainable. Projects in unfamiliar environments where culture, limited resources, and accumulated pressure tested not only technical ability, but patience, humility, and endurance. Those seasons were hard. I would not romanticize them. But they also changed me. They stripped away some illusions about control and taught me to value steadiness, respect, and learning under strain in a much deeper way.

What stayed behind from those seasons was not pride in the hardship itself. It was the wisdom they forced into the way I lead. I learned to care more about sustainability, because I had seen what unsustainable effort can cost even when the outcome succeeds. I learned to respect culture more deeply, because leadership without cultural humility eventually becomes brittle. I learned to value preparation, documentation, and shared ownership more intensely, because I had seen what happens when too much depends on a few people carrying too much for too long. And perhaps most importantly, I learned that some of the hardest seasons in a leader's life are not only tests of endurance. They become part of what the leader leaves behind in the institution: stronger judgment, deeper empathy, and a more disciplined commitment to building environments that do not require the next generation to carry quite the same burden.

The Conversation After the Hard Season

There is a particular kind of conversation that happens only after a hard season has finally begun to loosen its grip. The launch is behind you. The crisis has passed. The project that once seemed unmanageable is no longer consuming every hour. And then, usually in a quieter room than the one where the pressure unfolded, people begin naming what the season actually cost. Someone says how close they were to exhaustion. Someone admits what they were carrying without saying it at the time. Someone else describes the moment they almost stopped believing the work would come together. I have learned to respect those conversations because they tell the truth that success alone often hides. They remind leaders that endurance may have been necessary, but it should never become the only story we keep about what happened.

What matters in those moments is not only relief. It is interpretation. What did this season teach us that should remain. What should we strengthen, document, or redesign so the next difficult chapter does not extract the same price. What kind of leadership did we practice under strain, and what kind do we want to become because of it. In my experience, those reflections are part of what makes hardship meaningful instead of merely survivable. They turn endurance into wisdom. They help the institution carry forward better judgment rather than only better stories. And they reinforce something I have come to believe deeply. What endures best after a hard season is not pride in how much we endured, but the discipline to build a future that does not require quite the same kind of suffering to succeed.

The Quiet Sign That the Culture Had Changed

One of the clearest signs that a culture has changed is often so quiet that it would be easy to miss if you were only looking for dramatic proof. It appears in ordinary moments. A team raises an issue earlier than it used to. A manager brings forward a metric with more confidence because the definition is now stable. A handover happens more smoothly because someone took the time to document what used to live only in memory. A meeting ends with less confusion because the decision path is clearer than it once was. None of these moments would make a presentation headline. But together they tell a deeper story. They say the organization is beginning to carry itself differently.

I have come to value those signs more than the louder ones because they usually endure longer. A visible success can be celebrated quickly and forgotten just as quickly. But when a culture begins to reduce ambiguity, surface truth earlier, protect focus more naturally, and trust its own systems more consistently, the institution itself feels different. That difference is one of the quiet forms of legacy that matters most to me. It is evidence that leadership did not only produce a result. It helped shape a better way for the organization to live its work after the original moment of effort has passed.

If there is one idea I hope remains, it is that leadership is not what we announce. It is what we practice when no one is watching. It is there in the discipline to tell the truth early, the humility to build others up, the steadiness to protect continuity, and the patience to value what endures over what merely impresses. These habits rarely feel theatrical, but they are often the very reason an institution keeps moving with strength after the visible chapter of the work is over.

What Endures When the Tools Keep Changing

There has never been a moment when this chapter's question mattered more, because there has rarely been a technology shift as fast or as sweeping as the one now underway. AI is changing tools, workflows, and expectations at remarkable speed, and that speed makes it tempting to believe that everything is being reinvented, including the fundamentals of leadership. I have come to believe the opposite. The faster the tools change, the more valuable the things that do not change become. Trust does not become obsolete because a model improved. Accountability does not expire because a process was automated. Clarity, governance, judgment, and developed people do not lose their value in the age of AI. They gain it, because they are exactly what an organization needs to adopt powerful new tools without losing itself.

This is the reassurance and the challenge at the close of the book. AI will change a great deal about how work is done, but it does not change what makes an institution worth trusting. An enterprise still endures on the strength of its trust, the honesty of its accountability, the discipline of its governance, and the judgment of its people. A leader who builds those things is building what will still matter after this technology wave, and after the next one, because those foundations are not tied to any particular tool. They are what allow an institution to keep absorbing change without being scattered by it.

So the most durable contribution a leader can make in this era is not to chase every capability, but to strengthen the things that endure beneath all of them. The tools will keep arriving and keep being replaced. What will still be standing is the institution's capacity to think clearly, decide responsibly, and work with trust, no matter what technology it holds in its hands. That capacity is the deepest form of what endures, and building it is the same stewardship this book has described from the first chapter to this one. The technology of leadership will keep changing. The character of leadership does not.

A Note on Real-World Results

One point matters to me in this book. The ideas in these chapters are not theoretical to me. They were formed in real enterprise conditions, and many of them have already produced visible results in practice. Across every part of my own work, the same pattern appears again and again. Stronger governance, clearer priorities, disciplined execution, trusted data, and steadier operating rhythms do not just sound compelling in a leadership book. They work. In my own CIO journey, those principles helped turn around a struggling IT organization, improve delivery confidence, strengthen reliability, modernize the platform landscape, and reduce unnecessary cost while increasing strategic value.

The evidence is concrete. Project success improved from below fifty-five percent into the mid-nineties, while enterprise uptime remained in the high nines even during major systems rollouts and transformation work. Capital discipline and vendor rationalization produced roughly a million dollars in optimization, with additional operating savings from platform retirements and contract renegotiations. Core platforms were modernized through cloud migration, manufacturing execution expansion, HRIS rollout, electronic data interchange progress, productivity platform standardization, intranet improvement, and the strengthening of Data-Lake and BI-based analytics. AI and assistant adoption also moved from discussion into practical enablement through training, tips, and use-case development, including chatbot work and self-service analytics expansion. Just as important, these outcomes were achieved while governance matured, culture strengthened, and IT moved from a support function toward a strategic business partner.

I want the reader to know that these principles have been tested in real work, not only described in reflection. At the same time, no book can guarantee another leader the exact same outcome, because every institution carries its own history, constraints, and people. But I do believe this. Leaders who apply these disciplines seriously, clearly, and consistently give themselves a far better chance of building the same kind of trust, steadiness, and institutional strength these accomplishments represent. That is the practical invitation of this book. Not to copy my path exactly, but to apply the same disciplines with enough conviction that your own enterprise becomes measurably stronger because you led.

When I think about what endures now, I think less about how a role was described and more about what it quietly made possible. Public descriptions of a CIO can focus on strategy, transformation, and technology modernization. Those are real responsibilities. In my own role as Chief Information Officer at a global automotive and industrial coatings company and its family of brands, that scope is real. But what endures most in leadership is usually quieter than any formal description suggests. It is the steadier operating model, the clearer decision rhythm, the stronger governance habits, the better-developed people, and the trust the institution now has in its ability to carry difficult work without losing itself. That is the leadership I hope remains after the visible chapter of the role has ended.

This is also why I believe the deepest leadership legacy is institutional, not personal. Over the course of this book, I have written about accountability, data truth, speed, integration, transformation, trust, governance, calm under pressure, disciplined restraint, clarity, resilience, memory, durability, and the responsibility to leave an enterprise better than you found it. Those themes are not separate. They are different expressions of the same stewardship question: what are you building that will still help people think clearly, decide responsibly, and work with trust after you are no longer the one in the room. For students, faculty, and practicing executives, that is the lasting leadership challenge. Titles end. Projects close. Metrics move on. What endures is what the institution can now carry because someone chose to lead beyond themselves.

Why This Chapter Matters

The practical value of this chapter is that it gives a leader a way to think about success that outlasts the next performance cycle. Most measures reward what is visible now. This chapter argues for a longer scoreboard, one that asks what will still be working better a year or five years after the leader has moved on. That longer view changes present decisions, because a leader who is building for endurance invests differently in people, systems, and trust than one building for the next review. The reason this belongs at the close of the book is that it reframes every discipline that came before it. Each was, in the end, a way of building something that lasts.

The lesson reads differently depending on the reader's seat. For the practicing CIO and the IT leader, the message is operational. Measure your work by continuity rather than applause, and invest in the trust, clarity, and capability that survive your tenure. For the consultant, the message is diagnostic. The truest test of a leader's contribution is what still functions well without extraordinary intervention, so look past the visible wins to the durable capability underneath. And for the faculty member and the graduate student, the message is conceptual. This is a chance to study leadership by what endures rather than what impresses, and to recognize that in a fast-changing technological era, the things that do not change are exactly what make change survivable.

Boardroom Perspective: Endurance Is Measured After the Applause

Boards should care about what endures because the true quality of leadership often becomes most visible after the visible pressure has passed. A mature board should ask what capabilities still function well without extraordinary intervention, what lessons have been preserved rather than repeatedly relearned, and whether the institution has become less fragile over time. Those are not sentimental questions. They are strategic ones. Endurance is measured in whether trust still holds, whether governance still helps the business choose clearly, and whether continuity survives beyond the personalities who once held the work together.

A mature board should therefore look past the achievements of any single cycle and ask how the institution is aging as a whole. Is it becoming steadier and less dependent on heroics over time, or merely busier. Are the lessons of hard seasons being preserved or repeatedly relearned. And as AI reshapes the tools, is the enterprise strengthening the enduring foundations, trust, governance, judgment, developed people, that will let it adopt new technology without losing itself. These questions protect a board from mistaking visible motion for durable strength, which is one of the most expensive errors an institution can make.

From the CIO's Desk

If there is one lesson I value deeply now, it is that leadership becomes clearer with time, not because the work gets simpler, but because the noise around what matters starts to fall away. You begin to see that not everything important is visible in the moment. Some of the most meaningful work is the work that helps the enterprise function more naturally, recover more steadily, and learn more faithfully after you are no longer in the center of the story. That is why I have come to respect what endures more than what merely impresses. Endurance is one of the clearest signs that stewardship has done its work.

The longer I have led, the more I have come to trust ordinary evidence over dramatic proof. I trust the meeting that no longer needs rescue. I trust the team that raises the issue early because it expects honesty to be met with clarity. I trust the handoff that works because someone cared enough to document what used to live only in memory. I trust the calmer room, the cleaner metric, the better question, the stronger backup path, and the manager who now leads with steadiness rather than noise. These are the signs that leadership has moved beyond presentation and into the fabric of the institution. They do not usually attract immediate praise, but they are often the clearest evidence that something enduring has been built.

If I had to summarize my own view simply, it would be this. Stewardship gives leaders a way to think about success that is larger than visibility and more durable than applause. It asks whether your choices made trust easier, clarity stronger, resilience more real, and the next leader's work a little less burdened than it would have been otherwise. That is the question I hope remains with the reader. Not only what people will remember about your leadership, but what will still be working better because you led with continuity, discipline, and care.

Five Leadership Rules for Building What Endures

These are the rules I keep returning to. They are simple to state and demanding to live, which is usually the mark of a principle worth keeping.

First, build capability that can survive your absence. If the enterprise still needs your constant presence to stay coherent, the work is not yet complete. What endures is what keeps functioning well after the leader has moved on.

Second, preserve the lessons that cost the most to learn. Institutions grow stronger when hard-earned wisdom is not lost to turnover or time. The most expensive knowledge is the kind an organization has to keep relearning because it was never preserved.

Third, make trust and clarity part of the operating model. What endures is often not a single project, but a healthier way of working together. Trust and clarity outlast any platform, because they shape how the institution thinks and decides.

Fourth, invest in systems and people at the same time. Platforms matter, but they endure best when leadership capability grows alongside them. Developed people carry the institution's strength into a future the leader will not be present to see.

Fifth, measure success by continuity, not applause, especially as the tools change. The enterprise is stronger when it can keep moving wisely after the spotlight has moved on, and the foundations that endure are what let it adopt new technology without losing itself.

Leadership Lessons

- Technology keeps changing, but trust, accountability, governance, and clarity endure across every era.

- What remains after the work is done is the condition of the system, the confidence of the people, and the trust the organization has in itself.
- The leadership that stays behind lives in standards, habits, and developed people, not in titles.
- Hard seasons leave their most valuable mark as wisdom, not as pride in the endurance itself.
- A changed culture shows up in quiet signs, the early-raised issue and the smooth handoff, long before it shows up in headlines.
- The faster the tools change, the more valuable the things that do not change become.
- The deepest leadership legacy is institutional, not personal, measured by what the enterprise can carry after the leader is gone.

Discussion Questions

- What leadership qualities are most likely to endure after projects, titles, and visible milestones have passed?
- How does stewardship differ from performance-focused leadership, and why does that distinction matter?
- Why are continuity, trust, and operating stability often more important than visibility in senior leadership roles?
- Why do the enduring foundations of leadership become more valuable rather than less in a fast-changing technological era such as the age of AI?
- As a consultant, how would you assess what truly endures in a client organization beyond its visible recent achievements?
- If you were using this chapter in a graduate leadership program, what would you identify as the most important lesson about what truly lasts?

Application for Practice

- For the practicing leader: reflect on the last three major initiatives you led, and judge which outcomes are most likely to endure after the visible project work is forgotten, and why.
- For the IT leader: identify one way your leadership currently creates continuity, reliability, or clarity for others, even if that work is not especially visible, and one way to strengthen it.
- For the consultant: assess a client organization for the durable foundations, trust, governance, preserved lessons, developed people, that will outlast its current leaders and its current tools.
- For the faculty member or facilitator: design a short exercise in which students distinguish a leader's enduring contributions from their visible but temporary ones, using a described case.
- For any reader: think about a leader you respect, and identify what made their impact endure beyond titles, projects, or personality.
- For reflection: write a short personal stewardship statement describing what you want your leadership to leave behind in systems, people, and organizational culture.

Chapter 17: People First

Opening

After everything this book has said about systems, governance, data, and durability, it ends where it should have been understood to begin all along, with people. Every discipline in these chapters finally runs through human beings. Governance only works if people trust it. Data is only trustworthy if people maintain it with care. Resilience is only real if people have been developed enough to carry the institution when pressure arrives. Strip away the platforms and the frameworks, and what is left is the oldest truth in leadership. Institutions are made of people, and they rise or fall on whether those people were developed or merely used. That is why this chapter matters for practicing CIOs, IT leaders, consultants, and graduate leadership programs alike. It names the human core that everything else depends on.

This chapter is closely related to the one on leaving the enterprise better, but it is not the same. That chapter was about legacy and succession, about what a leader hands to whoever comes next. This chapter is about the daily, present-tense work of developing people while you lead them, the mentorship, the trust, the conditions that let human beings grow into their fullest capability. One looks at the end of a leader's tenure. This one looks at every ordinary day of it. Putting people first is not a sentiment to be expressed in a farewell. It is a discipline to be practiced in how a leader communicates, delegates, corrects, and grows the people around them, week after week, long before any handoff is in view.

Over time, I learned that durability is not only a technical idea. It is a human one. It shows up in whether people can trust the workflow on an ordinary Tuesday, whether a younger leader can carry more responsibility without fear, whether a system can survive change in personnel, and whether the enterprise still knows how to think clearly when the room gets tired. Those are not small things. They are the quiet evidence that stewardship has become real, and every one of them depends on people who were invested in rather than spent.

What My Own Journey Kept Proving

My own career kept proving this in different forms. The Y2K and early ERP years taught me that systems shape trust, but people decide whether that trust takes hold. The outsourcing and layoff period at a global electronics components manufacturer taught me that leadership decisions reach human lives before they ever reach a slide deck. Global consulting and ERP work taught me how often institutions mistake implementation for maturity, when the real difference was always the people carrying the work. The coatings world taught me that industrial reality does not reward fashionable complexity for very long, and that capable, developed teams outperform clever tools that no one fully owns. International development project work taught me that leadership must survive culture, distance, fatigue, and imperfect conditions if it is to become real, and that it survives through people more than through plans. By the time those lessons converged in my current role, the conclusion was settled. The work was never simply to modernize. The work was to leave the institution stronger, and institutions become stronger through people.

This is where my experience with ERP, manufacturing execution, BI, HRIS, Data-Lake modernization, quality and maintenance systems, service management, expense management, financial consolidation, and reporting environments began to converge into one larger leadership lesson. Each of these domains can produce visible wins, but they only become transformative when the enterprise is disciplined enough to connect them into a coherent operating model, and that discipline lives in people. The temptation in modern organizations is to discuss these as separate programs. In reality, the business experiences them as one lived environment, navigated every day by human beings. If those people are growing in judgment and confidence, the environment becomes cleaner, more reliable, and easier to trust. If they are not, the enterprise stays more fragile than it needs to be, no matter how modern the tools.

That is why I have become more committed to leadership development than I was earlier in my career. Publicly and privately, I keep returning to the same truth. Organizations change most deeply when leaders invest in people, not only in systems. Systems matter. But if the people around those systems are not growing in judgment, confidence, communication, and ownership, the enterprise will remain more fragile than it needs to be. I learned this the hard way. A successful go-live does not guarantee a stronger institution. A more developed team does.

Stop Building Platforms Only, Build People Too

One of the clearest convictions I carry now is that leaders make a mistake when they invest in systems while underinvesting in the people who must live inside the change. Early in my career, I thought a strong implementation meant clean design, stable infrastructure, and a successful cutover. Those things matter, but they are not the whole story. Projects rarely fail only because the technology is weak. More often, they weaken because communication was too thin, trust was too low, ownership was too unclear, or the team was too overloaded to carry the work with enough confidence. In other words, transformation often fails for human reasons while looking like a technical problem on the surface.

That is why I have come to value mentorship over micromanagement, development over dependence, and clarity over complexity. If people are afraid to speak, afraid to fail, or too tired to think clearly, no platform will save the institution from the cost of that environment. Leadership has to create conditions where people can tell the truth early, learn quickly, and grow into broader responsibility without feeling that every mistake will be held against them forever. In my experience, that is one of the quiet ways trust becomes structural. It stops being a slogan and becomes part of how the enterprise works.

Why Transformation Fails for Human Reasons

The longer I have led, the more convinced I have become that most failed transformations are human failures wearing technical costumes. The post-mortem will often blame the platform, the integration, or the timeline, because those are easier to name. But underneath, the real causes are usually human. Communication was too thin, so people filled the gaps with rumor and anxiety. Trust was too low, so people protected themselves instead of the project. Ownership was unclear, so important work fell between roles. The team was overloaded, so quality quietly eroded under the weight of too much at once. None of these show up cleanly in a technical diagram, but all of them decide whether a transformation succeeds.

This is why I have learned to diagnose struggling efforts by looking at the human conditions first. When a project is in trouble, I do not begin by asking what is wrong with the technology. I begin by asking whether people understand the goal, whether they trust the leadership behind it, whether ownership is clear enough that no one is guessing, and whether the team has the capacity to carry the work without burning through its own judgment. More often than not, the technical symptoms trace back to one of those human conditions. Fixing the human factors does not solve every technical problem, but neglecting them guarantees that the technical fixes will not hold.

The practical implication is that leaders who want durable transformation have to invest in the human side with the same seriousness they bring to the technical side. That means communicating more than feels necessary, clarifying ownership before work begins, protecting teams from the overload that erodes quality, and building enough trust that people surface problems early rather than hiding them until they become crises. These are not soft additions to the real work. In my experience, they are the difference between a transformation that lasts and one that looks successful at go-live and quietly unravels in the months that follow.

Mentorship Over Micromanagement

When I say I value mentorship over micromanagement, I mean something specific about how a leader spends their attention. Micromanagement invests attention in controlling the task. Mentorship invests attention in developing the person. The micromanager produces work that is only as good as their own oversight and people who never quite learn to think for themselves. The mentor produces people who grow more capable over time, which means the quality of the work rises even in the leader's absence. Over a career, the difference between these two postures is enormous, because one concentrates capability in the leader while the other distributes it throughout the institution.

Developing people is not the same as being permissive with them. It means giving people real responsibility, with enough support that they can succeed and enough room that they can learn from the parts they get wrong. It means explaining the reasoning behind decisions so that judgment transfers, not only instructions. It means letting capable people make calls you could make faster, because the point is not speed in this instance but growth over many instances. And it means resisting the temptation to step in and rescue every difficulty, because a person who is always rescued never develops the confidence that comes from carrying something hard to completion themselves.

The hardest part of mentorship is that it asks the leader to tolerate a slower, less perfect present in exchange for a stronger future. It is almost always faster, in the moment, to do the work yourself or to dictate exactly how it should be done. Choosing instead to develop the person costs time and patience now and pays off later, often after the leader has moved on. That is precisely why it is an act of stewardship. The leader is investing in capability that serves the institution more than it serves their own immediate convenience, which is one of the clearest signs that someone is leading for something larger than themselves.

Psychological Safety and Telling the Truth Early

People cannot be developed in an environment where they are afraid. Fear is one of the most expensive conditions a leader can allow, because it quietly degrades everything that matters. Afraid people do not surface problems early, so small issues grow into large ones. Afraid people do not admit uncertainty, so decisions get made on false confidence. Afraid people do not take the risks that growth requires, so they stay smaller than they could be. An organization where people are afraid to speak, afraid to fail, or afraid to be honest about what they do not know is an organization that has capped its own capability, no matter how talented its people are.

This is why I connect people development so closely to honesty and safety. The condition that lets people grow is the same one that lets the truth move freely, a confidence that telling a hard truth early will be met with clarity rather than blame. When people trust that raising a problem will be treated as responsible rather than punished, they raise problems early, when they are still small. When they trust that admitting a mistake will lead to learning rather than humiliation, they admit mistakes honestly, and the institution learns. Safety is not the absence of accountability. It is the presence of enough trust that accountability can be honest rather than defensive.

Leaders create this condition less through what they say than through how they respond in the difficult moment. The first time someone brings bad news and is met with composure and clarity, the organization learns that honesty is safe. The first time someone admits a mistake and is helped to fix it rather than made an example of, the organization learns that learning is welcome. Those responses, repeated over time, are what build a culture where people can be developed, because people only grow where they are not busy protecting themselves. In my experience, that kind of safety is one of the most practical investments a leader can make in human capability.

Enterprise Case Study: Building Capability Through People, Not Around a Title

Context. In a large enterprise transformation environment, a leader can become central very quickly. The organization may depend on the executive for prioritization, translation, credibility, and momentum. That centrality can be useful for a season, but it becomes dangerous if the system never grows beyond it. The deeper leadership challenge is to use that visibility to build human capability across the institution, not to concentrate capability in a single role.

Tension. The tension is that executives are often rewarded for being indispensable while genuine people development requires the opposite. In the underlying enterprise journey, role clarity, governance discipline, communication rhythms, platform modernization, project rigor, and team development all had to improve at once. The visible leader mattered, but the deeper requirement was to ensure that leadership capability, system knowledge, and operational confidence would spread across many people instead of collecting around one title. That meant deliberately developing others even when doing the work personally would have been faster.

Leadership Decision and Teaching Value. The leadership move was to invest in people as the primary strategy, through clearer ownership, mentorship, stronger communication, and the steady transfer of judgment and responsibility to a growing group of capable contributors. The teaching value is significant for CIOs, consultants, and faculty because it reframes transformation as a people-development effort as much as a technical one. Students and executives can explore a practical question: how does a leader build capability in others fast enough that the institution grows stronger rather than merely more dependent on the person at the center. That question sits at the heart of people-first leadership.

Putting People First in the Age of AI

AI raises the stakes of people-first leadership rather than lowering them, and how a leader responds will reveal a great deal about what they truly value. There is a version of the AI era that treats people primarily as costs to be reduced, capabilities to be replaced, and headcount to be optimized away. And there is a version that treats AI as a tool to elevate people, to remove drudgery so human judgment can focus on what matters, to give capable people more leverage, and to develop a workforce that works skillfully alongside increasingly capable tools. Both versions use similar technology. They reflect profoundly different beliefs about whether people come first, and they produce profoundly different institutions.

I hold the conviction that putting people first in the age of AI means developing people to work with these tools, not discarding people because of them. The judgment to know when an AI output is wrong, the accountability to own a decision the tool informed, the trust that holds a team together, and the wisdom to apply a capability well rather than blindly, these remain human, and they become more valuable as the tools grow more powerful. A leader who invests in growing those human capacities is building an enterprise that can use AI well. A leader who treats people as the expendable part of the equation is hollowing out the very judgment that makes AI safe to rely on.

There is also a matter of dignity that I do not think leaders can responsibly ignore. The people inside an organization are watching how their leaders talk about AI and about them. If the message they receive is that they are liabilities awaiting replacement, trust erodes, the best people leave, and the culture turns defensive at exactly the moment it needs to be adaptive. If the message is that the organization intends to grow them, equip them, and elevate their work, they engage with the technology honestly and help the enterprise adopt it well. People-first leadership in this era is not naive about what AI can do. It is clear-eyed that an institution's enduring strength still lives in its people, and that how a leader treats them through this transition is one of the most consequential choices they will make.

Why This Chapter Matters

The practical value of this chapter is that it corrects the most common imbalance in technology leadership, the tendency to invest heavily in systems while underinvesting in the people who must live inside them. A leader who internalizes this chapter allocates attention differently. They treat communication, trust, mentorship, and human capability as core deliverables rather than soft extras, because they understand that these are what actually determine whether the technical work succeeds. That reallocation of attention is the difference between a leader who produces go-lives and one who produces a stronger institution.

The lesson reads differently depending on the reader's seat. For the practicing CIO and the IT leader, the message is operational. Diagnose struggling efforts by their human conditions first, invest in mentorship over control, and build the psychological safety that lets truth move early. For the consultant, the message is diagnostic. When a client's transformation is struggling, look past the technical symptoms to the human causes, thin communication, low trust, unclear ownership, overload, because that is usually where the real failure lives. And for the faculty member and the graduate student, the message is conceptual. This is a chance to study transformation as a fundamentally human undertaking, and to examine why developing people is not a complement to leadership but its most durable form.

Boardroom Perspective: People Are the Enterprise's Durable Capability

Boards rightly focus on strategy, risk, and performance, but those outcomes all rest on a foundation that is easy to overlook in a board deck: the capability and trust of the organization's people. A board that attends only to systems and metrics can miss the human conditions that actually determine whether strategy gets executed and whether performance lasts. Developed people, healthy trust, and a culture where truth moves early are not soft concerns. They are the durable capability on which everything else depends, and they deserve board-level attention precisely because they are hard to rebuild once lost.

A mature board should therefore ask the questions that surface the health of the human enterprise. Is the organization developing its people or merely using them. Is there a deepening bench of capable leaders, or does too much depend on a few individuals. Does the culture surface problems early, or does fear keep bad news hidden until it becomes expensive. And as AI reshapes the work, is the enterprise developing its people to work with these tools and treating them as durable capability, or treating them as costs to be removed at the expense of the judgment the institution will still need. These are not sentimental questions. They are questions about the most durable asset the enterprise has, which is its people.

From the CIO's Desk

If I have learned anything worth carrying into the closing chapters of this book, it is that leadership is at its best when it develops people more than it directs them. I do not say that lightly. It is genuinely faster, in the moment, to control the work or to do it yourself. But the leader who only directs produces work that depends on their oversight and people who never fully grow. The leader who develops produces capable people whose judgment serves the institution long after any single project, and often long after the leader themselves. In my experience, that is the choice that matters most over a career, and it is made not once but in countless ordinary moments.

I have lived enough of the journey now to know that the most meaningful work is often quieter than outsiders assume. It is the younger leader who now carries more judgment than they did a year ago. It is the team member who learned to raise a hard issue early because they trusted the response. It is the analyst who grew into an owner, the manager who learned to lead with steadiness rather than noise, the colleague who became more capable because someone took the time to develop them rather than merely use them. That growth, distributed across many people, is what actually makes an institution strong. It is also the kind of leadership I most hope this book helps others practice.

If I had to summarize my own view simply, it would be this. Institutions are made of people, and they become stronger only when their people do. A leader can modernize every system and still leave the enterprise fragile if the people were spent rather than grown. But a leader who puts people first, who develops judgment, protects trust, and treats human capability as the real work, builds something that lasts, because the strength lives in people who carry it forward into every room they enter. That, to me, is the human heart of stewardship, and it is where the deepest leadership work has been all along.

Five Leadership Rules for Putting People First

These are the rules I keep returning to. They are simple to state and demanding to live, which is usually the mark of a principle worth keeping.

First, diagnose human conditions before technical ones. Most struggling transformations fail for human reasons wearing technical costumes. Ask first whether people understand the goal, trust the leadership, know who owns what, and have the capacity to carry the work.

Second, choose mentorship over micromanagement. Micromanagement invests attention in controlling the task and produces dependence. Mentorship invests attention in developing the person and produces capability that grows even in your absence.

Third, build the safety that lets truth move early. People cannot grow where they are afraid, and problems cannot be solved where they are hidden. Respond to bad news with composure and to mistakes with learning, and honesty becomes structural.

Fourth, develop people rather than merely using them. Delivering the result and growing the person are the same work done well. The institution gains both the outcome and a more capable contributor whose growth compounds far beyond the moment.

Fifth, put people first in the age of AI by elevating them, not discarding them. Use AI to remove drudgery and amplify human judgment, and develop people to work skillfully alongside the tools, because an institution's enduring strength still lives in its people.

Leadership Lessons

- Every discipline in leadership finally runs through people, who rise or fall on whether they were developed or merely used.
- Most failed transformations are human failures wearing technical costumes, traceable to communication, trust, ownership, or overload.
- Micromanagement concentrates capability in the leader, while mentorship distributes it throughout the institution.
- People cannot grow where they are afraid, so safety and honesty are preconditions for development.
- Developing people costs time now and pays off later, which is exactly what makes it an act of stewardship.
- AI raises the stakes of people-first leadership, because the judgment that makes AI safe to rely on remains human.
- Institutions become stronger only when their people do, no matter how modern the systems.

Discussion Questions

- Why do so many transformations that fail for human reasons get diagnosed as technical failures, and how can leaders see past that?
- What is the practical difference between mentorship and micromanagement, and how does each shape the institution over time?
- How does psychological safety enable both people development and the early surfacing of problems?
- What does it mean to put people first in the age of AI, and how does that choice shape an organization's culture and capability?
- As a consultant, how would you identify the human conditions behind a client's struggling transformation?

- If you were teaching this chapter, what would you identify as the hardest part of choosing to develop people when doing the work yourself would be faster?

Application for Practice

- For the practicing leader: think of a current or recent struggling effort, and diagnose its human conditions, communication, trust, ownership, capacity, before its technical ones.
- For the IT leader: identify one person you have been managing rather than developing, and outline how you would transfer more real responsibility and judgment to them.
- For the consultant: in a client engagement, assess whether the organization develops or merely uses its people, and identify the human factors most affecting its results.
- For the faculty member or facilitator: design a short exercise in which students must respond to bad news or a mistake in a way that builds psychological safety rather than fear.
- For any reader: reflect on whether your current environment treats AI as a way to elevate people or to replace them, and identify one way to put people first in how the tools are adopted.
- For reflection: think of a leader who developed you rather than merely used you. Identify what they did, and how it shaped the leader you became.

Chapter 18: Conclusion, Stewardship in Motion

When I began this journey during the Y2K era, I could not have predicted that a path starting in accounting and early ERP work would eventually become a life in CIO leadership, enterprise transformation, and stewardship. I did not know then how much the harder seasons would matter. I did not know how much the outsourcing years, the layoff at a global electronics components manufacturer, the consulting seasons at a global firm, the coatings world, the internationally funded development work across different parts of Africa, and the long modernization arc through ERP, manufacturing execution, BI, HRIS, Data-Lake, quality and maintenance systems, service management, expense management, financial consolidation, and reporting would shape the kind of leader I would become. But looking back now, I can see the thread clearly. Every chapter was teaching the same deeper lesson in a different form. Leadership is stewardship under pressure.

That lesson came fully into view in my current role as CIO. By then, the work was no longer simply about systems. It was about helping an enterprise become more coherent, more disciplined, more resilient, and easier to trust. It was about making modernization serve the business instead of forcing the business to serve modernization. It was about connecting ambition with governance, change with continuity, and innovation with responsibility. It was about building teams, not only platforms. It was about helping the enterprise move with greater clarity and less confusion. In other words, it was about stewardship in motion.

This conclusion is not a summary, because a summary would only repeat what the chapters already said. It is an attempt to show how they were never really separate. Each chapter examined one discipline, but all of them were describing the same underlying responsibility from different angles. What follows is the thread that connects them, the story that tested them most directly in my own career, and the reason I believe this work matters more now, in the age of AI, than at any point I have lived through.

The Thread Through Every Chapter

The book began with accountability, because everything else depends on it. The first chapter argued that tools, including the most powerful new ones, amplify whatever leadership already is. That is the seed of the whole book. Technology does not rescue a weak operating model. It scales it. From there, the early chapters built the foundation: data has to be trustworthy enough to serve as institutional memory, because an enterprise that cannot trust its own numbers cannot decide with confidence, and a tool trained on confused data only learns the confusion faster.

The middle chapters were about the disciplines of execution, and they share a single concern, that good intentions are not enough without structure. Speed has to be designed rather than demanded, because rushing past the foundation produces motion without progress. The enterprise has to be understood as one integrated system rather than a collection of functions, because the seams between them are where work quietly fails. Transformation fails quietly, not loudly, when adoption is assumed rather than earned. Governance, far from being the enemy of speed, is one of its most reliable sources, because it converts ambiguity into sequence before ambiguity becomes rework. Calm under pressure is a designed capability, not a temperament. Saying no is a discipline that protects the credibility of every yes. And indecision is rarely neutral, because the silence left by an unmade decision fills with drift, assumption, and hidden labor. Running underneath all of these was trust, the operating asset that makes coordination cheap, and the recognition that legacy thinking, not legacy systems, is the harder thing to modernize.

The later chapters turned to what endures, and they converge on a single conviction that I hold more strongly than any other. The strongest organizations are not built on heroes. Resilience is the institution's ability to keep its shape without depending on one indispensable person. Organizational memory preserves not only what was decided but why, so the enterprise does not keep relearning what it already paid to know. Durability means choosing what will still serve the business after the excitement fades, rather than what merely impresses in the demonstration. Leaving the enterprise better means building capability into people and systems so the institution can thrive without you. And people, in the end, are the human core that every other discipline depends on, because institutions become stronger only when their people do.

Set side by side, these are not eighteen separate topics. They are one idea expressed eighteen ways. Leadership is the stewardship of something that will outlast you, practiced under the pressure of a present that never stops moving. That is the thread, and once you see it, you cannot unsee it in any of the chapters.

The Turnaround That Tested Everything

If there is one season of my career that tested every principle in this book at once, it was the work of restructuring a struggling IT organization, and I want to close with it because it is where the ideas stopped being theory.

One of the hardest leadership seasons of my career came when I stepped into the responsibility of restructuring an IT department of more than fifty people after years of failed projects and roughly fifty percent project success before the reorganization. The work was not only operational. It was emotional, cultural, and deeply political. I was stepping into a leadership environment where some people had been with the company for nearly forty years. The organization had seen disappointment before. Promises had been made before. And now I was expected to convince people that this time, change would actually work. To do that, I first had to believe it myself. Then I had to help the people inside IT believe it. Then I had to help the executive team, the board, and the private equity owners believe it as well. That was the burden of the role before the results had given anyone permission to trust it.

The restructure required much more than a new organization chart. We had to redesign the structure around customer needs while still leveraging economies of scale. We rewrote job descriptions, clarified roles and responsibilities, and made difficult decisions about right-sizing the team and addressing the weak performance that had gone unaddressed for too long. We introduced daily huddles, town halls, and monthly governance meetings with the executive team. We established a clearer vision and began building a performance culture grounded in objective measures rather than personality or habit. None of that work felt dramatic in a single moment, but together it began changing the operating rhythm of the department.

I learned that culture does not change when people merely understand the message. It changes when they begin to trust the repetition behind it. They watch whether accountability stays visible after the meeting. They watch whether standards still hold when pressure rises. They watch whether leadership remains calm, fair, and consistent when the room is no longer being formally addressed. I remember the first town hall after the restructure had begun to take shape. The room was attentive, but not yet trusting. People were listening for more than the message on the slide. They were trying to decide whether this was another temporary program that would fade once the pressure changed, or whether something deeper was actually happening. Some had lived through too many disappointments to give belief away easily. What stayed with me was not whether the message landed perfectly. It was that belief had started becoming visible, even if it was still fragile. People asked harder questions, and they asked them as participants rather than observers. Skepticism becomes productive the moment people care enough to help shape the future instead of standing back to see whether it fails.

There was a week during that season when I was no longer wondering whether the plan was right. I was wondering whether the team would still be willing to keep carrying it with me. The pressure had been high for a long time. Decisions had consequences for roles, workload, and the emotional future of the department. Some people were tired. Some were skeptical. Some were watching to see whether the conviction leadership had shown at the beginning would remain steady once the cost of change became more personal. I remember the weight of that week clearly, because leadership in those moments is not abstract. You can sense whether belief is hardening, whether fear is spreading, and whether the room is still willing to trust that the harder path may yet become the stronger one. What helped us through was not perfect confidence. It was visible consistency. The standards did not move to protect comfort. The communication did not disappear when the questions got harder. The governance routines kept holding. And the people who chose to stay and build began to recognize one another as believers rather than bystanders.

Fifteen months later, the restructure did work. The project success rate improved dramatically, governance was stronger, execution was steadier, and the function became more aligned to business priorities. I am proud of that outcome, and I am also honest about what it cost. It demanded conviction before evidence, consistency before applause, and a team willing to carry the work long enough for the new culture to become real. That experience taught me that leadership sometimes means asking people to walk with you toward a result they cannot yet see, while making sure your actions give them enough reason to keep believing it is possible.

But the outcome I value most was not the metric. It was that the organization no longer depended on momentum or personality to perform. The system itself had become more stable, more understandable, and more capable of sustaining performance. That is the deeper meaning of the whole book in a single experience. The goal was never to be the leader the department could not do without. The goal was to help it become an institution that could carry more of itself, so that its strength would remain after any single leader, including me, had moved on.

What made that durable was not the reorganization chart. It was that the new rhythm became something the institution could hold on its own. The weekly meetings, the regular governance, the clearer roles, and the visible measures were not decorations added after confidence returned. They were how confidence was rebuilt in the first place, and because they were built into the operating model rather than carried in my presence, they kept working when I was not in the room. That is the quiet test of whether a turnaround is real. Not whether the numbers improved while the leader pushed, but whether the standards still hold, the meetings still have shape, and the decisions still move once the leader steps back. A turnaround that depends on one person is not finished. A turnaround that the institution can sustain without that person is what stewardship was aiming at all along.

Stewardship in the Age of AI

I am finishing this book at a moment when the ground is shifting faster than at any point in my career. AI is changing what tools can do, what work looks like, and what leaders are being asked to promise. It would be easy to treat that as a reason to set aside everything written here and start over with a new playbook. I believe the opposite is true. The arrival of AI does not retire the disciplines in this book. It raises their value, because they are exactly what an institution needs to meet a powerful and unfamiliar technology without losing itself.

Consider how directly the threads of this book apply. AI amplifies whatever operating model it enters, which makes accountability more important, not less. AI inherits the quality of the data it learns from, which makes trusted institutional memory a precondition rather than a nicety. AI is unusually prone to quiet failure, fluent and confident in the demonstration and unreliable in the corner cases, which makes the discipline of earning trust before extending it essential. AI raises the temptation to chase novelty, which makes the discipline of choosing durable value over impressive demonstrations more valuable than ever. AI tempts organizations to defer the hard governance decisions, which lets ungoverned adoption fill the silence. And AI can become a new single point of dependence, a tool the enterprise forgets how to operate without. Every one of these is a problem this book already described. AI is not a new subject. It is the most demanding test yet of the subjects we have covered all along.

This is why I have come to believe that the most important thing a leader can do about AI is not to chase every capability, but to build the institution that can adopt it wisely. That means leaving behind judgment, not only tools. It means an enterprise with the accountability to own what AI produces, the data foundation to use it safely, the governance to adopt it responsibly, the restraint to decline what merely dazzles, and the developed people to apply wisdom to what it generates. The specific tools will keep changing, faster here than anywhere I have seen. What will still be standing is an institution's capacity to think clearly, decide responsibly, and work with trust, no matter what technology it holds. Building that capacity is not separate from stewardship. It is stewardship, practiced in the conditions of our moment.

There is also a human dimension to this that I do not think leaders can responsibly set aside. The people inside our organizations are watching how we talk about AI and about them. There is a version of this era that treats people mainly as costs to be removed, and a version that treats AI as a way to elevate people, to free their judgment for what matters most and to equip them to work skillfully alongside increasingly capable tools. Both use similar technology. They reflect very different beliefs about whether people come first, and they leave behind very different institutions. The judgment to know when an output is wrong, the accountability to own a decision the tool informed, and the trust that holds a team together all remain human, and they become more valuable as the tools grow more powerful. A steward meets the AI era by developing people for it, not by discarding the very judgment the institution will still need.

Stewardship in Motion

I called this book Stewardship in Motion for a reason. Stewardship is not a destination a leader reaches and then rests. It is a discipline practiced continuously, because the enterprise never stops moving and neither does the pressure on it. The systems keep changing. The people keep changing. The technologies, as we are seeing now, can change with startling speed. Through all of it, the steward's responsibility remains the same, to leave the institution steadier, clearer, and more capable than it was, and to keep doing so even though the work is never finished. The motion is the point. There is no final state of stewardship, only the ongoing practice of it.

There is also a sense in which stewardship is always a relay. No leader carries an institution from beginning to end. Each of us inherits something built by those who came before and hands it to those who come after, ideally a little stronger than we received it. That framing has changed how I think about my own work. I am not trying to build something that depends on me. I am trying to strengthen something that will outlast me, and then pass it on in good condition. The leaders who came before me did not finish the work, and neither will I. What we can do is take our turn seriously, leave the institution more capable than we found it, and prepare the people who will carry it next. That is what it means for stewardship to be in motion. It moves through people and through time, never resting in any single one of us.

That is also why this book was written to be used, not only read. If you are a practicing CIO, I hope it has given language to responsibilities you already feel and perhaps carry more quietly than people around you realize. If you are an IT leader growing toward broader executive responsibility, I hope it has made the role feel both more serious and more human. If you are a consultant, I hope it has reinforced that the most durable change is the kind that leaves the client institution stronger after you are gone. And if you are a faculty member, facilitator, instructor, or graduate student, I hope these pages have shown that leadership theory becomes most useful when it is tested in the lived complexity of real institutions under pressure. The case studies, discussion questions, and application prompts throughout the book exist for that purpose, to be taught, argued with, and applied in your own context.

In the end, leadership is not mainly about being noticed. It is about what endures because you led. It is about whether people trust the institution more, whether the systems are cleaner, whether the teams are stronger, whether the decisions are wiser, and whether the enterprise can move into the future, including this uncertain AI future, with more steadiness than it had before. That is the work I have tried to do. It is the work I continue to respect. And it is the work I hope more leaders will choose, in their own way, in their own institutions, and in their own time. Because when stewardship is taken seriously, leadership becomes more than a position. It becomes a contribution that keeps serving long after the visible chapter has ended.

Boardroom Perspective: The Enduring Question

Boards spend most of their attention on what is current, the quarter, the initiative, the risk in front of them. Those things matter. But the deepest question a board can hold about leadership is quieter and more enduring. Is the institution becoming stronger, steadier, and less fragile over time, or merely busier and more dependent on the people who currently hold it together. That question cannot be answered by a single metric or a successful launch. It is answered by whether trust is rising, whether lessons are being kept rather than relearned, whether capable people are being developed, and whether the enterprise could absorb a change in leadership without losing its discipline.

A mature board should therefore keep returning to the enduring question beneath every strategy discussion. What is becoming more durable here, and what is becoming more dependent. And as AI reshapes the tools, is the enterprise building the lasting judgment to govern it well, or accumulating capabilities that will become someone else's problem. These are stewardship questions, and they are ultimately the board's most important ones, because they determine whether the institution has been built to last beyond any leader, any project, or any technology of the moment.

From the CIO's Desk

If I had to name the single conviction that has grown strongest over my career, it is that the role is temporary but the responsibility is enduring. Titles fade. Systems remain. People remember whether they were developed, trusted, and prepared. The institution remembers whether it was strengthened or merely carried. That is why I no longer measure leadership mainly by what I could personally accomplish in the seat. I measure it by what the enterprise became more capable of carrying because I was there.

I have also learned that the most meaningful work is often the quietest. The stronger team. The clearer governance. The steadier systems. The more trusted data. The younger leader who now carries more judgment than they did a year ago. The institution that can absorb pressure with less drama because leadership was serious enough to build for continuity rather than applause. None of that earns the recognition that a dramatic launch does, but it is what actually endures.

If I had to summarize the whole book in a sentence, it would be this. The highest form of leadership is not becoming indispensable. It is making the organization more resilient without you, and then having the humility to be glad when it no longer needs you the way it once did. That is stewardship. It is the work I believe in, and it is the work I hope this book helps more leaders choose.

Stewardship Playbook: Building What Endures

The principles in this book reduce to a small set of practical commitments. They are simple to state and demanding to live, which is the mark of a discipline worth keeping.

Build systems, not dependence. Reduce the enterprise's reliance on any single individual, including yourself, so strength lives in the institution rather than in a person.

Clarify roles and ownership. Make accountability visible and transferable, so the next person can see who decides and why.

Establish a governance rhythm. Consistency creates stability, and a predictable cadence is what lets people stop guessing whether today's standards will hold tomorrow.

Choose durability over novelty. Evaluate every capability by what it will still be worth after the excitement fades and the support burden becomes visible.

Develop people continuously. Strong, developed teams outlast strong individuals, and growing people is the most durable contribution a leader makes.

Preserve reasoning, not only outcomes. Document why decisions were made, so future leaders inherit understanding rather than a museum of unexplained choices.

Tell the truth early. Trust is built through repeated honesty under pressure, and it is the asset that makes everything else cheaper.

Build the judgment to govern new technology, especially AI. Leave behind an institution that can adopt powerful tools wisely, not merely a collection of tools no one fully understands.

The reminder beneath all of them is the same. The best leaders make themselves less necessary over time, because durability is a form of respect for the future.

Enterprise Case Study: The IT Turnaround

Context. An IT organization was struggling, with low project success, weak governance, and limited confidence from the business. The operating model depended too heavily on momentum and individual effort, and years of disappointment had eroded the organization's belief that change would hold.

Tension. The defining difficulty was that change required belief before results were visible. Convincing the team, the executives, the board, and the owners to trust a new direction had to happen before any metric could justify that trust. The leadership challenge was to sustain conviction, consistency, and communication through the long stretch when only effort, not success, was visible.

Leadership Decision and Teaching Value. The turnaround focused on fundamentals rather than heroics: role clarity, governance routines, visible performance measures, and disciplined communication through regular huddles, town halls, and governance meetings. Over roughly fifteen months, project success improved dramatically, alignment with the business strengthened, and trust in IT grew. The deeper outcome was that the function no longer depended on personality to perform. This makes the case valuable for graduate leadership programs, executive education, and CIO development because it demonstrates the book's central claim in a single arc: leadership endures when the system becomes stronger than the leader, and culture changes through repetition that earns belief over time.

Leadership Lessons

- Every discipline in this book is one idea expressed many ways: leadership is the stewardship of something that will outlast you, practiced under pressure.
- Technology, including AI, amplifies whatever the operating model already is, so the foundations matter more than the tools.
- Culture changes not when people understand the message, but when they trust the repetition behind it.
- The hardest seasons demand conviction before evidence and consistency before applause.
- The strongest organizations are not built on heroes, and the highest maturity is making the institution resilient without you.
- The arrival of AI raises the value of the enduring disciplines rather than retiring them.
- Stewardship is never finished, because the enterprise never stops moving, which is why it is stewardship in motion.

Discussion Questions

- What does it mean to say that the disciplines across this book are different expressions of a single idea, and do you find that claim convincing?
- What does it mean to leave an enterprise better, and how is that different from simply delivering strong short-term results?
- Why does culture change require belief before proof, and what does that demand of a leader during the period when only effort is visible?
- Why do the enduring disciplines in this book become more valuable rather than less in the age of AI?

- As a consultant, how would you help a client build the lasting judgment to govern AI rather than merely adopt AI tools?
- What evidence would show that leadership has become portable inside an organization, so that the institution could absorb a change at the top without losing its discipline?

Application for Practice

- For the practicing leader: identify what it would mean, in concrete terms, to leave your team or organization better than you found it, and name the single change that would matter most.
- For the IT leader: identify one area where your organization still depends too heavily on a single person, and outline the governance, documentation, or development that would make that strength portable.
- For the consultant: in a client engagement, assess whether recent modernization has produced durable capability or attractive complexity, and recommend where coherence should be restored.
- For the faculty member or facilitator: design a capstone exercise in which students trace one of the book's disciplines, such as accountability or trust, through a transformation case from beginning to lasting outcome.
- For any reader: review how success is measured in your environment, and judge how much of that measurement reflects short-term delivery versus long-term continuity.
- For reflection: write a short statement of one change you could make now that would still strengthen your organization even if you were no longer in the role a year from today.

Chapter 19: Final Synthesis, Stewardship in Motion

Opening

This book began with questions about accountability, trust, governance, data, execution, pressure, resilience, and what it means to lead well in environments where technology is no longer separate from the business. As the chapters unfolded, a deeper pattern became clear. These ideas are not separate leadership topics. They are connected expressions of stewardship. Stewardship is the discipline of strengthening an institution so it can continue learning, deciding, serving, and adapting after the current urgency has passed and after the current leader has moved on. That is why this final chapter is not a summary alone. It is a synthesis. It is meant to bring the whole argument back together in one place and make visible the central thread running through every chapter: technology changes, but the responsibility to build trust, protect continuity, and leave the enterprise stronger than we found it does not.

The Pattern Beneath the Chapters

Chapter 1 argued that AI does not remove responsibility. It intensifies the need for judgment. Chapters 2 and 13 showed that data and organizational memory are not technical conveniences. They are how institutions remember what they have already learned well enough to act with confidence. Chapters 3, 8, 10, and 11 made a related point from another direction: speed, governance, prioritization, and timely decisions all determine whether the enterprise moves with credibility or merely with noise. Chapters 4, 5, and 6 demonstrated that integration, transformation, and modernization only become durable when the operating model changes along with the platform. Chapters 7, 9, 12, 14, 15, 16, and 17 brought the argument to its deeper human level: trust, calm, resilience, durability, legacy, what endures, and the people who carry the work are the conditions under which leadership becomes institutional rather than merely personal. Seen together, these chapters do not describe a collection of techniques. They describe a way of leading.

The Thread of AI Beneath the Argument

One thread deserves to be named on its own, because it runs quietly through every chapter rather than living in only one. Artificial intelligence appears throughout this book not as a separate subject but as the sharpest current test of each discipline. AI amplifies whatever operating model it enters, so it raises the stakes of accountability. It inherits the quality of the data it learns from, so it depends on trusted institutional memory. It is unusually prone to confident, fluent failure, so it demands that trust be earned before it is extended. It tempts organizations toward novelty and toward deferring hard governance decisions, so it rewards restraint and timely clarity. And it can become a new single point of dependence, so it tests resilience in an unfamiliar form. The synthesis here is simple. AI does not replace the disciplines of stewardship. It makes them more valuable, because they are exactly what an institution needs to adopt powerful new tools without losing itself.

What Stewardship Looks Like in Practice

In practice, stewardship is not abstract. It is visible in the design choices leaders make every day. It is visible in whether ownership is clear, whether data can be trusted, whether priorities are disciplined, whether systems are supported well enough to be relied upon, and whether people are being developed strongly enough that the institution can continue without depending on one heroic individual. It is visible in whether the enterprise knows how to say not now when capacity is finite, whether governance reduces confusion before confusion becomes rework, whether pressure is managed in a way that helps people think, and whether transformation is followed long enough for trust to transfer into the new environment. These are not side issues around technology leadership. They are the operating realities that determine whether technology strengthens the institution or simply adds more movement to an already strained system.

Boardroom Perspective: The CIO as Steward of Institutional Capability

Boards should not think of the CIO only as the leader responsible for platforms, security, and delivery. The modern CIO is increasingly a steward of institutional capability. The role touches resilience, trust, data integrity, governance quality, operational coherence, AI accountability, and the development of future leadership capacity. A mature board therefore evaluates technology leadership not only by implementation progress or cost discipline, but by whether the institution is becoming more understandable, more durable, and less dependent on hidden workarounds and individual memory. In that sense, the CIO role is becoming one of the places where enterprise stewardship becomes most visible. Technology is the environment. The institution is the responsibility.

From the CIO's Desk

If there is one lesson I value most at this stage of my journey, it is that leadership becomes more meaningful when it stops being mainly about being needed and starts becoming about leaving the institution less burdened by needing you personally. Some of the most valuable work I have ever done will never look dramatic on a résumé. It lives in cleaner handoffs, stronger people, calmer operations, clearer governance, better memory, and a business that can continue moving with confidence because the underlying system has become healthier. That is why stewardship matters so much to me. It gives leadership a direction beyond visibility. It asks what is becoming more trustworthy, more durable, and more useful because we were here. For me, that is the question worth carrying into every chapter of leadership that still lies ahead.

Five Capstone Rules for Stewardship in Motion

First, build trust before you ask for speed. Institutions move well when people believe the environment is disciplined enough to support responsible action. **Second, turn knowledge into memory.** What the enterprise learns should not have to be paid for again simply because the people in the room have changed. **Third, let governance reduce hidden labor.** Good governance protects attention by converting ambiguity into sequence early enough that work can still be done well. **Fourth, design for continuity, not heroics.** A resilient institution should be able to carry important work even when key individuals are absent. **Fifth, measure leadership by what endures.** The deepest work of stewardship is not what looks most impressive in the moment. It is what leaves the enterprise stronger after the moment has passed.

Discussion Questions

- How does stewardship unify the themes of trust, governance, resilience, memory, and leadership legacy across the book?
- How does AI function as a test of each discipline in the book rather than as a separate subject, and why does that matter?
- What would it mean for a board or executive team to evaluate a CIO primarily as a steward of institutional capability rather than only as a technology executive?
- Which chapter ideas in this book feel most connected in your own leadership context, and why?
- If you were teaching this synthesis chapter, what evidence would you use to show that stewardship is a practical discipline rather than a leadership slogan?

Application for Practice

- Write a short stewardship statement for your own leadership role. What are you trying to leave stronger than you found it?
- Identify one area in your organization where trust, clarity, or resilience still depends too heavily on a person rather than on a system. What would it take to transfer that strength into the institution?
- Choose one lesson from this book that your current team most needs to apply. What practical action could begin that shift within the next thirty days?
- Create a one-page reflection on what you want your leadership to make more durable over the next five years.

Chapter 20: Instructor / Facilitator Guide

This guide is designed to help faculty members, facilitators, executive coaches, and program leaders use *Stewardship in Motion* in structured learning environments. The book was written to function not only as a leadership text for individual readers, but also as a practical resource for graduate leadership courses, MBA and executive education programs, CIO development cohorts, organizational change seminars, and facilitated reflection settings. The case studies, discussion questions, and application prompts built into the chapters are intended to support rigorous dialogue, thoughtful analysis, and practical application.

Ideal Audiences for Instruction

The book is especially well suited for graduate leadership programs, MBA and executive leadership courses, organizational behavior classes, digital transformation seminars, governance and strategy modules, CIO or senior technology leadership cohorts, and interdisciplinary programs examining leadership under complexity. It can also be used effectively with senior managers, directors, and cross-functional leaders who need a framework for stewardship, execution, trust, resilience, and enterprise change.

How to Use This Book in Courses and Programs

Each chapter can be taught as a standalone session or combined into broader thematic modules. A typical session can use four components in sequence: assigned chapter reading, enterprise case study discussion, review of the discussion questions, and completion of the Application for Practice prompts. In executive settings, facilitators may choose to shorten the discussion portion and spend more time on applied reflection. In graduate classrooms, instructors may want to encourage students to compare the chapter ideas with their own professional environments, internships, research, or prior cases from other courses.

Sample Teaching Formats

- Single-session chapter discussion with advance reading and guided dialogue
- Multi-week module pairing several chapters around a central leadership theme
- Executive workshop format using case studies and application prompts for peer reflection
- Leadership cohort format where participants journal responses and discuss patterns across chapters
- Capstone reflection assignment asking students to define their own stewardship philosophy

Recommended Chapter Groupings

- **Leadership, AI, and Judgment:** Chapters 1 through 3
- **Integration and Transformation:** Chapters 4 through 6
- **Trust, Governance, and Calm Execution:** Chapters 7 through 10
- **Decision Clarity and Resilience:** Chapters 11 and 12

- **Memory, Durability, and What Endures:** Chapters 13 through 16
- **People, Legacy, and Stewardship in Motion:** Chapter 17, with the closing synthesis in Chapters 18 and 19

A Note on the AI Through-Line

One theme runs through every chapter rather than living in only one, and it can be taught as a thread across the whole book. Artificial intelligence appears in each chapter not as a separate topic but as the current test of that chapter's discipline, from accountability and trusted data to governance, restraint, resilience, and what endures. Instructors may find it valuable to assign a cross-chapter exercise in which students trace how the book treats AI from beginning to end, and then articulate the book's central claim about it: that AI raises the value of the enduring leadership disciplines rather than replacing them. This works well as a synthesis assignment near the end of a course.

Sample Assignment Ideas

- Write a short case reflection comparing one chapter to a real leadership situation in your organization.
- Analyze an enterprise case study from the book and identify the central leadership tension, decision, and lesson.
- Create a personal leadership memo explaining how one chapter changes your approach to governance, execution, or stewardship.
- Develop an application plan using one chapter's prompts to improve a real process, team practice, or operating model.
- Trace the AI through-line across several chapters and argue for what the book claims AI does and does not change about leadership.

- Draft a final stewardship statement summarizing what you want your leadership to leave behind.

Facilitation Tips

Encourage participants to move beyond agreement and into analysis. The strongest discussions usually happen when readers compare the chapter's ideas with real organizational trade-offs, not when they simply restate the text. Invite students or participants to identify tensions, assumptions, and leadership trade-offs. Keep the conversation practical. Ask what would happen if the chapter's ideas were ignored, misapplied, or overapplied. Encourage reflection on both systems and human behavior, since the book is intentionally written at the intersection of operations, leadership, and enterprise design.

Suggested Discussion Norms

- Discuss ideas generously, but challenge assumptions directly.
- Connect abstract leadership language to observable organizational behavior.
- Respect confidentiality when using live workplace examples.
- Distinguish between what is technically possible and what is organizationally sustainable.
- Use the Application for Practice prompts to move from theory into action.

Final Note to Instructors and Facilitators

At its best, this book should help readers think more clearly about how leadership actually works inside complex organizations. It is meant to support reflection, challenge, and practical application. If used well, it can help students and practitioners alike develop a deeper understanding of stewardship, discipline, trust, and continuity, not only as ideas, but as lived leadership responsibilities.

Chapter 21: Board Retreat / CIO Leadership Workshop Format

Purpose

This format is designed for board retreats, executive leadership off-sites, CIO forums, and consultant-led leadership workshops where the goal is not simply to discuss technology, but to examine how leadership, governance, trust, resilience, and institutional readiness shape the enterprise over time. The material is especially suited for groups wrestling with digital transformation, ERP or HRIS modernization, AI accountability, board communication, enterprise integration, cybersecurity, and operating-model maturity.

The workshop should not be approached as a technical briefing. It works best as a **leadership and stewardship session**. The deeper question is never only what tool the organization has adopted. The deeper question is what kind of institution the organization is becoming because of the way leaders are choosing, governing, communicating, and building trust around that work.

Recommended Audience

This format works especially well for:

- **Board members**
- **CIOs and senior IT leaders**
- **Executive leadership teams**
- **Consultants facilitating governance or strategy discussions**
- **Cross-functional transformation leaders**
- **Graduate or executive leadership cohorts in applied workshop settings**

Recommended Format

Length

- Half-day retreat: **3.5 to 4 hours**
- Full-day retreat: **6 to 7 hours**
- Executive workshop series: **2 to 3 shorter sessions**

Structure

A typical workshop may include:

- **Opening framing**
- **Leadership case discussion**
- **Thematic breakout or board-level dialogue**
- **Practical playbook review**
- **Application to the organization's own context**
- **Closing commitments and reflections**

Half-Day Board Retreat Format

Opening Framing (20 to 30 minutes)

The facilitator should begin by positioning the session around a simple idea. Technology leadership is no longer only about systems. It is about **institutional readiness, trust, resilience, governance, and stewardship**.

A strong opening framing might include:

- how the CIO role evolved from systems leadership into enterprise stewardship
- why this matters now, in the age of AI, cyber risk, ERP, HRIS, BI, and Data-Lake modernization, and rising cross-functional complexity

- why boards should care not only about initiatives, but about what the institution is becoming underneath them

Opening prompt for the room

- *What does this board or leadership team most need from a CIO now that it did not need ten years ago?*

Module 1: Governance, Clarity, and the Cost of Drift (45 minutes)

Suggested chapters

- Chapter 8: Governance as Accelerator
- Chapter 10: What Great CIOs Say No To
- Chapter 11: The Cost of Indecision

Discussion focus

This segment explores why governance is not bureaucracy when it is done well, how weak prioritization quietly damages execution, why indecision becomes an operating-model problem, and why a disciplined not now is often better leadership than an overcommitted yes.

Board and executive prompts

- Where is our organization currently paying the cost of weak prioritization?
- What decisions are drifting longer than they should?
- Where are we still confusing activity with progress?
- What requests or initiatives are being kept alive without enough clarity about cost, sequencing, or capacity?

Facilitator emphasis

Keep the discussion at the level of stewardship, trade-offs, operating-model credibility, and institutional trust, rather than at the level of project mechanics alone.

Module 2: Trust, Resilience, and Leadership Under Pressure (45 minutes)

Suggested chapters

- Chapter 7: Stewardship and Organizational Trust
- Chapter 9: Calm Under Pressure
- Chapter 12: Institutional Resilience

Discussion focus

This segment explores trust as an operating asset, why calm under pressure is a leadership discipline, how resilience differs from heroics, and why reliable systems and clear communication reduce institutional fragility.

Board and executive prompts

- What in our organization currently depends too much on heroics?
- Where does trust remain more dependent on individuals than on the institution?
- How does pressure currently affect the quality of our communication and decision-making?
- Are we building systems people can trust, or just expecting people to work harder around weak ones?

Facilitator emphasis

Invite the room to think beyond technical uptime, service metrics, and incident recovery, and toward credibility, emotional climate, leadership behavior under strain, and the design of the operating model.

Module 3: Board Communication, AI, and Institutional Readiness (60 minutes)

Suggested chapters

- Chapter 1: Leadership in the Age of AI Accountability
- Chapter 17: People First
- Chapter 18: Conclusion, Stewardship in Motion

Discussion focus

This segment helps boards and executives reflect on what the CIO should translate into board language, what AI changes and what it cannot replace, why AI governance belongs inside enterprise stewardship, and what institutional readiness actually means.

Board and executive prompts

- Are we treating AI as a capability to govern or as a novelty to admire?
- What decisions in this organization should remain visibly human?
- What kind of future leadership will this institution actually require?
- Where does leadership still need stronger clarity around ERP, HRIS, BI, Data-Lake, cybersecurity, AI, and enterprise integration?

Facilitator emphasis

The board should leave this segment asking one question. *What must remain human, visible, and accountable as capability expands?*

Closing Reflection and Commitments (20 to 30 minutes)

The workshop should close with reflection, not just summary.

Closing prompts

- What leadership discipline does our institution most need to strengthen now?
- What are we trying to leave stronger than we found it?
- What should this leadership team stop tolerating because it quietly weakens the enterprise?
- What one commitment should come out of today's discussion?

Optional written exercise

Ask each participant to complete this sentence: *The institution will be stronger in twelve months if we become more disciplined about...*

Full-Day Retreat Format

A full-day version can deepen the same ideas and add breakout work.

Morning

Session 1: Stewardship as Leadership Framework

- introduction framing
- themes from Chapters 1 through 4
- the leadership arc from ERP and systems work into enterprise stewardship

Session 2: Governance, Capacity, and Decision Quality

- Chapters 8, 10, and 11
- case discussion and board dialogue

Afternoon

Session 3: Trust, Resilience, and Cyber and AI Readiness

- Chapters 1, 7, 9, 12, and 17

- breakout discussion on resilience and governance

Session 4: The Enterprise, the Board, and the Future Institution

- Chapters 16, 18, and 19
- board communication and the future of enterprise stewardship
- closing action commitments

Suggested Breakout Exercise

Exercise: What Is the Institution Becoming?

Ask participants to work in small groups and discuss:

- Which current initiatives are strengthening the institution?
- Which are adding capability without enough governance or clarity?
- Where is complexity growing faster than trust?
- What does the organization most need from leadership now: more speed, more clarity, more discipline, or more courage to stop, simplify, or decide?

This exercise works well because it moves the room from project discussion to institutional reflection.

Suggested Materials for the Workshop

Facilitators may choose a focused set of materials such as one or two chapter excerpts, one enterprise case study, one playbook, a few selected discussion questions, and a short written reflection prompt.

For a board-focused version, the strongest chapters are:

- **Chapter 1: Leadership in the Age of AI Accountability**
- **Chapter 16: What Endures**
- **Chapter 17: People First**

- **Chapter 18: Conclusion, Stewardship in Motion**

For a CIO or IT leadership workshop, strong groupings include:

- **Chapters 7, 9, and 10**
- **Chapters 11, 12, and 13**
- **Chapters 14, 15, and 16**

Facilitator Guidance

What to avoid

- turning the session into a technical presentation
- over-focusing on tools rather than leadership consequence
- allowing the conversation to stay too abstract
- letting participants discuss best practices without confronting trade-offs

What to reinforce

- stewardship, institutional consequence, trust, readiness, and visible ownership
- the difference between speed and clarity, between capability and maturity, between transformation and trust, and between systems change and leadership change

Why this format works

This format helps the book function as a graduate-level teaching text, a practical leadership guide, a boardroom discussion resource, a CIO development tool, and a consulting facilitation framework. It also preserves the author's CIO voice, because the themes are still grounded in lived lessons drawn from:

- ERP work beginning in the Y2K period
- outsourcing and organizational disruption
- ERP consulting and cross-company pattern recognition

- internationally funded development work and cultural adaptation
- coatings, automotive, manufacturing, and enterprise transformation
- and the full-circle CIO role where governance, trust, resilience, AI, BI, Data-Lake, HRIS, ERP, and institutional readiness all come together

About the Author

Francis Mushi, PhD, MBA, is the Chief Information Officer of a global automotive and industrial coatings company, where he leads strategic and operational technology functions across the organization and its family of brands. He is a senior technology executive with more than twenty-five years of experience leading enterprise transformation across manufacturing, automotive, industrial, chemical, and coatings environments. His career spans accounting, enterprise systems, ERP consulting, project leadership, global delivery, and executive technology strategy.

He began his professional journey during the Y2K era, transitioning from accounting into enterprise technology, and has since led complex transformation efforts across ERP, manufacturing execution, BI, HRIS, Data-Lake modernization, governance, and digital operating-model design. His experience also includes internationally funded global project leadership and the cross-company pattern recognition that comes from years of consulting.

He is known for turning around underperforming technology organizations, strengthening governance, raising delivery performance, and aligning technology more closely with business outcomes. His recent CIO experience includes improving project success from below fifty-five percent into the mid-nineties, maintaining strong system reliability, modernizing enterprise platforms, improving data quality and visibility, and delivering measurable cost savings through disciplined optimization and strategic execution. That work has included modernizing ERP environments, expanding manufacturing execution capabilities, implementing HRIS platforms, strengthening data and BI capabilities, improving cybersecurity posture, enabling platform consolidation, and helping organizations scale with stronger governance, clearer accountability, and better operational discipline.

Francis holds a PhD in IT Project Management, an MBA in Technology Management, and a bachelor's degree in Accounting, along with professional certifications in project management and major enterprise systems. He is known for his approachable leadership style, his ability to communicate from the shop floor to the boardroom, and his belief that the best leaders leave the enterprise steadier, wiser, and easier to trust.

Stewardship in Motion reflects the lessons of that journey and his conviction that the strongest leaders build systems, teams, and institutions that remain steady long after the visible work is done.

www.ingramcontent.com/pod-product-compliance
Lightning Source LLC
LaVergne TN
LVHW052035200926
848481LV00005B/1683